School Accountability

The SSRC Cambridge Accountability Project

John Elliott, David Bridges, Dave Ebbutt, Rex Gibson & Jennifer Nias

GRANT
McINTYRE

First published in 1981 by Grant McIntyre Limited
90/91 Great Russell Street, London WC1B 3PY

British Library Cataloguing in Publication Data

The Self-accounting school.
  1. Great Britain. *Social Science Research Council.*
  Cambridge Accounting Project
  2. Educational accountability—England
  I. Elliott, John   II. Great Britain. *Social Science*
  Research Council. Cambridge Accountability Project
  379.1'5'0942   LBZ806
  ISBN 0-86216-074-X

Photoset in 9/11pt Times by
Rowland Phototypesetting Limited,
Bury St Edmunds, Suffolk
Printed in Great Britain by St Edmundsbury Press
Bury St Edmunds, Suffolk

Contents

Acknowledgements

The authors owe a tremendous debt to Jean Graham-Cameron, the Project Secretary. With tact and good humour she effectively liaised between the research team and the project schools, and demonstrated just how much can be accomplished 'between secretaries'. With the tolerant and hardworking assistance of Patricia Still, she typed the six case studies, each of which was drafted at least twice. She was also largely responsible for typing the papers in this book as they moved through various drafts. It was largely due to her firm but tactful coordination that deadlines were met, some of our worst illiteracies rectified, and many obscurely expressed 'insights' rendered intelligible for the reader.

We are also heavily indebted to the Headteachers and staff of the six schools featured in this book, for their willingness to submit their accounting practices to scrutiny, for the time they gave up to be interviewed, and for reading and discussing the case studies. We would also like to thank all the LEA officials, governors, parents, pupils and local employers, who supported and participated in the research. A special word of appreciation is due to the secretaries of the schools involved, for the cheerful tact and skill they displayed in securing our access to busy heads and staff.

We would like to acknowledge the constant support and encouragement provided by Joyce Skinner (ex-Director, Cambridge Institute), Howard Bradley (present Director), members of the Institute's Research Committee, Alison Shrubsole (Principal, Homerton College) and the Academic Board of Homerton College.

Barry MacDonald (University of East Anglia), John Child (Secretary of the Cambridge Institute) and Ian Lewis (visiting scholar from the University of York) have at various points made special contributions to the research. Barry was especially helpful at the initial stages of research design; John provided invaluable critiques of some of the case studies from the position of an intelligent layman, and supervised their publication by the Institute; Ian provided us with a penetrating and helpful critique of the contents of this book shortly before the final manuscript was sent to the publishers.

We would also like to acknowledge the active and constant support given by the past and present secretaries of the Social Science Research Council's Educational Research Board. Both Glyn Davies and John Smith attended seminars between the research team and participating schools; the latter taking a special interest in our efforts to involve teachers in the process of research and its dissemination. Finally, thanks are due to Aileen Webber, teacher and part-time student at the Cambridge Institute, for preparing the index.

John Elliott
August 1981

Introduction

The Context   John Elliott

In 1976 the then Labour Prime Minister Jim Callaghan initiated the 'Great Debate' on Education in a speech at Ruskin College, Oxford. It seemed there had been 'a wobble of public confidence' in the capacity of our educational system to meet the needs of British society in the latter half of the twentieth century. The main themes in Callaghan's speech were 'the need for a common core curriculum', 'the monitoring of standards' and 'the relationship between schools and industry'.

The Great Debate did not exactly emerge as a surprise. For some time the media, stimulated by the publication of the 'Black Papers', had speculated about the possibility of declining educational standards. In 1974 the government established its Assessment of Performance Unit (APU) and charged it with responsibility for monitoring the effectiveness of the educational system by 'defining identifiable areas of pupils' achievement and developing criteria for their assessment'. The areas were English and Foreign Languages, Maths, Science, Personal and Social Development, Aesthetics, Physical Development. Criteria for assessment were only developed for the first three. Monitoring in the other 'exploratory areas' has not yet got off the ground; indeed the Personal and Social Development panel was closed down when monitoring in this area was criticised as unwarranted interference in private morality.

The APU's first director, Brian Kay, claimed (1976) that the Unit's existence 'represents part of the response of the DES to demands for greater accountability by the educational service for the resources it consumes'. The spate of government reports which followed in the wake of Callaghan's speech could be interpreted as an attempt to implement the other part of the response; namely, to

standardise a national curriculum in terms of the APU's operation-
al categories, and thereby make it possible for central government
to control, rationalise and evaluate the provision of educational
resources. And so seven years after the setting up of the APU we
find the latest government report, *The School Curriculum* (1981),
recommending a national core heavily weighted towards (wait for
it) Maths, English, Science, Modern Languages and Technology.
One might indeed describe this core as 'the industrialists' curriculum' and infer that from the standpoint of the Department of
Education and Science (DES) the chief function of the educational
service today is the revival of our nation's declining industrial base.

The goals of education become synonymous with the goal of the
state; namely, 'to promote industrial efficiency'. The intention
tacitly embodied in the creation of the APU, to subordinate
educational practice in schools to state goals, was little modified by
the Great Debate. Although the spate of official government
reports had the manifest function of stimulating free discussion
between professionals and public about the aims and content of
education, their latent function has been to manufacture the
appearance of a democratically derived consensus in order to
legitimate greater state control over educational policy.

Of course, in the UK the statutory powers of the state with
respect to education are an insufficient basis for the exercise of
direct control. It is the local education authorities (LEAs) who
carry formal responsibility for educational provision. At least since
the 1944 Education Act, LEAs have tended to view this responsibility as a matter of administering resources rather than pre-
scribing their use. The latter has largely been the prerogative of
headteachers and their professional staff in schools. However, the
power that central government currently wields over local government expenditure through the rate support grant enables it to
pressurise the latter into exercising more control over the uses to
which resources are put. In this way it becomes possible for the state
indirectly to shape educational policy as an instrument for achieving its goals. We only have to turn to the final page of *The School
Curriculum* for examples of this strategy for transferring power
over educational decision-making from the professional staff of
schools to the state.

The improvements in the curriculum sought by the Secretaries

of State fall to be achieved mainly by local education authorities and schools within the constraints set by limited resources. The Secretaries of State believe that each authority
should have a clear policy for the curriculum in its schools and
make it known to all concerned; be aware of the extent to
which its schools are able, within the resources available to
them, to make curricular provision which is consistent with
that policy; and plan future developments accordingly, in
consultation with teachers and others concerned in their
areas.

The Secretaries of State will wish to inform themselves in due
course about the action which, within the resources available
to them, local authorities are taking in the light of the guidance in this paper.

The idea which is increasingly used to justify this transference of
power from the professionals to the state is that of *public accountability*. In the USA the accountability movement was well underway
by the early 1970s. Commentators such as House (1972, 1973) and
Atkin (1979) attributed its root causes to factors which are not
dissimilar to those suggested by my account of the Great Debate;
namely, economic decline and the growth of value pluralism in
society concerning the aims and purposes of education. House
(1972) argued that the rhetoric of public accountability masked a
covert intent to maximise utility for the most powerful interest
groups in the society and in no way reflected an authentic social
consensus. Indeed he claimed that the accountability movement in
the USA failed to do justice to all the legitimate interests represented amongst the clientele of schools; particularly those of
parents belonging to underprivileged minority groups.

According to House, the pressure on schools to maximise
productivity – by raising test scores – for the most powerful interest groups limited their responsiveness to the needs of less
powerful groups, such as under-privileged minority communities.
He contrasted 'responsive accountability' to the dominant bureau-
cratically-controlled 'productivity' model. The 'responsively
accountable school', and here I am somewhat elaborating and
perhaps reinterpreting House's idea, enters into free and open
communication with a variety of interest groups about the aims
and nature of the education it provides. The relationships through
which influence is exerted are characterised by dialogue rather than

power, and therefore must operate at the local rather than the more remote bureaucratised level of the state. The 'responsive model' suggests that schools ought to be *self-accounting*; generating and communicating information about themselves in the light of interests and concerns expressed by local 'audiences'. This can be contrasted with the 'control' or 'productivity' model where the accounting is done by some external monitoring agency.

In 1978 the Social Science Research Council sponsored a seminar on accountability in Cambridge with a view to launching a research initiative in this area. At this seminar Barry MacDonald (1978) outlined in considerable detail an alternative model of accountability to the technocratic 'product' model which appeared to be emerging in this country. MacDonald's 'process' model, although more detailed, varied little from House's idea of 'responsive accountability', and was quite explicitly grounded on it. MacDonald emphasised the need for schools to develop self-reporting procedures for the local community which rendered educational practice 'open to view and responsive to critique'.

The Cambridge Accountability Project

Following the Cambridge Seminar the Education Research Board of the SSRC established an Accountability Panel which undertook a number of research initiatives, including studies of the APU based at the University of London Institute of Education and *Accountability in the Middle Years of Schooling* (East Sussex, 1979) based at the University of Sussex in collaboration with East Sussex LEA. As a member of the original seminar I became interested in 'The Problems and Effects of Developing Self-Accounting Procedures in Secondary Schools' and submitted a proposal for case study research along these lines to the SSRC Educational Research Board in the summer of 1978. At that time the special initiative panel had not been fully established so the proposal went through 'the ordinary channels', and was accepted.

The Cambridge Accountability Project (CAP), as we came to call it, was funded from 1 January 1979 to 31 December 1980, and was based at the Cambridge Institute of Education (CIE) in association with Homerton College, Cambridge. The research team consisted of myself as Director (CIE), David Bridges

(Homerton), Dave Ebbutt (Full-time Research Fellow, CIE), Rex Gibson (CIE) and Jennifer Nias (CIE). Six secondary schools located in three local authorities agreed to participate in the research. They were selected because they all claimed they were trying to be more responsive to the interests and concerns of external groups (or 'audiences' as we were to call them) within their localities, and developing their self-accounting procedures to this end.

In an initial document circulated to LEAs and prospective schools, we sketched two alternative views of school account-ability, together with the research approach that we would be adopting.

> Currently there appear to be two main views of school accountability representing different ideas about how school-ing might be improved. One view is that improvement comes with greater public control over decisions about school orga-nisation, teaching methods and the curriculum. The other view is that schooling is more readily improved when the school retains control over decisions but becomes more responsive to those whose interests are affected by those decisions.
>
> Such responsiveness is demonstrated by a school's ability to communicate and discuss its activities with outside groups in ways which enable these groups to influence rather than control decisions. Such groups could include: parents, gov-ernors, representatives of local industry and the community.
>
> Of course, many schools already have procedures through which they offer some explanation of their work to people who have a legitimate interest in it. The kind of procedures through which schools offer accounts of their work include written documents of one kind or another, oral reports and meetings of different types. The extent and detail of the information provided in these accounts varies greatly from school to school. So, too, does the range of people to whom they are made available.
>
> An increasing number of these schools are attempting to improve their lines of communication and to involve more people in a discussion of what does, and should, go on in school. The Cambridge Project will try to understand the problems which arise when schools adopt this 'responsive' approach, and its potential for influencing decision making in schools.

During 1979/80 the project team will be working in close association with a group of secondary schools (mainly located in the Eastern region of the country) which are already accepting responsibility for providing information about, and discussing, their work with various external groups. It is hoped that case studies compiled by the project team will be used by participating schools in the further development of their own procedures. The team will also derive from these case studies suggestions as to how other schools might develop their own 'responsive' approach.

The project will focus on the problems and potential of the 'responsive' rather than the 'control' approach to account-ability issues simply because the former has received less attention in the public debate.

There were two reasons for adopting a case study approach: first, we wanted our research to contribute to the development of self-accounting practices in participating schools. This action-research orientation in the area of 'responsive accountability' appeared to necessitate a case study approach. 'Responsiveness' requires schools to be sensitive to the attitudes, values and beliefs which structure their audience's interactions with them under the particular social and political conditions which prevail in their local settings. If the project was to help schools in developing their responsiveness to local audiences then it needed to understand the problems and effects of self-accounting in the light of the particular circumstances they faced.

Secondly, since the self-accounting procedures adopted by schools, and the problems and effects which arise as a result, will depend on their own situation, we were sceptical about the possibility of producing a definitive set of 'research findings' in the form of generalisations which could be applied to all schools irrespective of the settings in which they operated. However, we felt that by comparing and contrasting the 'problems and effects' of self-accounting across a small number of cases, and explaining them in terms of similarities and differences between settings, we could generate some ideas and hypotheses which staff in schools outside the project could usefully explore and examine in relation to their own circumstances.

The research therefore basically consisted of two main phases. The first was the production of case studies on each school. Each team member undertook responsibility for a particular school, except Dave Ebbutt, who was responsible for two. After approximately a year of research, each school received a first draft of its case study for it to discuss. This strategy enabled us in the second year to monitor the impact of our case studies on staff thinking about accountability and its practice in the schools. It also enabled us to discuss the relevance and validity of the contents of our studies with Headteachers and their staff. Were the issues we addressed relevant to accountability in the school and had we explored them in a way which illuminated its practice? The answers to such questions largely depended on the extent to which our understandings of the phenomenon of accountability were shared with the staff. From the beginning we were concerned to elicit teachers' interpretations of their accountability and to allow this data to influence the development of our thinking on the subject. But the introduction of the first-draft case studies enabled us to identify similarities and differences in perspectives on accountability more precisely, both amongst staff and between staff and the external researchers.

Staff reactions to the first drafts allowed the project team to be more responsive to teachers' perceptions and understandings of 'problems and effects' during the second year. We found ourselves either collecting data around new theories which teachers felt we had neglected, or probing certain issues more deeply, or trying to clarify new concepts and ideas which had arisen from our discussions with teachers. Towards the end of the second year we produced revised drafts of the case studies which, after further discussion with staff, and with their permission, have now been published by the Cambridge Institute of Education in three volumes under the general title of *Case Studies in School Accountability* (1981).

After the first-draft studies were introduced the project team moved into the very important phase of comparing and contrasting themes across the six schools. From an initial list of across-site themes each member of the team selected three to write about. The themes tended to fall into two broad categories; 'practical' and 'theoretical'. A practical issue was defined in terms of its focus rather than its method of treatment. It centred attention on a practical theme – for example, the non-involved parent – while the theoretical issues focussed attention on general concepts and

ideas which had emerged during the course of our research. The
method of treatment, however, was analytical for both types. In
dealing with the practical issues we tried to explain similarities and
differences between schools in certain respects; for instance, the
presence or absence of a particular problem. Thus the treatment if
not the focus was theoretical; in the Glaser and Strauss (1967) sense
of 'grounded theory'. In writing the theoretical issues papers we
attempted to clarify some of the key concepts and ideas we had
used in writing the practical papers, and show how they had
emerged from interviews with teachers, parents, governors, employers, etc. during the course of our research.

As first drafts were written they were discussed with other
project researchers at team meetings and, following the clearance
of the case studies, revised for publication in this book. We hope
that, in conjunction with the case studies, they will prove a useful
source of information, ideas and hypotheses about the problems
and possibilities of self-accounting.

The authors feel that this collection could be useful not only as a
means of exploring accountability issues in such professional
contexts as school-based and school-focussed inservice sessions,
but it could also be profitably used as a basis for seminars involving
governors, parents, local employers, and LEA officials.

The reader will notice that the collection is heavily weighted
towards 'accountability to parents', although he or she will find
papers concerned with other audiences, particularly governors and
local employers. The reason for this apparent bias is simply that it
reflected the accountability priorities of the schools who participated. We felt that it was not our responsibility as researchers to
suggest what the self-accounting priorities of our schools ought to
be, but rather to simply reflect in our research those priorities we
found to exist.

All the names of the project's schools, and the individuals
associated with them, have been fictionalised both in this book and
in the case studies. The pseudonyms plus brief descriptions of the
schools are as follows:

Highstones (HI): a new 13–18 co-educational upper school in a
predominantly rural area two miles outside a market town.

Holbein (HO): a purpose built 13–18 co-educational upper
school set in an industrialised large market town within easy

access of two major industrial and commercial centres of the country. It was opened in 1976.

Old Town Girls (OT): Located on the outer London fringe, it opened in 1960 as a grammar school for girls. It is now a girls' 11–18 comprehensive school with approximately 750 pupils on the roll.

Robert Peel (RP): a new 13–18 co-educational upper school in a London over-spill town.

Springdale (S): Built in 1954 as a secondary modern school it became an 11–18 county comprehensive in 1964, and finally evolved in 1972 into a 13–18 upper school. Set in a market town, it has over 1,000 pupils on the roll.

Uplands (U): built in the mid-1960s as a purpose built 11–18 co-educational comprehensive school. It is set in a high technology industrial area.

Where quotations are made from the case studies in this book, the name of the particular school is given in abbreviated form as shown above, and is followed by the appropriate chapter or section number.

1

Teachers' perspectives on school accountability

John Elliott

To whom do teachers see themselves accountable?

For what do they see themselves accountable?

What do they mean by 'accountability'?

During the course of the CAP research we explored such questions as these with teachers, hoping to throw light on the practice of accountability within our schools.

At Uplands, my interviews with fifteen staff yielded a range of responses to these questions. This chapter is organised around my analysis of those responses, and I have tried to explore the extent to which the perspectives on accountability held by the teachers at Uplands were reflected by the comments of staff in other CAP schools.

To whom?

1. *The majority of teachers tend to select multiple audiences, which can be grouped into two categories:*
   (a) Accountability to others within the producer (or profession-al) system of the school, e.g. the Head, Heads of Section (Upper, Middle, Lower School), Heads of Department and other staff.
   (b) Accountability to clients, i.e. to children and their parents.

   John Elliott: Finally, as a teacher – who do you see yourself as primarily accountable to?

Janet Johnson: I see myself directly accountable to the Head. A little bit in here within the Science Department. But because I have got a department within a department, for which I am not really accountable to the HOD, I see myself to be in the Head's 'department'. And to the Deputy Head as the Head's representative. And to the Head of Upper School in certain respects. But really more or less directly with the Head.

John Elliott: And who would you see the School as account-able to as opposed to you as an individual teacher?

Janet Johnson: I think . . . directly to the parents. It doesn't seem to me that the county shows much interest in holding us accountable. The Governors do a little bit but there I would have said it was as much a matter of personalities amongst the Governors rather than the Governors as a group . . . one never sees the Governing Body as exerting an influence. They are receivers rather than givers. Possibly to be manipulated. (U, 22)

Although the vast majority of teachers in Uplands and other CAP schools tended to cite a cluster of 'audiences', the membership of these clusters varied somewhat between teachers, as did the rank order in which teachers placed their 'audiences' within a cluster. Whereas 'children', or 'myself', do not appear in Janet Johnson's list they do in other teachers' lists quite frequently. While some teachers tended to exclude clients (parents, children, employers) from their cluster, others excluded colleagues within the pro-fessional staff of their school.

In spite of this element of variability there was a tendency for many staff to select at least one audience from both the 'pro-fessional' and 'client' categories. In Figure 1 I have summarised the frequency and range of citations within a sample of 10 teachers interviewed at Uplands. It can be seen that half of the sample cited audiences from both the 'professional' and the 'client' categories. These are audiences they felt directly accountable to as individual teachers. If one includes audiences they felt indirectly accountable to – direct accountability being exercised by the school staff as a whole, e.g. to parents – then 7 of the 10 staff cite audiences from each category. These 'results' from interviews in one school do, I feel, reflect a general trend within the schools we looked at.

The frequently cited audiences across all the CAP schools were:

Oneself (sometimes also one's subject)
Head

	CR	AB	RS	AS	DR	JJ	MS	PC	SC	JR	Number of citations
Self	✓	✓	✓	✓							3
Head		✓	✓	✓		✓		✓			7
Other staff (in superordinate roles)										✓	1
Professional system — Other staff	✓	✓					✓				2
Other staff (in subordinate roles)									✓	✓	2
Students	✓	✓	✓	✓	✓		✓		✓		7
Client System — Parents		✓	✓	(indirectly)				✓			7
Employers					✓ (indirectly)			✓			1
Political/ Administrative System — Governors											1
LEA					✓			✓			1
Society as a whole											

Figure 1.

Teachers' views of clients to whom they are accountable (sample: teachers at Uplands School)

Other school staff (super-ordinates, sub-ordinates, peers)
Children
Parents

Since the project set out to study how schools account to external groups it is no wonder that school–parent relations dominate the six case studies, with the possible exception of Robert Peel where the headteacher of this new school was particularly concerned to establish an accountable relationship with employers.

In comparison, the case studies generally contain less material on relations with governors, LEAs and employers. School–LEA relationships are perhaps represented least. There is little mention of teacher–LEA adviser relationships, with the exception of Rex Gibson's account of the Holbein 'accountability exercise' with advisers. After parents, governors get the most attention because they tend to relate closely with heads. This lack of 'balance' in the attention our case studies give to relations with various groups outside schools is no accident. We set out to reflect in our research the accountability priorities of the schools involved. The interview data we collected on 'teachers' perspectives' therefore tends to confirm our perceptions of accountability practices in the schools.

2. *Many teachers see themselves to be individually, rather than collectively, accountable to clients.*
At Uplands half of the 10 teachers in my sample felt themselves to be directly accountable to the parents of the children they taught, and 7 to the children. The fact that many viewed their accountability to consumers in these individualistic terms perhaps reflects a relative lack of strong collegial ties and shared professional norms, a product of the isolation in which teachers carry out their classroom tasks.

> I would think it probably happens in other departments too – each teacher becomes very much an individual and there is very little group activity. I think many of the individuals are going their own separate ways, and this can be positive. There are dangers, however; the theory that 'each teacher is account-able to himself' poses grave problems to the organised edu-cational system. (Alan Sorrell, talking about internal account-ability in his subject department. U, 21)

If common professional norms were stronger one would expect teachers to view their individual accountability as an intra-professional matter.

This *individualistic perspective* on accountability to children and parents was by no means unique to staff at Uplands.

> I am as a teacher accountable to the people in my charge and through them their parents. I don't have a larger account-ability than that. (S, 1)

> The children. Basically before anybody else it is to the children. (S, 1)

At Uplands there were certainly a number of teachers who saw their accountability to clients as a collective obligation, in-terpreting their individual accountability primarily in intra-professional terms. We found no evidence in any of our schools to suggest that there is a typical staff perspective on the question of whether individual accountability is primarily a matter of obliga-tion to professional colleagues or of obligation to clients. In any school one may find areas of collective endeavour where teachers are made to feel accountable to each other, and areas of solitary effort where they feel individually accountable to their immediate clients.

3. *A sense of intra-professional accountability is indicated by a tendency for teachers to cite peers and subordinates in addition to super-ordinates as significant 'audiences'.*

> Thinking about it, one is accountable in a much wider sense to all the other staff. Whether, if you like, they are above you in the pecking order or below. For example, the people who work in your department, you should be accountable to them for the way in which you lead it. (John Ray, Head of Geography. U, 21)

> I feel accountable to the staff . . . in that what I'm setting up in Middle School options ought to be acceptable to them. I'm working within the limits of what the Head allows me to do. I am also working within the limits of what is possible on the timetable, but at the same time I like to feel that I'm accountable to staff in that they are having a say in what is

being set up and what is being studied and the size of the groups that are set up, and so on. (Celia Riley, Head of Middle School. U, 21)

Consultation amongst the staff, I think, is important. . . . I hope it's a team here. I think it is and we run the management as openly as we possibly can. (Headteacher. HI, Sec. 1)

Intra-professional accountability must be distinguished from hierarchical accountability. In the latter, the information flow is strictly one-way, up 'the chain of command'. The more one moves up the hierarchy the more people know about the activities of those below, and the more one moves down it the less people know about the activities of those above them. Hierarchical accountability facilitates social control over an organisation by a powerful elite at the top of the pyramid. It is indicative of a bureaucratised school organisation and is concerned with achieving the goals of the organisation most effectively and efficiently.

Intra-professional accountability does not preclude the existence of differentiated administrative responsibilities. But it does entail a certain view of those responsibilities. Those affected by the organisation's policies should be provided with opportunities for shaping them. It is more a responsibility for co-ordinating the formulation and implementation of policy at different levels than a responsibility for making policies which are then imposed on others without adequate consultation and discussion. An intra-professional system of teacher accountability must ultimately be grounded in what the headteacher at Highstones called 'open management'; that is, where teachers feel they have a collective responsibility for articulating and implementing policies. In this context teachers with responsibility for administering policies will feel as accountable to the teachers affected by them, as the latter will feel to them.

The Sussex report on *Accountability in the Middle Years of Schooling* (East Sussex, 1979) draws a distinction similar to the one I have drawn between intra-professional and hierarchical accountability. It contrasts a professional with a managerial system of relationships in schools. The latter involves a considerable specialisation of responsibilities for different tasks which are strongly hierarchalised. The former is ultimately grounded in a collegial sense of responsibility for the formulation and execution of the school's tasks.

4. *The more hierarchical the school organisation the less individual teachers will feel either accountable to each other, or collectively accountable to client groups.*
The problem of teacher individualism, noted in (2) above, can be resolved in two ways. The first involves the development of scientific management in schools with its rigid standardisation, specialisation and hierarchalisation of tasks and roles. The second involves the development of organisational structures which foster a sense of collective responsibility for tasks, and discussions about the best ways to carry them out. The first generates feelings of hierarchical accountability to immediate superiors within the chain of command, the second feelings of intra-professional account-ability. The more successful scientific management strategies become, the less teachers will feel individually accountable to themselves, the subjects they teach, or the children directly in their care and their parents; the state of affairs widely represented in our case studies. But this erosion of teacher individualism will also impose constraints on the development of intra-professional accountability among individual teachers, and on the development of client-oriented accountability to children and parents at the corporate staff level. A sense of professional obligation to account to each other, and a corporate sense of moral obligation to account to children and parents, will be replaced by a sense of contractual obligation to account to those occupying superordinate positions in the hierarchy. When individual teacher accountability becomes bureaucratised in this way local government administration is able to increase its capacity to control task performance at the classroom level. For once the school as a unit of organisation is made contractually accountable through its headteacher to its local government employer, an impetus is provided for extending the system of contractual obligation into the organisation of the school. The chain of command from local government policy-making to policy-implementation within the school is then complete. There is a 'top-down' system of social control over the activities of individual teachers, which makes it increasingly difficult for client groups within the local community to influence what happens in schools, and for the schools to be responsive to their clients' needs.

Some teachers in our CAP schools emphasised their hierarchical accountability but we did not gather sufficient evidence to place the schools on a spectrum from strong to weak hierarchalisation with respect to their internal accountability systems.

According to Jennifer Nias, there was some conflict at Highstones between the headteacher's attempts to institute open management (and by implication a system of intra-professional accountability) and the preference of some of his staff for a hierarchical chain of command. She writes:

> It is by no means clear, however, that the staff wanted then, or want now, a policy of dispersed responsibility or participation in decision-making. In the initial interviews . . . many staff listed the Head amongst those to whom they felt primarily accountable. Sometimes this was based on a sense of individual responsibility to him as a person. . . . Equally often, however, it stemmed from an awareness of his bureaucratic position. He was 'the boss', 'the end of the line', 'the buffer between us and everyone else', 'the one who ultimately carries the can'. (HI, Sec. 1)

At Uplands, few staff longed for a strong system of hierarchical control. The individualistic perspective of some teachers was tempered by those who clearly articulated a sense of collective responsibility and feelings of being collegially accountable to each other. This is not unconnected with the school's reputation for 'approachability' amongst parents.

5. *The more the staff of a school feel collectively responsible for the work of the school as a whole, and therefore accountable to each other, the more they can begin to feel collectively accountable to client groups, for instance parents and children.*
Interviews with parents revealed that most of the CAP schools were perceived to be very 'approachable' by parents. The term 'approachability' was used to signify ease of access; an absence of 'red-tape', delay and formality in contacting someone who can listen and respond appropriately to the parents' queries and comments.

The following comments by Cllr John Dodd, Chairman of Governors and a parent at Uplands, clearly reveals the connection between the approachability of a school and a sense of collective responsibility amongst its staff. In this respect he contrasts Uplands with another school in which responsibilities appear to be strongly hierarchalised:

> I was talking to one parent who had moved here, only a fortnight ago, . . . and they said they went up to another school and were invited round. And the chap asked one question, and that was 'could you tell me what specific information you have on pass marks in examinations?', and the Assistant Head said, 'Oh, I don't think I know, I'd better ask the Headmaster before I can give you that information', and the parent said to me, 'That was enough, I don't think there's any point in me staying', and he came away. Now he came to Uplands and he asked the same question of one of the teachers who was showing him around and they were readily able to give him, not dead accurate, but at least information that he was looking for. As far as he was concerned that is where his daughter and son go to now, and I think it is this involvement of all the staff within the running of the school which rubs off on a lot of parents certainly. (U, 7)

In an approachable school individuals have access to the information that parents want and are entrusted to convey it. In a hierarchical system the flow of information within schools and out of it is controlled by those at the top of the pyramid. Such a system neither encourages teachers to feel accountable to each other as professional colleagues, except in a hierarchical sense, nor collectively accountable to parents. Indeed, I suggest that hierarchalised schools do not act accountably to their parents. Instead the staff at the top of the school pyramid will see themselves as contractually accountable to the next link in the bureaucratic chain of command, to the Divisional or Chief Education Officer.

If 'approachability' is indicative of a school's capacity to be accountable or answerable to its parents, then I would argue that this kind of accountability can only be exercised by a school where internal accountability is collegial rather than hierarchical. The reputation for approachability enjoyed by the majority of CAP schools is a strong indication that internal accountability has developed along collegial rather than hierarchical lines. However, since the latter development seems to be an inevitable consequence of strong contractual accountability to local government, I would argue that approachability to parents is incompatible with strong contractual accountability.

6.   *The majority of teachers in CAP schools felt neither individually nor collectively accountable to governors and local government officials.*

In the light of my previous remarks this should come as no surprise. When the staff of a school feel primarily accountable to one another and collectively accountable to clients they will lack any strong sense of contractual obligation to their LEA or its representatives. It was rare indeed to come across staff, even heads, who felt hierarchically accountable in this way.

Some teachers acknowledged a distinction between 'the official', 'formal' system of accountability and the 'unofficial', 'informal' system operating in practice.

> J.E.: If you take accountability to children, parents, govern-
> ors, and local authority. How do you rate these in order of
> priority.
>
> M.S.: Formally, I would rank them in one order. Informally I
> would rank them entirely differently. (U, 22)

The formal system corresponds to an official 'chain of command' stretching from classroom teacher to head of department to governors to LEA. Some representatives of local government on governing bodies interpreted educational accountability primarily in terms of this official 'chain of command':

> My own view is that teachers should be accountable to the
> Headmaster and the Headmaster to the Board of Governors
> and the County Education people . . . (Cllr Mike Drake;
> U, 21)

Governors who adopted this point of view understood its logic and therefore disagreed with the view that schools were accountable to parents and their children:

> . . . a school must consider its pupils and parents as customers
> . . . but I don't see that they are accountable to them, and
> possibly if the parent is aggrieved by some action of a teacher

then they should take it to the Head or the Governors, and let
the chain of command take over. (Cllr Mike Drake; U, 21)

. . . in my view they [parents] are so close to the action that
often they can't see the overall picture which many, many
decisions are going to be fitted into. . . . Now what are the
LEA representatives there to do? Let's take out the political
overtone altogether. Basically they are there to represent the
community at large. And they have a very important role to
play in my view because they ought not to be partisan.
(Chairman of Governors; S, 5)

The view that governors must articulate a non-partisan point of
view, detached from the partial interests invested in a school by a
particular group of clients like parents, is echoed in another
governor's objection to school accountability to parents:

I think there is an awful danger – because there is such a broad
spectrum of opinion among parents – there will be one parent
who will say one thing and another will say precisely the
opposite and you will never get away from the situation will
you? It will always be the case. So what happens? The
Headmaster can never satisfy the lot. (Vice-Chairman; U, 21)

From the 'chain of command perspective', what the school is
accountable for can only be assessed by those at the top of the chain;
only they are in a position to adopt a disinterested, broader
viewpoint. The hierarchical chain of accountability implies a
hierarchy of credible knowledge. The LEA is not simply one
interest group amongst many. Only it can represent the interests of
the total community. The chain of command perspective abstracts
the interests and needs of the total community from the particular
interests and needs articulated by sections within it, and in doing so
sets them in opposition to the latter. Contractual, formal, hierarchical accountability can be understood as a device for handling
pluralism within the community. As Atkin (1979) has argued, the
emergence of bureaucratic 'contractual' accountability is a response to increasing social pluralism.
   Now there is an alternative view of 'accountability to governors'
articulated in the Taylor Report on school government. This is the
view that a governing body is representative of all the different
groups which have an interest in the work of the school. The report

recommended equal representation for LEA, parents, teachers and pupils. In this scheme the LEA is merely one interest group amongst others. It implies that pluralism on the question of what the school is accountable for should be resolved through dialogue, rather than through the hierarchy of knowledge presupposed by contractual accountability along a chain of command. As the governors committed to the chain of command system recognised, the Taylor Report threatened to undermine it, reducing the hierarchical control of LEAs over their schools and of head-teachers over their staff and parents.

Nevertheless there were signs that many of the heads of CAP schools had manipulated the membership of their governing bodies to conform to something like the Taylor recommendations. But even in this context, where the constitution of governing bodies imposed constraints on the effectiveness of the chain of command, one major obstacle had to be overcome before teachers could begin to feel accountable to governors.

7. *Many teachers view their accountability and the obligations it entails to flow out of sustained face-to-face interactions with others. The more 'remote' they felt others to be from their day to day work the less accountability they felt towards them.*

M.S. (talking about his accountability priorities):

The pupils. After that the hierarchical positions in the staff. The heads of upper, lower and middle schools. I think they seem to be team leaders, for whom one does all this work on behalf of the kids. After that colleagues in the department. After that the Head, who tends to be remote. I think I will put the Deputy Head with the team leaders. After that we have got parents and governors. I think the governors are more remote than the parents. That is the way it actually works to me. (U, 22)

Teacher (of Assistant Education Officer in the LEA):

I wouldn't accept his word as law because he happens to be the education officer for our particular area. This is what I mean by distance. We don't have any direct contact with these people. I don't know what he is thinking, whether he thinks that we are succeeding or failing. I'm pretty sure he doesn't know that I exist. (HI, 3A)

From the chain of command perspective, face-to-face interaction is not a necessary condition of being accountable.

Well, I don't think you have to know people to be accountable to them do you – most of us are accountable to somebody that we don't know. (Cllr Mike Drake; U, 22)

The amount and intensity of social interaction probably accounts more than anything else for the order of priority in which the teachers placed their audiences. Hence children and parents tend to be placed high on the list because teachers are in constant contact with them, whilst governors and LEAs tend to be placed very low because they are perceived to be 'remote'.

In the Uplands Case Study (ch. 20), I have indicated some of the ways in which the school tried to increase the amount of social interaction staff have with governors, such as regular visits to classrooms and conferences in the school, and through the institution of informal governors' meetings which all staff were free to attend. The Holbein 'Accountability Exercise' with LEA advisers (see HO, 4) can also be viewed as an attempt to increase the amount of social interaction, this time with LEA personnel.

For What?

Simply asking teachers who they feel 'accountable to' may well mask the fact that they feel accountable to different audiences for different things. In this section I shall explore different views teachers have of what they are accountable for to parents, since this particular audience tends to have high priority for many of them.

Having interviewed staff at Uplands and observed various 'accountability events' in the school I felt able to classify the range of things teachers cited as follows:

Accountability to parents for:

a. Their children's progress
b. Children's option choices

    c. Public examination entries

    d. Provision of extra-curricular activities

    e. Provision for sick and injured children

    f. Standards of discipline and dress

    g. The subjects on the school curriculum

    h. Teaching methods

The elaborate and painstaking way the schools planned consultation evenings for parents indicated the extent to which staff felt accountable to parents for their children's progress.

In a survey of fourth year parents at Uplands, 77 per cent and 46 per cent of the sample claimed they had a considerable say with respect to 'option subjects' and 'examination entries' respectively (see U, 17). But only 20 per cent and 6 per cent of the sample felt they had a considerable say in what was taught to their children (g) and how this was taught (h) respectively.

The way teachers rank their priorities appears partly to depend on how they view accountability in relation to the idea of 'professional expertise'. Some perceived little contradiction in the idea that teachers can be experts at making curriculum decisions and yet at the same time feel accountable to parents for them. Others tended to draw a boundary between professional expertise and accountability to extra-professional groups when it comes to decisions about content and methods:

> If a parent says to you, 'You have got a duty to provide an education', well yes, I have obviously, and that is what I am paid for. But I don't think it should go much further than that. I think the nature of that education should be determined by people who work in and have experience of it. (John Ray; U, 22)

> I see it very much as a professional matter. I would be reluctant to see increased parental representation in that aspect of one's work . . . we provide the menu and parents choose the dishes – if I may put it like that. (HO, 2)

> Head: Of course I think I know best. (HI, 3A (10))

For some teachers the territory of teacher professionalism did not even extend to curriculum decisions; it was confined to teaching methods alone:

> Jim Clark: I would like to think that what I am doing the parents agree with, and that we can have some communication about it if they don't.
>
> J.E.: So you see parents as having some sort of right, with the teachers, to determine the overall policy about maths teaching . . .
>
> J.C.: But not how it's done, because they are not in a position to make such a decision. (U, 22)

How then do we understand what is at stake between those teachers who feel accountability is a threat to their professional prerogatives and those who view them as compatible? The issue lies, I believe, in rather different interpretations of what accountability involves.

What is Accountability?

Those teachers who view accountability to parents as a threat to their professionalism tend to understand accountability to mean:

Interpretation A: 'Fitting in' with role expectations pre-determined by others
The comments cited at the end of the last section indicate the major assumption which underlies drawing a boundary between what teachers are accountable for and what they are professionally responsible for. The assumption is that accountability involves conformity to external prescription, thus leaving little room for the exercise of professional discretion. Thus we find Dick Reid, a teacher at Uplands, claiming that teachers ought not to be held extra-professionally accountable for teaching methods since each classroom situation is unique and decisions about them should appropriately rest with the teacher 'on the spot':

> . . . I think teaching is a profession. What you cannot say, even though we work to a time-table, is that every lesson is the same. No two lessons are the same. Even if you are teaching the same

subject, even if you are writing the same numbers on the board, weather conditions outside can make a difference to the atmosphere in the classroom. All these sorts of things that we have to take into consideration makes the task of being able to pin-point accountability very difficult indeed. (U, 22)

Reid's view of accountability assumes that it involves doing things prescribed by others. This assumption is, I believe, taken from 'the chain of command' use of the term to describe the process by which those in superordinate roles in the hierarchy assess the extent to which subordinates have carried out their tasks in accordance with pre-standardised rules of procedure. In other words, accountability is associated with systems of contractual obligation. This was made very clear by another Uplands teacher, a recruit from industry, when trying to relate his experience of industrial accountability to school:

Steve Carpenter: How do my colleagues see the relationship in a school, because I think this is where I find it difficult to understand the difference between the industrial scene. It is this immediate supervision, the immediate hierarchy seem to have very little interest – is that the word? – knowledge, perhaps, of the situation that pertains in the classroom. . . . You see, I perhaps am a bit naive on this word accountability, but I look on it as a straightforward he-and-you-and-I. Now suppose you say to me, 'I want you to do some craft work for me – this is it', and from then on in, I am accountable to you for doing that work. In other words I very much see accountability as a form of commission. (U, 22)

The problem then for teachers who employ Interpretation A is that accountability appears to limit their discretionary powers to exercise judgement and take decisions about the ways they carry out their responsibilities as teachers. On this interpretation, accountability to client groups can only be given a 'soft' sense if teachers' discretionary powers are not to be undermined.

On the basis of his interviews with Old Town teachers, Dave Ebbutt (OT, 2) drew a distinction between *giving an account* (which refers to a context of trust in which accounts are fully rendered; the recipient is expected to listen to but not take issue with what is provided) and *being called to account* (which, in contrast, involves a more investigative stance on the part of the audience). Other CAP researchers made similar distinctions. In her Highstones Study (2Bb), Jennifer Nias contrasted teachers who expect parents to listen to their accounts and those who listen to parents.

At Uplands I discovered a tension in staff–parent communication. I gained the impression that the dominant mode was one in which the teachers went to great lengths to explain and justify their policies to parents on the assumption of the latter's ignorance. I called it *paternalistic accountability*. I contrasted it with an alternative mode of communication which was emerging in which parents were encouraged not simply to *ask questions* but *to question* and criticise the school's policies.

Eileen Green, a teacher at Uplands, articulated very clearly the context of mutual trust in which giving an account, accountability in a soft sense, operates:

> Eileen Green: I think in my dealings with parents I sort of feel accountable to them for the progress of their child or their child's lack of progress. I feel it myself. They don't make me feel it. I very often get the feeling from parents that they are almost hanging on your every word. They believe every word that you say. And more often than not, I think that parents are – a great many of them – are more than happy to be told what their child should be doing. They accept what the school says too easily perhaps in the case of some parents. (U, 22)

It is precisely because the teacher is trusted as a professional expert that he or she feels obliged to give an account. Observations in CAP schools indicated that the schools were generally very accountable to parents in this soft sense for curriculum and even teaching methods. Interviews with teachers across the schools certainly revealed plenty of staff very willing to *give accounts*, but when it came to willingness to *being called to account* it was a different matter.

> I think they should know what we do because they are tax-payers. They should have some idea where their money is going and how it is distributed in the school . . . whether it would be a good idea for them to complain and say, 'My money should go on so and so . . .', I don't think that's a good idea. (HI, 2B3)

Even Jim Clark, the Uplands teacher who objected to being accountable to parents for his teaching methods, was willing to give them accounts of his methods:

> Well all those [parents] who really come and talk to me always seem much happier when they have taken the trouble to find out how we do these things. I don't mean what modern maths are but the methods of teaching. Because a lot of them, if you are not standing in front of the board with a piece of chalk, don't think you are teaching. (U, 22)

However, some teachers in CAP schools welcomed being called to account by parents:

> It's very nice the parents are [patient and trusting] but there may come a time when they say, 'Look, what is this that's going on in your school? You're not doing anything about it, now, what about it?'
> Holbein parents trust us over curriculum and careers and it is justified trust over discipline etc. I sense they are not entirely happy but are being patient with us. But my nose tells me there may soon be a protest from some of the more knowledgeable parents – and those who listen to and rely on their kids' comments at home. (HO, 2)

For such teachers there was little danger of having their professionalism undermined:

> I've always felt that I could stand and must answer whatever charge they're [parents] making, it might be a charge of not enough homework set, or children not being prepared properly for an exam; or a recent example is a child who wasn't entered for an exam.' (Celia Riley, Head of Middle School; U, 22)

Here the 'must answer' is an imperative which seems to flow from a sense of moral rather than contractual obligation to clients. I suggest that teachers like Celia Riley tend to understand their accountability in the moral sense of *answerability*, and that being called to account in contrast to simply giving an account in this context is perfectly intelligible and quite reconcilable with a teacher's professional rights. This is because it stems from personal interaction rather than contractual relations with others. I now want to clarify the interpretation of 'accountability' which underlies the views of those teachers who use it as a moral term.

Interpretation B: Explaining and justifying to others the decisions and actions one has undertaken
Of course, what I called the 'soft sense' of the term is perfectly compatible with this interpretation. But so also is *being called to account* by clients. Bob Sands, a head of Maths, claimed:

> . . . this school is different from any school I've been in. The children seem much more forward or rather less backward in coming forward. If they are dissatisfied with something, they will say so. Whether you like it or not, you are forced to be accountable to the child. You get the age-old question 'Why are we doing this?' (U, 22)

This excerpt reveals the social interaction context in which Interpretation B operates. It thus clearly distinguishes it from being called to account in a context of contractual, hierarchalised relations, where accountability is expressed in terms of a standardised, impersonal and formal procedure independent of the persons involved. For Bob Sands' feelings of accountability were contingent upon the quality of the face-to-face encounters he had. As a teacher at Springdale remarked:

> Accountability is something brought about by interaction between me and somebody else.

It rests on moral rather than legal obligation. In this context, being called to account involves being obliged to answer a challenge about the point or value of one's actions by giving reasons intended to explain their point or value and thereby justify them in the eyes of one's audience. It may not presume trust in one's professional judgements and decisions, but it does presume that one's actions flow from personal judgement and decision rather than external prescription. On Interpretation B, 'accountability' implies responsibility for judgement and decision, while on Interpretation A it implies responsibility for acting in conformity to the judgements and decisions of others. On Interpretation B one is accountable for the decisions and judgements one makes rather than for the extent to which one fits in with other people's. The following interview excerpt makes this quite clear:

> Yes, I think if I make decisions about children, something simple like marking, I feel I need to explain something that may seem ambiguous to a child. (Pauline Chappell; U, 22)

Pauline went on to explain why she didn't feel accountable for 'what' rather than 'how' she taught.

> I feel directly accountable to parents for *how* I teach, but it is difficult for me to feel accountable for all of *what* I teach. I suppose I feel like that because basically speaking the Head made a policy decision before I came to the school and said integrated science will be taught . . .

On Interpretation A Pauline would have to draw the reverse conclusion; namely, because the head prescribed the curriculum she taught she should feel accountable to him for it.

If calling teachers to account is not to secure conformity to externally prescribed rules of conduct, what is its function? I would claim that its function is to render professional decisions and judgement responsive to public criticism. The function of clients calling teachers to account is to engage them in a dialogue about their activities. The ideal outcome is not the imposition of sanctions aimed at compelling teachers to conform to a set of externally prescribed rules, but the exertion of rational influence.

We can therefore contrast a control model of accountability in which *calling to account* is a power-coercive strategy for changing teachers' behaviour in conformity with an externally imposed contract, with a dialogue model of accountability in which *calling to account* aims at rationally resolving judgements and decisions perceived to be in some way problematic. In a context of free and open dialogue with clients, *being called to account* carries no implication of external compulsion, of being compelled to accept the client's judgement. The only force which has to be acknowledged is that of argument.

Habermas (1968) contrasts impersonal and standardised administrative systems of 'purposive-rational' action with communicative interaction 'governed by binding consensual norms, which define reciprocal expectations about behaviour'. He argues that:

> While the validity of technical rules and strategies depends on that of empirically true or analytically correct propositions, the validity of social norms is grounded only in the inter-subjectivity of the mutual understanding of intentions and secured by the general recognition of obligations.

In other words the validity of the rules which govern 'purposive-rational' action depends on their proven effectiveness in achieving the objectives of the system, not on their subjective validity for those whose actions are regulated by them. In contrast the norms which govern communicative interaction depend for their validity on the willingness of participants to be bound by them.

According to Habermas, communicative interaction normally proceeds smoothly and unreflectively; the norms which govern it remaining tacit and unexamined by those involved. But when this tacit consensus breaks down and makes normal communication difficult one may begin to call the other norms into question and thereby render them problematic. The mutual trust implicit in normal interaction is suspended and the level of communication shifts to take the form of practical discourse or dialogue. According to Habermas (1973) dialogue aims to re-establish a genuine consensus so that normal interaction can proceed.

He poses the problem of how to distinguish a warranted consensus from an unwarranted one; one which is imposed on one party by another. Habermas resolves this in terms of the formal properties of dialogue. Dialogue presupposes, he claims, an absence of all constraints on people's thinking and reasoning save 'the force of the better argument'. Participants must have equal freedom to adopt dialogue roles, 'to put forward, call into question, and give reasons for and against statements, explanations, interpretations and justifications'. Thus dialogue presupposes the liberal-democratic values of 'equality', 'freedom' and 'justice'. The presence of these conditions, according to Habermas, ensures that any consensus which results will be a warranted one, undistorted by the imposition of power constraints. 'The better argument' is simply the one which carries the greatest inter-subjective force under conditions of free and open dialogue.

Thus for Habermas practical discourse or dialogue arises out of a situation of accountability in which the norms which govern social interaction are challenged or questioned. His account very much reflects Interpretation B and the commonsense understanding of those teachers who failed to perceive any conflict between their professional prerogatives and their accountability to parents and children.

Now we can reserve the term *accountability* to cover the control model only (Interpretation A), and call the dialogue model (Interpretation B) *answerability*. But I prefer to see *answerability* as one mode of accountability and *contractual accountability* as another; the term 'accountability' referring to any mode of evaluating and influencing human action. In the contractual mode the criteria for evaluation are standardised and responsibility for evaluation hierarchalised. In the *answerable* mode the criteria evolve as the negotiated outcomes of free and open social interaction, in which all parties have equal opportunities to put forward, defend and criticise arguments.

The two modes of accountability which have emerged are functional to different systems of social relationships. Contractual accountability is a way of establishing control over people's actions in bureaucratised social systems where relationships are governed by impersonal and standardised roles. Answerability enables people to influence rationally the conduct of others through inter-personal communication free from constraints imposed by the adoption of special statuses and roles. Answerability as a mode of teacher accountability therefore presupposes a social context in which human relationships are not too formalised, standardised and hierarchalised. It can express itself both as intra-professional accountability between individual teachers operating in open management system, and as collective accountability to client groups operating in a situation of moral obligation.

Contractual accountability to local government employers and answerability to client groups are alternative ways of handling the breakdown of any social consensus about the aims and purposes of education. Such issues can either be resolved centrally through a bureaucratically imposed solution or resolved locally by increasing opportunities for dialogue between schools and their clients. Contractual accountability, by removing the locus of decision-making from the schools to government, makes it far more difficult for parents to influence directly the educational practices of the schools their children attend. The extent to which schools can be answerable to parents depends on the extent to which responsibility for educational decision-making is devolved to them. Only in such a devolved system can parents exert any direct influence over their children's schooling.

Heads and staff in CAP schools were becoming increasingly aware of the alternative paths along which school accountability can develop in the future. Faced with a choice between greater contractual accountability to the LEA and greater answerability to their clients there was little doubt that they would opt for the latter. In fact, there was evidence that they were consciously trying to become more answerable to parents in order to counter pressures towards greater contractual accountability already being exerted 'from above'.

2

Types of school and accountability

Dave Ebbutt

This chapter explores a set of related ideas which I have been developing over the two years of the project. Partly they represent an attempt to grapple with a foreshadowed problem (Hammersley 1979; Stake *et al*. 1978).

This chapter does not address the issue of what school account-ability is, or should be. Rather it assumes that school accountability has a great deal to do with communication, about how a school presents itself to its various audiences, and about how it is perceived by those audiences. What follows depends on the realisation that the type of a school is embedded in its geographical, historical, social and psychological context. The type of school and the nature of its relationship with the context in which it is set are significant determinants of accountability issues and priorities; a clearer understanding of the differences between schools will contribute usefully to the accountability debate.

This chapter depends upon a classification of school ideal types which transcend the official titles such as high school or upper school which mask the significant differences between schools. The ideal types range from the Neighbourhood Catchment School (subsequently referred to as the *Neighbourhood School*) at one end of a spectrum, through to *Extended Catchment Schools* at the other. The classification is developed step by step, and a diagram summarising the various dimensions along which the ideal types differ is presented at the end of the chapter. I have adopted the term Neighbourhood School because it was in current usage by many of those interviewed in the project, and because it avoids confusion with titles such as Community Schools and Village Colleges. In this respect, as throughout the book, this discussion of school differences is grounded in the CAP case studies.

The CAP school which occupies a position close to the Neighbourhood School end of the spectrum is Springdale. This school has a roll of 1130 with an annual intake of approximately 210 from two middle schools, one in the same township, the other close by. Strict zoning means in effect that many parents have no choice over the selection of secondary school for their offspring. By way of contrast Old Town Girls' school occupies a position at the opposite end. Old Town has a roll of 743 with an annual intake of 120 coming from some forty feeder schools across a wide swathe of the central area of the same county. Parents in this authority have a wide choice of secondary schools. In the case of Springdale the use of the label Neighbourhood School was not mine; several people associated with it saw it in a similar manner:

> Dave Ebbutt: You used the term neighbourhood school, what is it about a school that makes it a neighbourhood school?
>
> Teacher A: I don't know. This is definitely the school of this neighbourhood, and this neighbourhood is definitely the villages of Antheath, Flatwill, Clopton. Although Clopton isn't in our catchment any more, it's still considered to be . . . almost the community which uses Antheath as a market town. (S, 3)

Both the head of that school and one of its governors agreed in essence with this label, but made the distinction between Springdale as a Neighbourhood School, and a 'true' Neighbourhood School. A 'true' Neighbourhood School was seen by them as one where a 'whole patch identifies with the school', irrespective of the ability of the pupils. Daily bussing of pupils from outlying rural villages was seen as a factor which prevented Springdale being a *true* Neighbourhood School. Thus, while I choose to place Springdale close to the Neighbourhood School on the spectrum, it does not precisely represent the ideal type and is perhaps best described as 'neighbourhood-oriented'.

Interestingly, whilst the research at Springdale was in progress the boundaries of its catchment area were redrawn by the LEA. The result of this exercise was to divert pupils from one village middle school (not one of the villages mentioned in the preceding extract) away from Springdale. An LEA officer explained the lack of any parental criticism of this in terms of the village being situated 'on the other side of the hill'. The implication was that the hill forms a natural barrier such that the village in question is considered to be outside the historically and geographically accepted neighbour-hood of Springdale. On a far grander scale House (1974), focussing on the diffusion of educational innovation, shows how, in the United States, the spread of educational innovations tends to be obstructed or delayed by geographical barriers such as mountain ranges and major rivers. He maintains that innovations 'hop' from one centre of population to another along major highways or following river valleys.

I have so far suggested that the labels Neighbourhood and Extended Catchment merely refer to geographical (and perhaps historical) differences. Differences, that is, in terms of the size of the catchment from which the schools draw their pupils and the logistics of travel. On this definition alone almost all primary, junior or first schools are candidates for the label Neighbourhood Schools. However, I suggest that in the case of secondary schools this spatial/historical distinction is insufficient. This is because the spatial dimension is sustained through administrative arrange-ments made by the LEAs with respect to allocating pupils to schools. In the case of the Neighbourhood School this is achieved through LEA zoning. In contrast, pupils enter the Extended Catchment School as a result of parents exercising their choice.

I have already implied that *the number of feeder schools* is a useful dimension by which one can differentiate Neighbourhood and Extended Catchment Schools. The Neighbourhood School I have identified has two contributory middle schools. There are curric-ular consequences which flow from this simple observation. From within the Neighbourhood Secondary School, differing curricular experiences of pupils coming from each of the contributory schools are readily apparent to teaching staff. Consequently liaison and curriculum consultation (or lack of it) between the tiers of the system are major issues. By the same token pupils from the few feeder schools will have an expectation of the Neighbourhood School based on social interaction with past pupils. Such factors do not operate to the same degree in Extended Catchment Schools. In my example, liaison between the Extended Catchment School and its forty contributory schools necessarily becomes a bureaucratic exercise, largely mediated by officers of the LEA. Individual feeder schools, because of the vicissitudes of parental choice, may only contribute one pupil every three years or so to the Extended Catchment School. Consequently pupils' expectations, as a result of transmitted knowledge or information, will be minimal.

A further dimension along which contextual differences between the two schools are apparent is socio-economic. The Neighbourhood School in the project draws up to half its intake from agricultural village communities. (It might well be asked to what extent these separate village communities form a neighbourhood? As I stated earlier, Springdale is not a *true* Neighbourhood School and does not illustrate all the typical features.) Nevertheless there is a form of zoning so that no other state secondary school is in competition for these pupils.

An Education Welfare Officer remarked about some of the rural parents:

> . . . I find fathers who perhaps work on the land, who are lorry drivers [for farmers], admit that their schooling was not good in their day and age, and would like to see their child do better, but they don't seem to have the encouragement to make them come . . . there isn't the push there to make them come. (S, 3)

She went on to indicate how she found self employed parents, or parents working in industry, to be much more appreciative of the involvement of the EWO.

On the other hand the Extended Catchment School is situated in an area which just entitles its staff to the additional outer London allowance. The locale has a large number of service industries together with electronics, aerospace design and manufacturing and a polytechnic. Many parents in this school hold professional and managerial posts, and many also commute into central London. The parents of this school describe themselves (some coyly apologetic) as middle class, and to some extent see themselves as a self selected group. Said two parents who are also governors:

> . . . and this is where the whole business of accountability is so interesting at that school, because we know before we send our girls there exactly what sort of school they are going to, so it is as it were a self selected group – right? (OT, 6)

> Now whether that's to do with the fact that in a sense we are a
> self selected lot – we like the school we chose it. And by and
> large we go along with and we actively support what goes on in
> the school. (OT, 6)

It can be inferred from the last two quotations that the exercise of
free parental choice of school has resulted in the Extended
Catchment School being populated in the main by children of
middle class parents who travel from far across the middle of the
county.

Surprisingly Springdale, with its carefully drawn catchment
boundaries, nevertheless does not take in all the pupils from within
its catchment (another reason for denying it the label of a true
Neighbourhood School). There are within travelling distance of
Springdale four selective independent schools (another variety of
extended catchment school?) which were taking (by means of a
computerised selection procedure) some of the top 30 per cent of
the ability range who might otherwise have attended Springdale.
Furthermore, the very existence of these four schools allows other
middle class parents, unlucky in this lottery, to buy an alternative
education for their children. As one of the teachers in the
Neighbourhood School remarked:

> As it turns out – certainly the computer [computerised selec-
> tion procedure] doesn't remove the cream from us . . . I think
> that the middle/upper class cream may have gone. But we do
> have bright customers. Our biggest problem is trying to show
> the population that we are doing the right thing by these
> customers, and the mere fact that we don't get them in
> sufficient numbers in any one year group means that whereas
> the [Independent] School boasts its 16 to 20 to Oxford or
> Cambridge every year, we boast [about] one or two . . . (S, 3)

The irony of the two situations is that similar factors – concern by
largely middle class parents to obtain what they see as the best
education for their children – have helped to confirm Springdale in
its role as a Neighbourhood orientated school, whilst contributing
significantly to Old Town's continuation as an Extended Catchment School.

An important, possibly crucial, dimension underlying this
ascription of the terms Neighbourhood and Extended Catchment

school depends to some extent on whether or not a significant number of middle class parents exercise choice – either through the state system (OTGS) or outside it (Springdale) – choice, that is, which results in their selection of distant schools. I am not saying that Neighbourhood Schools are necessarily synonymous with working class schools, rather that a focus of articulate middle class parent-concern about education, outside the neighbourhood, has effects.

There is another dimension which further distinguishes between Neighbourhood and Extended Catchment schools. This is a psychological dimension which reflects a heightened identification between a Neighbourhood School and its environment and vice versa. Atkin (1979), writing about factors which have contributed to the accountability debate in the United States, catches something of the essence of what I have in mind:

> Sometimes education experts promote a change in educational policy that modifies community structure in ways that are seen by the public as destructive. In the 1960s, small secondary schools in remote areas all over the country were closed, and youngsters were sent by bus to nearby towns where new 'consolidated' schools had been built. The reasons supporting this shift, primarily, were those associated with economy of scale and an enriched set of educational offerings. High schools of 200 and 300 students were not in a position to offer the array of courses that would be possible in a school of 1000. Four secondary schools might be closed and one new one built.
>
> Again and again, however, there was marked deterioration of the small towns and villages in which the schools were closed. Americans understood poorly (and perhaps still understand poorly) the function of a school in sustaining a sense of community, but it seems that secondary schools particularly, through athletic contests and other events that lead them to be natural meeting places for people of all ages, provide a powerful cohesive element in American small towns. Everyone seems to identify in some profound sense with the school in a stable community. It is difficult to find adequate substitutes. When the school is closed, there often is a deep sense of loss.

I suggest that in England this psychological identification is perhaps less than in the United States, and is generated not so much from the school as a natural meeting place but out of the visibility of the Neighbourhood School. The table below examines the *informal* ways in which schools are visible to parents and prospective parents, and is based on material from *Accountability in the Middle Years of Schooling* (East Sussex EA, 1979) as well as data from CAP case studies.

Figure 1

Visibility of Schools to Parents and Prospective Parents through Incidental Information (no order of importance intended)

Staff and Head Teachers' dress, public behaviour and life style (entertainment, sport, consumer habits, etc.)
Teachers' control of children in public
The staff car park
Media reports of teacher union action
Comments of ancillaries
Comments of pupils and former pupils
Comments of other parents
Myths/folk tales regarding long serving teachers

Pupils Random observation of pupils travelling to and from school (their behaviour, uniform, etc.)
Random observation of pupils at bus stops, on buses
Comments of ancillaries
Comments of pupils and former pupils
Comments of shopkeepers, bank managers
Media coverage of school successes, e.g. Oxbridge
Exam results
Media coverage of school miscreants, e.g. court cases, probation, etc.
Gossip about pregnancies, drugs, etc.
Random observation of playground
Observation at sporting events
Observation of babysitters

Curriculum	Casual observation of children out of school: traffic surveys, mini field trips, community service, Work Experience Scheme
	Comments from parents, pupils, former pupils
	Media coverage of curriculum issues (e.g. standards)
	Involvement in local drama, music, fetes, etc.
Teaching	Pupil reports of classroom events
	Ancillaries' reports of classrooms (graffiti, discipline, etc.)
Individual Progress of Pupils	Random observation of pupil progress
	Inter-pupil comparisons
	Perception of pupil progress against own perception when pupil
	Inter-school comparisons

This list is not meant to be exclusive to either Neighbourhood Schools or Extended Catchment Schools. Nevertheless the proximity of the school to its neighbourhood makes the Neighbourhood School especially vulnerable to instant evaluation by parents or prospective parents based on incidental informal evidence, which is disseminated unmonitored. The corollary is that, with its more diffuse catchments, the Extended Catchment School's day to day business is relatively invisible to its consumers or potential consumers. Low social visibility means it is less exposed to instant evaluation based on such 'grapevine' information. Such relative invisibility means that the Extended Catchment School does not need to identify the neighbourhood as a psychological entity. Such evaluations as parents or prospective parents make are more likely to be on the basis of the school's planned, formal information flow. Audience evaluation of the Extended Catchment School is altogether more subject to control by the school itself.

The Neighbourhood School is visible to audiences other than those so far discussed. Within its immediate environment many, if not the majority, of ex-pupils are likely to find employment in favourable times. They are equally likely, as in the present economic climate, to find unemployment. Thus not only are the surface features of the process of schooling readily visible and thus prone to instant evaluation but so also are the products of that process; either by the community at large (passing the Post Office or other focal points where the young unemployed gather) or, more specifically, by employers. Such instant and identifiable 'product evaluation' would be virtually impossible for an Extended Catchment School.

Before turning to consider the accountability implications of what has been said, it is useful at this point to bear in mind one other point based on Atkin's comments and on Jennifer Nias' Highstones study. (Highstones is a rural school similar in many respects, in particular its neighbourhood orientation, to Springdale.) The idea is a simple one. It is that personnel of a school gain acceptance within a school, and presumably also within the neighbourhood, by their ability to 'fit in'. Jennifer Nias found 'fitting in' to be a key notion shared by faculty heads, the chairman of governors and others involved in interviewing candidates for teaching posts in her study school. It was an important notion behind employers' willingness to take part in work experience, for it enabled them to see whether potential employees would 'fit in' to the world of work. It was a phrase often used also by parents in talking about teachers:

> Parent: We want to know – do they fit in with the sort of school we should like to see? (H, 2A2)

> Governor: We look for people who are going to fit in. It would be no good to have a way out progressive for example *in this context*. It just wouldn't have been on. It's far better to have a competent person who is going to pay a lot of attention to standards and so on. (H, 3A7; my italics)

In the same study Jennifer Nias goes on to show how the head of that school demonstrated to prospective parents in three separate middle schools that he 'fitted in' and could be 'trusted'. He did this, she observes, by unconsciously varying his presentation to take account of each audience's special anxieties (H, 2B1).

Practical Implications for Accountability
I suggest that the accountability implications for a Neighbourhood School derive from:

    a. the existence and acceptance of the neighbourhood as a psychological entity

b. the school's proximity and visibility to instant evaluation by the neighbourhood

c. the expectation exerted by the neighbourhood that the school should 'fit in' with their values

The combined effect of these influences are such that they force the Neighbourhood School to recognise neighbourhood values: to attempt to achieve a tacit trade off between its own values and those of the neighbourhood before appointing staff or implementing change in the organisation, policy or curriculum, or, at least, to couch its accounts of such changes in terms of neighbourhood values.

Lest this idea of schools engaging in a trade off in order to fit in with neighbourhood values should seem too fanciful, the following examples will illustrate my point. The first is documented in my case study of Springdale (Chapter One) and describes how the performance of the play 'Epsom Downs' at the school caused a considerable stir in the neighbourhood. The play was mounted not by the school but by the theatre workshop (a community group). However, the producer was a Springdale teacher; Springdale's head was in overall charge; and there were several sixth-formers in the cast. It was staged in the main hall of the school. Advance press advertisements indicated that the play contained some 'adult' language, and that it might be unsuitable for young children. The play was presented uncensored, but not before the press had carried reports and unfavourable correspondence. Furthermore, a letter condemning the performance, bearing a score of signatures, had gone to the Chief Education Officer who subsequently intervened to mollify the situation. There were rumours of threats from sections of the neighbourhood to disrupt the performance, but these were not carried out. In this example I feel the school, or at least those connected with the play, failed in some respects to take into consideration, or accommodate to, the rather parochial values of a section of the neighbourhood.

By way of contrast, my second example comes from my case study of Old Town (OT, 4), the Extended Catchment School. An Olde Tyme Music Hall was staged under the auspices of the Parents' Association. Using the services of a local amateur company, the evening was jolly, with red-nosed comedians and *doubles entendres* abounding, and risqué songs. Girls from the junior part of the school acted as wine waitresses. Nobody turned a hair. Admittedly the audiences for the two events were different – open to the neighbourhood in the first example, restricted to parents and staff in the second. But this difference in audience is significant because it emphasises the point made earlier, that in a sense the Extended Catchment School has no need to conceive of its immediate neighbourhood either as a psychological entity or as a potential audience – and thus no need to worry unduly about conforming to neighbourhood values. The Olde Tyme Music Hall was catering for a self selecting, sophisticated, predominantly middle class audience. It was a restricted community of parents and staff whose support could be virtually guaranteed.

There is another closely related accountability implication. Not only are 'the products' and physical details of the Neighbourhood School open to instant evaluation, but so also are accounts rendered by the school open to immediate validation by the neighbourhood. Thus having 'fitted in' with neighbourhood values, the school must be constantly alert to work to maintain 'the trust' which flows from such accommodation. Not only has the neighbourhood got its finger on the pulse of the school, but the school must be able to monitor the pulse of the neighbourhood accurately. This may have implications for where the staff of a Neighbourhood School choose to live, because it would be something of a contradiction if most staff of a Neighbourhood School lived outside the neighbourhood. It also suggests that a Neighbourhood School risks losing any 'good reputation' it may have more rapidly than an Extended Catchment School.

The parent from the neighbourhood, sending his or her child to the Neighbourhood School is, in consumer terms, buying an educational package which at least in its superficial surface features is more open to inspection. Before transfer, arrangements exist between the CAP example of such a school and its contributory schools, for prospective entrants to spend a day at their new school. In contrast, the parent who considers sending his or her offspring to an Extended Catchment School is buying an educational package in which the surface features are far less apparent. These parents are able to evaluate the school from the head's address on 'shopping' days, and from prospectuses or Open Evenings for prospective parents. But by and large all these events fall into the category of formal information transmitted and controlled by the school. This is not to be so naive as to suggest that such parents do not have their own informal networks; indeed, John Elliott's Uplands study contains evidence of work contacts and baby sitters being used in this manner. What I am suggesting is that the networks within the neighbourhood are characterised by immediacy. The networks of parents and potential parents of the Extended Catchment School are based on a set of shared values which they regard as important. In the case of parents from the CAP Extended Catchment School these values derive from their own experiences as pupils. As Atkin (1979) remarks:

> Thus many Americans have seen positive features of their publicly-supported schools weakened. Often they are upset; they want to re-establish the kind of educational institutions they remember. Many aspects of the accountability movement can be interpreted reasonably as reflections of the desire to return to a familiar and more dependable past.

In the Old Town Girls' School case study (Chapter Seven), I wrote:

> What then are the values underpinning the ethos of the [Extended Catchment] school? I summarised [earlier] the Head's view that these are essentially Christian vocational ideals of service, care, trust, fair play and accessibility. Governors have variously used the terms 'thorough', 'christian', 'middle class', and 'enormously caring'.

A parent governor, documented in the same chapter, said:

> But I think the other thing one has to bear in mind – I think the end product of the school is something that parents like. They like the fact that children have this sense – they get this sense of the individual being important. I think that comes through very strongly. And they like the fact that by and large the children work and are worked very hard. And the work actually cashes out in terms of very good results. So on all three counts it seems to be a working school and a caring school.

The prospectus published by the Extended Catchment School contains half a page of curricular information, and staff are listed without academic qualifications. The document is nevertheless packed with detail of organisation and procedure. I suggest that the curriculum and its efficient staffing are in this instance implicitly accepted by the Extended Catchment School parents. The Neighbourhood School publishes in its prospectus two pages on the academic curriculum and five pages of staff names and academic qualifications (the Neighbourhood School has a larger staff to match its larger roll).

Whilst Old Town Girls' School is extremely diligent in fostering its relationships with parents, in essence many aspects of this Extended Catchment School are, relatively speaking, taken implicitly on trust, whereas the Neighbourhood School has to work hard to create and earn trust. It does this by explicitly and formally exposing its academic curriculum and the qualifications of its staff to inspection, in the hope of encouraging serious evaluation by the neighbourhood as an alternative to superficial instant evaluations made on the basis of informal information.

Another aspect of 'working to earn trust' is evidenced by a teacher in the Neighbourhood School who bemoaned the fact that the school staff failed to grasp the importance of being represented on such local bodies as Church Committees or the Rotary Club. This he saw as being instrumental in generating unchallenged criticism of the Neighbourhood School.

It would seem to me that the relative exposure of the two schools each week in the press is an indicator of the distinction between what is 'explicit, earning trust' and the 'implicit, taken on trust'.

The CAP Neighbourhood School operates in a steady glare of publicity, some of it supportive and some highly critical; it is being made to work to earn trust explicitly, whereas the Extended Catchment School is 'taken on trust' to such an extent that any press publicity has to be actively solicited by the school.

I did not talk at length with enough parents of the Neighbourhood School to be able to list their values. Certainly Hoggart (1955) in writing, perhaps over-romantically, about northern working class values catches some of the resonances of the EWO I quoted earlier:

> And there is the ability to keep on 'putting up with things', not simply from a passivity but because that is where one starts from, from the expectation that one will have to put up with a lot; and the maintenance of the traditional corollary of this, to put up with things cheerfully.

Jennifer Nias, in her Highstones study of a school very similar in some aspects of its rural catchment to Springdale, lists the following teacher qualities as being valued by parents in all walks of life: teachers 'being bothered', teachers 'being straight' and teachers 'fitting in'. Elsewhere she cites 'directness' and 'fairness'.

A clutch of accountability implications surrounds this example of the Neighbourhood School because it is in competition with Extended Catchment Independent Schools. This element of competition might well in the future affect 'true' Neighbourhood Schools with the 1980 Education Act and its provision for greater parental choice of school. Does the Neighbourhood School when faced with this problem give precedence to the values of the neighbourhood, and reflect these in its curriculum? Or does the school pay them lip service and adopt the values and curriculum of the Extended Catchment School? The risk for the Neighbourhood School is perhaps to fall into the trap of attempting to be all things to all men. This is currently exemplified within my example of a Neighbourhood School, where a popular and successful work experience scheme has been operating for six years and has attracted academically able children, possibly to the detriment of future numbers entering the sixth form. The question facing the staff and head is, should work experience be restricted to the less able, for whom it was originally introduced, in order to obviate the risk of prospective sixth-formers leaving early? This is a particularly important issue, because a large viable sixth form is seen by many in that area to be one of the characteristic indicators of the successful Extended Catchment School. Or should the head bow to the concerns regarding economic forces as they are interpreted from within the neighbourhood, and cater for these in the curriculum?

Ironically, in order to resolve this particular dilemma which has its local roots, as I have said, in the distinction between Neighbourhood and Extended Catchment Schools, the head has invoked the wider nationally articulated accountability issue, that of inducing schools to consider their accountability to industry. The CAP Extended Catchment School is by contrast only now considering the feasibility of a work experience scheme.

Talk of competition leads on to a consideration of falling rolls. The two schools' LEAs have reacted differently to this development. In one the LEA has, as I have already mentioned, redrawn the catchment boundaries in order to ensure a minimum intake to each of its existing schools. The overall result has been to ensure that the Neighbourhood School survives but becomes even more neighbourhood orientated. The other LEA, meanwhile, has decided upon a more *laissez-faire* policy. Here the market economy will operate, probably resulting in some schools having to close. It is conceivable particularly under this policy that what were once successful Neighbourhood Schools may evolve into Extended Catchment Schools and that the opposite could also occur. It would seem that some schools are attempting to preclude this. The 'Battle of the Glossy Brochures', as documented in Part 1 of John Elliott's case study, I take to be the evidence of this. Meanwhile the CAP Extended Catchment School is over-subscribed and is taking on extra staff.

Talk of competition between secondary schools for a falling population of school students presages the time (1982) when legislation in England and Wales will oblige schools to make their examination results publicly accessible. There are justifiable fears voiced from within the education service that this could lead to the publication of league tables of schools located in the same area, based on a single criterion of examination success. League tables of this nature would be blunt instruments indeed upon which to base decisions about schools. They fail to discriminate between schools doing an excellent job against the contextual current, from those which are doing a poor job swimming with it. I have attempted to show in this chapter how the priorities and practices of different types of school differ along a series of dimensions rather than on a single criterion. It is my contention that use of the descriptors Neighbourhood School and Extended Catchment School are useful in helping to encapsulate some of this detail and its consequences. I would further suggest that an understanding of the subtlety and complexity underlying these descriptors will provide a helpful perspective for parents, school staff, governors, administrators and elected representatives in forming the difficult decisions they will have to make about schools over the coming years.

I have attempted to summarise the discussion in Figure 2. I should emphasise that it needs to be seen as descriptive rather than prescriptive. Few state secondary schools will exactly fit the ideal-type polarity of each dimension. Nevertheless, consideration of where and with what implications individual schools are placed on the various dimensions should serve to generate fruitful discussion.

True Neighbourhood Secondary School Pole		Extended Catchment Secondary School Pole
Strictly delimited catchment	……	Diffuse/indeterminate catchment
No parental choice of school	……	Wide parental choice of school
Few contributory schools	……	Many contributory schools
Consultation/liaison with contributory schools	……	Little consultation with contributory schools
No 'bussing'	……	'Bussing'
Parents not predominantly middle class	……	Parents predominantly middle class
School psychologically identifies with locale (i.e. requirements to 'fit in', explicitly earn trust)	……	Little identification with locale (i.e. no need to 'fit in'; implicitly taken on trust)
Exposed to immediate surface evaluation	……	Surface evaluation controlled
Exposed to product evaluation by consumers	……	Product evaluation obscured

Figure 2.
The dimensions of the distinction between Neighbourhood Schools and Extended Catchment Schools

3

How do parents judge schools?

John Elliott

The new education act (1982) will make it obligatory for local authorities to publish the examination results of all their secondary schools, in a form which enables comparisons to be made between them. This legislation assumes that examination results are one of the most important indicators of the quality of a school, and provides the kind of information the consumers of edu-cation – parents – need as a basis for choosing one. But the evidence we have gathered of parental opinion in CAP schools suggests that a considerable number of parents value the *human qualities* of schools above their technological efficiency in maximis-ing examination success.

At Uplands I found that a number of teachers went along with the view that examination results rated high in parents' scale of priorities. Eventually I came to understand why. At an open evening I attended for parents out 'shopping for a school', question time was dominated by a parent who wanted to know about 'percentage pass rates' and those other two public indicators of quality, 'discipline' and 'uniform'. During coffee time I ap-proached this parent, who was closeted with a number of others at the back of the hall. Most in this group were leaving with a negative impression of the school, feeling that it gave insufficient priority to academic success (see U, 6). I left with the overwhelming con-viction that this parent represented the silent majority amongst the very large audience present at question time, and that the numbers on roll would fall even further next year than they had last year. In fact the school's intake increased considerably, in spite of its clearly articulated message that 'exams were not everything'. A question-naire for new parents, completed by representatives of 32 families a year after the open day/evening, revealed that this event was a major influence in helping them choose the school (see U, 9). Moreover, only a minority (19 per cent) cited 'good exam results' as a reason for choice, and less than half of these cited them as an important reason.

My observations and conversations with a small group of parents during that evening left me with a completely distorted impression of its impact and the spectrum of parental values represented in the audience. In the light of this experience I could understand how teachers' perceptions of parental values can become equally distorted. There is undoubtedly in any community a group of parents, varying perhaps in size, who stress *examination success*. They are always a very visible group, articulate at parents' evenings, forceful in individual approaches to teachers, prone to writing to the press and the local authority. Their high visibility gives teachers, administrators and the media the impression that they speak for parents generally. But in the light of our research in the CAP schools I would claim that every community has another, even sizeable, but more silent and less visible, group of parents.

These parents do not hold schools accountable against *product criteria* like examination results but against *process criteria* which pick out their capacities for human relations. Rather than adopting a *technological perspective* on schooling this invisible group of parents adopts a predominantly *humanistic* one. They are not unaware of the role played at parents' meetings by members of the more visible group. Moreover, they do not necessarily see members of this group as at all representative of parental attitudes to education. As one of them remarked:

> There is a vocal minority – I think it is a minority but you can't tell because the rest are not vocal – who have bright children, or think they have even if they haven't, because you can never be sure about your own children – who perhaps push for streaming for instance. . . . I don't think you would ever push for streaming if you felt your child would be in the bottom stream. (U, 8)

I shall use the CAP interview and questionnaire data to describe the cluster of concepts that parents who adopt a humanistic perspective tend to employ in making judgements about schools.

The key concepts

In his case study of Holbein School Rex Gibson comments:

> The yardstick by which they [parents] increasingly measure
> the school is the experience of their own children ('if he's
> happy, I'm happy').

He cites the following example from a parent interview:

> I came home with [another parent]. She was telling me about
> her [children]. They really hate it – so she doesn't like it – I
> couldn't say why – whether it's to do with a comparison with
> their previous school. I don't know. [This parent stressed her
> own child was happy at Holbein]. (HO, 2)

This theme of the child's *personal happiness* at school recurred
in other CAP case studies. David Bridges reported on the 'Classroom 79' event, organised by the PTA of Robert Peel Upper
School:

> The idea was that parents would be given the chance to find out
> something more about the school's approach to its main
> subject areas by actually participating in a lesson taught by one
> of the teachers.

At least one of the seventy parents attending was there to find out
more about a teacher her child hated.

> Mrs S.: There are two particular teachers, it's obviously a
> personality thing, he doesn't get on with them. One he does
> now, we ironed out the difficulties. The only way I could get to
> find out more about this particular teacher was to go – it was
> an excellent idea – they had the 'Classroom 79', that was
> marvellous, and in the two classes I chose to go to, I was really
> and truly trying to find out a little bit more about the teachers.
> Why does my son hate this particular man? I couldn't find any
> reason.

> David Bridges: But you felt it was a useful occasion for you to
> get to know these people a bit better anyway?

> Mrs S.: Yes, It was good in the other effect as well, the teaching
> point of view, to know exactly what's going on in the classroom

and how they are being taught. But I think, perhaps had it not been for this I might have chosen some other subjects.

If I would have taken an instant dislike to one of these two teachers, I might have been able to say 'Well that's it.' But 'no' it was nothing like this at all. I came back home and said 'What's wrong with the guy? He looks alright to me.' (RP, III2)

In my own initial interviews with Uplands' parents I was surprised by the extent to which some parents placed their children's personal happiness above academic success as measured by examination results:

. . . I think it's great if you can have a child who comes top in everything and wants to go on and do all these things, but to me it is much more important that they are happy at school. (Mrs Singleton; U, 8)

As they explained their objections to placing too much emphasis on examinations the parents often elaborated on the personal happiness theme by linking it with other concepts. Mrs Ryan, for example, associated happiness with children's personal and social development at school; their increasing capacity to communicate with others and thereby create satisfying personal and social relationships. Children became happy at school when it enabled them to engage in this kind of social learning, and for Mrs Ryan such learning was far more important than learning for exams.

. . . as Julius [her ex-husband who was also present] has said before, we are all going to have to rethink . . . I mean it is getting closer and closer, and we are going to have to stop it all – pitching ourselves forward to the cliff edge. Somebody has got to stop and say 'We have got it all wrong. We have got to have a different concept of what life is', and the thing that we want is communication . . . I mean you get a bloke who comes out of Cambridge and he can't talk to his mother or father – he can't relate or anything else. What good is he to anybody? So unless you get people who can relate, and who can laugh, and convey some kind of joy to their fellow men, you are not educating . . . parents need to be taught as well, that we can't waste education, this chance we have got of seeing what the solution is. (U, 8)

Mrs Ryan's comments suggest a reason why a significant group of middle class parents like herself give as much emphasis to their children's happiness at school and its *provision for their personal and social development* as to their success at examinations. (My own research at Uplands indicated that the humanistic outlook tended to be more widely shared by middle class than working class parents.) Such parents tend to be affluent, and the fathers particularly have 'got on'. Many of the Uplands fathers I interviewed occupy responsible managerial positions. Perhaps they had reached a vantage point from which they could understand that 'academic achievement', 'getting on', and 'material prosperity' did not necessarily bring personal happiness. Some may even feel they have paid a price for their 'achievements'. Such parents are not in romantic revolt against the competitive society and the 'rat race', but accept it and want their children to make their way in it; but not at the price of happiness. They do not despise examination success and the opportunities it brings, but they want schools to balance it against provision for personal and social development. During my research at Uplands I came to think that many parents interpreted the idea of 'the balanced curriculum' rather differently to teachers. It did not simply mean a balance of academic subjects, but rather a balance between the kind of academic knowledge assessed in examinations and socially useful knowledge. I was surprised by the number of Uplands parents who approved of the various 'integrated studies' schemes operating in the school. Could it be that they perceived integrated studies in terms of socially useful knowledge? Certainly Mrs Ryan did:

> I like the idea of it applied to the environment they [children] live in. It's all so reasonable and sensible.

Her view of worthwhile knowledge is perhaps echoed by this Holbein parent whom Rex Gibson interviewed:

> My criticism – and I make it of [the other school in the town] too – is that it's too geared to examinations and not enough to general knowledge. (HO, 2)

Some parents linked the 'personal happiness' theme with a view of learning as an enjoyable experience in its own right, and something which ought to continue throughout life. One parent, for example, argued that the publication of league tables of examination results would pressurise schools into stressing results to the exclusion of enjoyment, and thereby stifle any subsequent desire to learn after schooling was over:

> I think it can spoil the approach to education. I feel – perhaps I am not right, except that I would like all my children to receive some higher education – unless it is a reasonably enjoyable process, unless they find learning enjoyable, they will not wish to continue. And I have a horrible fear that if you start this result-chasing you turn the school – not into a crammer but in that direction – back to the old system of 'at the end of this year is the GCE. You will get your heads down. You will learn this that and the other thing. You will not look up or breathe or smile or do anything until you have learned that.' Obviously they have to pass exams – but I think it would be sad if the school became an exam passing machine. (Mr Bollinger; U, 8)

Mr Bollinger argued that the enjoyment of learning ought not to be sacrificed for the sake of maximising its utility for pupils on the job market. And in doing so he was aware that this is a difficult decision for teachers to take:

> I don't see how it could be otherwise if we get league tables of exam results, because I don't see how the school could fail to worry about getting the results home. In some ways it would be better – perhaps this is hard, I don't know – that a child failed his 'O' level at the first try and be sufficiently interested to go on into the sixth form to retake that 'O' level and get it without worrying about smashing 7–9 'O' levels through by the time they are 16, so that they can go out into the job market . . . (U, 8)

The idea of the *happy school* concerned about the *personal and social development* of its pupils is closely linked in many parents' minds with that of *the caring school*; in which the staff are more concerned about children as developing persons than their potential for maximising its examination results. It would be difficult indeed to imagine a school which catered for its pupils' personal and social development but showed little concern for them as individuals. Such concern would seem to be a necessary enabling condition for such development.

The image of Uplands School in its local community was largely constituted by the three qualities of 'children are happy there', 'it is concerned with children's personal and social development' and 'the teachers care about children as individuals'. Not all parents like this image. One I met described the school as 'trying to create a welfare state' (U, 6). She felt that the school had taken on responsibilities that properly belonged to parents, and she belonged to that highly visible group which emphasised exam results, streaming, traditional discipline and uniform. However, according to Raymond Large, a local primary school head, many of the parents who consulted him about their choice of secondary school were looking primarily for one which cared for the individual as a total person:

> . . . they are very concerned that their child is going to be an individual in the school – that they are not just going to have to go through as a total body. And that their particular child's strengths and weaknesses are going to be recognised and dealt with. (U, 7)

He also claimed that a school's examination record was rarely raised by the parents who came to him:

> . . . that doesn't usually come up as a topic.

> . . . certainly as an obvious subject for discussion it might be at the back of their minds.

Uplands established its 'caring' image when, as the first comprehensive school in the locality, it did not take many 'bright' children because they were 'creamed off' to the local grammar schools. However, this image remained long after all the local schools had gone comprehensive and the school had begun to take in the full spread of 'ability'. Recently falling rolls hit the area, and the staff at Uplands wondered whether the school's liberal, caring image would work against it in the parental choice stakes. But in spite of some wobbles the school is managing to sustain its numbers in this highly competitive situation. In order to do so it has had to attract the parents of children who are 'above average' academically. It seemed to be succeeding without compromising its original image overmuch. The parents I talked to felt that the school provided their children with adequate opportunity for examination success without losing its concern for them as individuals. We found that this value of 'concern for persons' lay at the heart of many parents' criticisms of schools they perceived to over-stress 'examinations':

> Some say – I don't mind – that it's more for the brighter children than the others. If you're okay at exams, you're okay, but if you're not they don't care so much – that's what some say I think. (HO, 2)

In her research at Highstones School Jennifer Nias discovered that:

> Parents are very sensitive as to whether or not teachers seem to 'be bothered about' their children. They frequently quoted to me instances from their previous experience of teachers 'who weren't bothered'. They made distinctions between individuals in this respect, and were appreciative of those who were 'bothered' . . . 'You can tell the ones to whom it's just a job . . .' (HI, 2A2)

Many of the instances of 'not being bothered' were cited by these parents in criticism of teachers who relate to pupils largely on the basis of their predicted performance in examinations:

> The teachers haven't given up. I'm afraid some of them at the last school had done that. They had decided that my lad wasn't in the top stream of anything, so he'd probably end up driving a tractor and they weren't going to bother to teach him anything but driving a tractor. I think this was their attitude. And they were very pleased if the children actually managed to get through their time in the school without breaking windows rather than teaching them anything. There is a complete transformation in his approach to work here. He is a lot happier and he has achieved a lot more.

It is interesting to note the way this parent links 'caring' with 'teaching' and 'learning'. It involves being concerned that pupils learn something 'worthwhile'. But the value of the learning is not to be measured exclusively in terms of its utility for passing examinations. Rather value resides in its significance for the personal development of the individual. 'Giving up' on teaching, on helping pupils to meet the challenge of real learning tasks in the classroom, is for many parents a sure sign that teachers are 'not bothered':

> If he's bored at school, the teachers aren't doing their job . . .
> They're not bothered about the in-betweeners. (HI, 2A2)

The link between 'caring' and 'learning' is clearly brought out in some of the indicators parents use to tell whether teachers are 'bothered' about their children. Jennifer Nias claims that the most common indicators are:

1 . . . the amount a teacher knew at an interview about an individual child

2 The concern for that child that they communicated by the way they spoke of him/her . . .

3 . . . their involvement in extra-curricular activities.

To this list I would add from my own case study research the following:

4 The amount of concrete diagnostic detail contained in written reports of children's performance. (U, 18)

5 'Telling the truth' about children's classroom performance and not 'glossing' over it (telling parents what you think they want to hear). (U, 18)

6 Making an effort to ensure that children make authentic choices in relation to option schemes. (U, 16)

7 Being prepared to consult a child's parents when he or she is having problems at school. (U, 16)

Many parents do not associate the *caring* and *happy* school with the school where pupils have an easy time. The humanistic ethos they value is not felt to be incompatible with hard work.

> I think it's a very good school where the pupils are *happy* and *hardworking*. (HO, 2)

From Old Town Girls' School, until recently a Grammar School with a good academic reputation, a parent and governor reported:

> They [parents] like the fact that the children have this sense – they get this sense of the individual being important. I think that comes through very strongly. And they like the fact by and large that the children are worked very hard. And the work actually cashes out in terms of very good results. So on all those three counts it seems to be a working school and a caring school. (OT, 7)

The concepts most frequently employed to link *caring* with *learning* were those of *stretching* and *pushing*. The humanistic aspect of these concepts was stressed by those parents who were careful to point out that in employing them they didn't mean 'bulldozing' children; forcing or compelling them to learn. Rather parents:

> . . . appeared to be referring to the provision of intellectually challenging tasks (stretch), and setting expectations which encouraged students to face rather than avoid such tasks (push). (U, 12)

Whereas 'compelling' removes responsibility for learning outcomes from the pupil to the teacher, 'stretching' and 'pushing' do not. They refer to *the process* of teaching and learning rather than its *outcome*. As I pointed out in the Uplands study this process orientation suggests:

> That many parents believe schools are responsible for the quality of the educational process rather than its outcome, i.e. what the child achieves as a result. The school can be blamed for not intellectually challenging a child but not always for a child's failure to meet such a challenge.

This view of what many parents hold a school accountable for was very much supported by one of Rex Gibson's findings at Holbein School:

> . . . it struck me forcibly that the parents seem to hold their children as responsible as they do the school ('he doesn't work as hard as he should', etc.). The longer the interviews went on,

the more the 'fairness' and 'understanding' of the parents – in
my judgement – was revealed to be. (HO, 2)

'Stretching' and 'pushing' can be regarded as part of the humanistic
ethic employed by many parents to evaluate schools. The use of
these concepts can carry the implication that teachers should not be
held totally accountable for 'results', since to do so is to dehumanise
the pupil's relationship to learning; viewing him or her as a passive
recipient of knowledge who cannot be held responsible for 'learning failure'.

These concepts were not only employed by parents of 'bright'
children:

> I just think they're not that *interested*. They just want the kid to
> come out and get a good job. They're not doing enough to *push*
> the kid. (U, 12)

This parent, like many others we talked to, quite explicitly links
'interest' or 'concern' with 'push' in the classroom. Those parents
who evaluate schools from a humanistic standpoint, with its focus
on the processes rather than the product of schooling, are con-
fronted with the problem of getting access to information about the
'secret garden' of the classroom:

> I think one would need a little more insight about what really
> happens in the working day of the teacher and the pupil, and
> quite frankly I must admit that was only raised because ever
> since our child has been there she has been bringing the
> homework home and working with cards and by the sound of it
> they always seem to work with cards in the classroom . . . it
> certainly raises doubt in your mind as to what type of teach-
> ing methods are used and are they adequate? (Mr Singleton;
> U, 15)

Many parents testified to the extent to which staff in the CAP
schools were able and willing to discuss their professional practices
with parents quite openly. This perceived capacity on the part of
the schools to engage in free and open discussion about educational
policies and processes was generally called *approachability*. The
term suggests a capacity for personal encounter, of being a person
within one's role rather than using that role as a defence against
inter-personal communication. In the context of teacher–parent

relations it refers to a capacity on the part of teachers for open and free discussion about their professional practices, and a relative absence of the kind of defensiveness which makes them resort to their 'professional expertise' as a protection against criticism.

> . . . the major impression I have is that the parents very typically think that Holbein is an *approachable* school – and that they would not feel hesitant about making contact with the school if they were concerned about their child's progress/behaviour/experience . . . nearly all parents seemed to feel that the school would take notice of their views . . . that they [parents] appeared to feel they had plenty of opportunity to make their views known . . . that parents felt that the school could be influenced. (HO, 2)

> John Dodd: I think Uplands' reputation comes from being fairly informative, and not only informative by putting out a lot of written information in the form of books, circulars, etc. They take time to say to parents 'OK, you want to choose a school, come in and have a look.' Now, yes, a lot of other schools do this, but I think that other schools . . . tend to do it with a certain amount of reticence. (U, 7)

Approachability as a concept picks out some of the elements in the CAP project's original notion of *responsive accountability*; the feasibility of which the project was established to explore. These elements might be summarised as:

a. a willingness to provide external audiences with information about professional policies and practices

b. a willingness to enter into a free and open discussion of this information

c. being open to changing and modifying policies and practices in the light of discussion

Although the concept of approachability differs from other evaluatory concepts I cited as elements within the humanistic perspective – picking out the quality of parent–teacher rather than teacher–pupil relations – it is not unconnected with them. If parents are to make sound judgements about educational processes in the light of such notions as 'personal happiness', 'enjoyment of lessons', 'care for individuals', 'opportunities for personal and social development', 'being stretched in the classroom', then they must have access to information about these processes and opportunities to discuss them with teachers. *Approachability* then is a condition of parents being able to make sound judgements about the *process* of schooling from a humanistic standpoint.

The school which distances itself from its parents by denying them access to the process of schooling renders itself vulnerable to political control, making its retreat behind a smokescreen of 'professional expertise' self-defeating. For the only way such a school can be made 'accountable' is via the publication of its quantifiable outputs (exam results); a mode of accountability which increases the possibility of political control over schools, and the deprofessionalisation of their staff.

The school which acquires a reputation for approachability amongst parents may be able to more easily resist current political pressures for schools to become 'examination factories', since parents have greater power to influence political decisions at the local level than the professionals.

In my list of humanistic concepts I have not so far mentioned *discipline*. Certainly all the CAP case studies cite it as a major consideration in parental assessments of schools. The Uplands case study (Chapter Twelve) in particular shows how parents can give the concept of discipline a humanistic interpretation, and can recognise other modes of ordering behaviour than the 'strict and disciplinarian' kind:

> The kids love it, they hate missing a day. The school is clean and bright. It smells good. I think the actual physical shape of it is quite good . . . and I like the atmosphere of freedom as opposed to Pilgrims' Rest which is strict and disciplinarian. Uplands is fairly free and they are flexible in their dress.
> (Third Year Parent)

> . . . it is a different kind of discipline. I couldn't honestly say if I went down there and just marched into the school that they have all got the same uniform on; but certainly I go in there and they seem to be quite smartly dressed. It's like most schools, they saunter along in the school you know, but you don't see too much rowdyism.
> (First Year Parent)

There is discipline, everybody argues about that with me, they say 'discipline is going down and down.' I always reply 'well if you have too much of everything that's not good.' Where you find too much discipline in a school you also find they have bigger problems. I always want to be in the middle you see. (Parent Governor)

Such parents acknowledge a form of discipline which, rather than over-riding the personal freedom and happiness of the child at school, arises out of it. They do not associate freedom with chaos.

How many parents employ these concepts?

Several of the CAP case studies testify to the existence of a significant number of parents who employ the cluster of concepts I have described in their judgements of schools.

Is this 'invisible' group larger for each school than the more obvious product-orientated group? The case studies provide few answers here. However, at Uplands I produced two questionnaires which provide a rough indication for one school where there is a free parental choice. The first was for parents who had chosen the school recently. I drew up a list of 'reasons for choice' based on comments parents made during my initial round of interviews. A sample of first year parents, one from each family represented at a 'new parents' evening', were asked to tick those items which they had considered in making their choice. They were also asked to rate the items they selected in order of importance. Those rated 1–3 and 4–6 I interpreted as very important and important reasons respectively. The size of the sample was small at 32, and probably skewed towards 'middle class' parents. At best the responses can only be indicative of a trend. They are summarised in Figure 1, and analysed in the following extract from the Uplands case study (Chapter Twelve).

The diagram shows that a large minority (28.5 per cent) cited 'the nearest school' as an important consideration, but only 12.5 per cent cited it amongst their 'top three' reasons for choice. This will surprise those who assume that most parents opt for 'convenience' rather than other considerations. However, one must remember that this questionnaire was completed at a formal evening for new parents, circumstances likely to attract more middle class than working class parents.

In Chapter 7 I suggested that working class parents tended to accept the advice of Primary Heads and send their children to the nearest school, and that positive choice would mainly be exercised by middle class parents. This would explain why only a small minority of respondents placed 'nearest school' amongst their top 3 reasons for choice.

'Our child wanted to go to the school' is revealed to be a *very important* reason for a large minority of parents (37.5 per cent). In fact it emerges as second in popularity within the 'top three' category. This result confirms an impression gained when interviewing existing middle class parents; that there is a substantial number of child-centred middle class parents in the Central Area community.

This diagram also reveals the extent to which 'opportunities for personal and social as well as academic development' (rated 1–3 by 28 per cent and 4–6 by 9 per cent) loom higher in respondents' scale of priorities in choosing a school than opportunities for exam success (rated 1–6 by 12 per cent) or the school's exam record (rated 1–6 by 9 per cent). The former consideration can be closely linked with 'provides a balanced, all-round education', the most popular consideration (rated 1–3 by 50 per cent and 4–6 by 19 per cent), and with 'the teachers care for children as individuals' (rated 1–3 by 12.5 per cent and 4–6 by 12.5 per cent) and 'the policy of teaching to mixed ability groups will benefit our child' (rated 1–3 by 12.5 per cent and 4–6 by 6 per cent).

'Children generally are happy at the school' (rated 1–3 by 22 per cent and 4–6 by 19 per cent) also emerged as a major reason for choice by a substantial number of respondents. A linked reason also frequently cited was 'new children enter a personal rather than impersonal atmosphere' (rated 1–3 by 19 per cent and 4–6 by 12.5 per cent).

A closer analysis of mothers' (15) and fathers' (17) reasons for choice revealed that one third of the mothers tended to rate 'children generally are happy here' amongst their 'top 3' reasons compared with about one eighth of the fathers. However, almost as many fathers as mothers cited this item as *a reason*. The questionnaire provided no evidence that this reason applied more to daughters than sons.

No difference in priorities between mothers and fathers was apparent with respect to 'opportunities for personal/social as well as academic development'. Interestingly more fathers did not, as I had anticipated, place 'good examination results' or 'opportunities to take exams' amongst the 'top 3'. In fact,

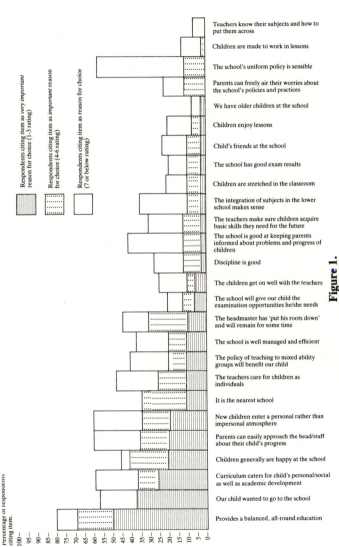

Figure 1.

Features considered by parents choosing Uplands school (sample: 32 first year parents)

although no differences in this respect were apparent, rather more mothers than fathers cited these reasons as *a reason*.

If any conclusion can be inferred from the questionnaire responses it is that there is, within the local community, a substantial number of middle class parents who place 'the development of the whole child, through an all-round education' and 'their child's personal happiness at school' above all other considerations when exercising choice. The liberal-progressive image of Uplands appears to match the educational values of a significant section of the local community. Such 'external support' could mean that the school does not have to change its ethos in order to survive in the market place.

If the original advocates of 'parental choice' intended it as a mechanism for bringing schools into line with a common set of community values, perhaps those which emphasise academic achievement, my interviews and the questionnaire responses suggest they may have seriously underestimated the extent to which value-pluralism exists in communities. However, it may well be that parents' value-priorities change as their children move up the secondary school age-range. From the standpoint of new parents, 'examinations' and 'employment prospects' are half a decade into the future. The 'New Education Act' in insisting that schools publish their examination results may have incorrectly assessed the kind of information many parents feel they need at the time of choice.

With respect to these last remarks I did in fact also circulate an inventory of statements to all fourth year (1980) parents, asking one from each family to complete it. Respondents were asked to place a tick beside each item, indicating whether they 'Strongly Agreed', 'Agreed', were 'Undecided', 'Disagreed' or 'Strongly Disagreed' with it. The response rate was 69 per cent (90 parents). Figure 2 summarises responses which are relevant to this discussion.

A large proportion of Uplands' parents appear to adopt a humanistic outlook on education. This may well be a consequence of thoroughgoing parental choice. When choice is restricted parents who share this outlook may get spread fairly thinly across schools. But the less the restrictions, the more concentrated they will become around certain schools rather than others; namely, those they perceive to match their values.

If this is so then one might expect more radical differences in

	Strongly Agree	Agree	Undecided	Disagree	Strongly Diagree
Children's personal and social development at school is at least as important as their academic development.	31	52	3	13	–
The most important thing about a school is whether the children are happy and enjoy their lessons	34	41	9	12	3
Schools should be judged according to their examination results	13	25	13	39	8

Figure 2.
Features considered important by Uplands parents (sample: 90 fourth-year parents, figures compiled as percentages)

ethos between schools in parental choice areas than between schools in restricted choice areas. The theory, that the 'liberal-progressive' school can be brought into line with the productivity ethic through competition in the educational market-place, is only sound if the vast majority of parents are mainly concerned about exam results. But when a significant number in an area balance 'results' against humanistic values, the 'liberal-progressive' ethos may flourish in certain schools. In fact I suspect parental choice can do more to safeguard this view of education than zoning polices which tacitly facilitate a reduction of parental influence and an increase in bureaucratic control over educational practices in schools.

4

Teacher-Parent Communication

Rex Gibson

Any school has three major ways of telling parents about its activities and beliefs: by inviting them to see what goes on, by talking with parents, and by writing to them. Most schools use all three methods and many, particularly at primary level, argue that it is through *involvement* and participation that parent-school relationships are most fruitfully developed. This chapter discusses only those written communications a school sends to all its parents. It is not concerned with pupils' reports or with correspondence about individual children; these are examined in Chapter Five. Rather, it confines itself to an examination of those booklets, brochures and newsletters which a school produces for all parents. It is therefore a study of how schools engage in (to use an unfortunately ambiguous term) mass communication.

Communications is one of those important-sounding words much in vogue. Marshall McLuhan wrote once fashionable books about it from which now only a few cliches remain; linguists such as Roman Jakobsen analyse it in ways impenetrable to laymen; in higher education it forms a distinct field of study; there exists a 'communication industry'. However, in spite of its apparent complexity there is a simple structure that underlies all communication: who tells what to whom, how, why, and with what effect? It is this deceptively simple six-point structure that will be used to analyse the written messages schools send to all parents.

1. Who?

'It's from the school' say the parents as the latest *Newsletter* or forty page *Sixth Form Booklet* is brought home by their child. But 'the school' is a convenient corporate fiction: the newsletter or booklet has been written by an individual or several individuals. Who actually writes what parents read? In many small schools the answer is straightforward: the headteacher. In large schools a variety of practices is to be found: a single individual, a team, a compiler of contributions from other teachers; invariably however the head retains responsibility for oversight, approval and usually signature, of each document.

Behind such an obvious and apparently trivial observation lie three important facts. First, that with the exceptions noted in section (4) below, whatever is communicated to parents is presented as a collective, corporate, school view, not an individual or sectional one; inter-staff disagreements have no place in such communications. Second, each document presents an image of the school to the parents, an image approved by the writer(s) and, by extension, all other members of the school staff. Third, that conscious choice is being exercised by someone over what to include and what to exclude.

2. What?

What do schools tell parents in writing? There is great variety of practice. Some schools tell a great deal, some very little. All six CAP schools provide much information for their parents. To take one example: at one school all parents of third year pupils could expect to receive, on a conservative estimate, communications totalling around 30,000 words during the course of the year.

It is useful to record what might be considered the minimum information that should be provided to all parents. In 1977 Shirley Williams, the then Secretary of State for Education and Science, set out the nature and extent of the information she considered should normally be available to parents in written form (in DES circular I5/77). Her recommendations were:

1. The name, address and telephone number of the school, the hours it is open and the dates of term times; the address and telephone number of the LEA and Divisional Education Office.

2. Characteristics: e.g. whether county or denominational, mixed or single sex, the age range covered and boarding provision, if any.

3. Names of the Head, and at least of the senior staff, and also the names and addresses of the Chairman of Governors and of any parent governors.

4. How parents should arrange to visit the school and the time at which the Head, senior staff members, class or subject teachers, year heads or pastoral tutors are normally available for consultation (bearing in mind the difficulties of working parents and the desirability of contact with the school for both parents).

5. Other arrangements to enable parents to be kept informed of their child's progress in school.

6. The number of pupils and the number normally admitted each year.

7. The basis on which places are normally allocated.

8. Arrangements for transfer between one stage of education and the next, including, where appropriate, details of the course options available in schools, tertiary or sixth form colleges, and in further education establishments.

9. Any special facilities offered in particular subjects or activities including facilities for careers advice.

10. Arrangements for religious education and for exemption from it.

11. (Secondary and upper schools only): Public examinations for which pupils are prepared, and the range of subjects and options available at the time when the information is issued, together with details of arrangements for consultation with parents on these matters.

12. A brief indication of the normal teaching organisation (including arrangements for teaching children of different abilities), of any special organisation or methods used, and of the school's policy on homework.

13. Clubs, societies, extra-curricular activities, including community service, normally available.

14. Organisation for pastoral care and discipline of pupils, including school rules and procedures.

15. Whether school uniform is required and if so the approximate cost, otherwise an indication of the type of clothing which is acceptable.

16. Whether any parents' or parent-teacher organisation exists, and if so the name and address of its secretary.

17. Local school transport arrangements.

18. The LEA's arrangements for the provision of free school meals.

19. The LEA's arrangements for the provision of free PE kit and the school clothing grants.

20. (Secondary and upper schools): The LEA's arrangements for the provision of educational maintenance allowances and discretionary awards.

Such a list is useful and apparently unexceptional. Regulations issued under the 1980 Education Act now make some items statutory requirements, but the amount of information the law demands to be published is small indeed, particularly that concerning governing bodies.

CAP evidence points to how greatly parents value written information about such matters as school uniform, bus times and school dinners. Parents wish to know the detail that will directly affect them and their children. One mother's remark about an 'Information for New Parents' booklet is typical:

> . . . you feel they want you to know about the place. 'Course you forget – I did read it all at the time and really the only thing I remember is things I wanted to know like school uniform – obviously the things I needed to know . . . Couldn't tell you about it now apart from those things, but I do know that I thought it was really good.

It is such practical, everyday matters that weigh heavily. They are not trivial but of great significance to almost all parents.

Usual practice in secondary schools is that such information as the DES advises is presented in booklets or brochures. One CAP school provides four brochures:

1. An introduction for Parents of Middle School Children (7 pages)

2. For New Parents and Students (21 pages)

3. Fourth Year Option Guide (14 pages)

4. The Sixth Form (39 pages)

In addition to such booklets, all the CAP schools issue newsletters several times per term or on a regular basis: fortnightly or even weekly. Newsletters contain a great miscellany of information about day-to-day school life; such topics include: Slide Evening, Can You Help?, Dates for Your Diary, County Hockey Honours, Reports, Meet Your Governors, Self Help, Charity Efforts, Public Examination Results, Road Safety. . . . The list, over a year, is very long.

There is a very wide range of opinion among teachers over what should be included in written information provided for all parents. Three items not mentioned in the DES list are worth remarking upon.

First: aims. It is a difficult exercise to convey to parents, pithily and in a non-banal way, what the aims of the school are. Lists that teachers draw up for themselves might sometimes seem inappropriate when committed to print. It is interesting that some schools which produce extensive brochures for parents do not specifically state their aims in a separate section. It would seem sensible to recommend that all schools should give thought to the question of how desirable and practical it is to include 'school aims' in their documents for parents.

Second: examination results. Project schools vary in the amount of information they provide to all parents about examination results. All give some information; at least one gives a complete breakdown by subjects and grades for both CSE and 'O' level. From 1982, legislation will compel all schools to make results available.

Third: rewards. Most schools make clear their expectations for behaviour in their written documents. Many set out details of their pastoral care and discipline organisation. One of the CAP schools lists its nine disciplinary measures (from 'setting of extra work' to 'suspension from school'). However, specific reference to 're-wards' is rare. Certainly, it is invariably easier to compile a list of a school's punishments. It is therefore well worth considering whether parents could not be more fully informed as to the manner in which a school rewards its pupils.

3. To Whom?

This might seem an unnecessary question. The answer is obvious: the parents. However, the question is well worth asking because it serves as a reminder that parents (like teachers) are not a homogeneous group. 'The parents' is as much a convenient and necessary fiction as 'the school' or 'the pupils'. Such labels conceal a diversity and richness of human qualities that defy aggregation. The only certain thing 'the parents' do have in common is that they have children who attend this school. Given that, each parent is unique; many may share expectations, perceptions, purposes, values; but it is certain that some will not. Awareness of such heterogeneity makes the task of addressing all parents difficult and demanding. It also reveals the danger of regarding parental contact simply as mass communication: the parents are never a 'mass'. Encouragingly, what the following sections show is that it is possible to succeed remarkably well in this potentially fraught enterprise.

4. How?

How does a school communicate with its parents? One obvious answer is that in every case the children take the documents home. But the 'How?' question raises much more subtle and important issues than this (although it should be recorded that some teachers are sceptical about how many children do actually deliver news-letters to their parents – a problem some schools resolve by including a tear-off reply/acknowledgement slip and the collection of these slips by form tutors).

Each of the CAP schools gives close attention to the presentation of its booklets and newsletters. Some have their booklets printed, others use offset litho or duplicating machine stencils. For news-letters the offset litho or stencil is employed. There is a very high quality of presentation: layout is attractive, letters and pictures clear cut, grammar and spelling impeccable. Whatever the mode of reproduction, the document received by the parent represents a model of what the school stands for and expects (see the many examples in Gibson 1980). Many of the resonances of McLuhan's deeply ambiguous 'the medium is the message' can be detected in these documents. Thus certain major assumptions underlying a particular school's approach to education often can be revealed by a consideration of the language, tone and style of its written communications.

The language of parental documents is a matter of concern for many teachers: 'Do they really understand what we write?' The answer to that frequently asked question, as will be shown in Section 6 below, is 'generally, yes'. Teachers nevertheless are much concerned whether some of the documents, particularly those relating to curriculum, go 'over the heads' of many parents. This concern is both genuine and realistic: how do you get over to all parents the curriculum structure of the school or something of the essence of Physics or Integrated Science? Such topics after all are not usually part of the everyday conversation of most homes, offices or factory floors. How can jargon be avoided and how can (say) curriculum choice be meaningfully presented? The success of the CAP schools is due to very conscious appreciation of the problem and a policy of keeping documents constantly under review, and a concern to ensure that written documents fit within a wider context of parent-teacher communications: meetings, visits, reports evenings and other events. The context of the written document is all important and no school relies solely on the written word but provides many opportunities for teachers and parents to meet face-to-face.

Style and tone are aspects of language that help to influence how a message is received. Immediately obvious in speech, they are no less present in writing, particularly when, as in newsletters, a steady flow proceeds from school to home over the year. Thus the ethos of every school is subtly reflected in the written documents provided for parents.

There is not room here to detail with accuracy how such differences are reflected in each school's booklets and newsletters.

What will be attempted is to sketch some of the common characteristics of the documents of all six CAP schools.

First, there is a friendly, welcoming tone:

> I am writing this letter on behalf of all the staff, to welcome you
> and your daughter to –.

> We look forward very much to getting to know you and to
> working with you in the years ahead.

> Welcome!

Second, a human, personal voice comes through, particularly in
newsletters and in heads' letters introducing the various major
documents. This is evidenced in a number of ways: for example, by
signing first name in addition to surname; by the occasional aside:

> We had another scramble to get ready for opening, but once
> again we managed to move all the furniture in time. It is
> rumoured that the idea is to retrain redundant headmasters as
> removal men!

And by direct acknowledgement of individuality:

> Whatever the need we try to meet it. . . . We are attempting to
> make the school fit the individual rather than force everyone
> into the same mould.

Although newsletters necessarily begin 'Dear Parents' (they
may go to over a thousand homes), it is clear that there is a concern
to establish direct, friendly contact, to acknowledge the unique-
ness of each parent and each pupil, and to show that teachers, too,
are human. One head signs, 'I look forward to meeting you
personally'.

Third, each school attempts to ensure that, as far as possible,
everyday, rather than technical, language characterises its documents. One school rewrote its introduction to curriculum choice
for the fourth and fifth years leaving out earlier reference to 'faculty
structure' as it felt that this hindered, rather than helped, parental
understanding. In the same school the Head of English periodically
carries out readability tests on parental documents.

Fourth, there is an enthusiasm, a vivacity and a feeling of

excitement in the documents. The implicit (sometimes explicit) message is that not only is the school an interesting, stimulating and lively place for pupils, but also that as parents become involved in school activities they too will find it both enriching to themselves and helpful to their children's education. The invitation for parents to participate in extra-curricular activities are legion: Summer Fayres, barbecues, open evenings, carol services, curriculum subject evenings, sales, careers conventions, slide shows, Caribbean evenings . . .

It could be said that the tone is one of sociability, of togetherness. The schools assert that they regard education as a joint enterprise, that success can only come through the cooperation of home and school. This concern to build and sustain a community is evidenced in the style of many of the documents.

Fifth, there is an underlying courtesy. Such concern for the dignity of others comes through in many ways, particularly in the very full and professional presentation of information on aspects of school life, and through a stated willingness to listen to individual parents.

Sixth, there is a strong tone of authority. Not authoritarianism, it must be stressed, because the invitation to discuss and the willingness to accommodate to children's needs is always present. Rather, it is authority in the sense that a very strong feeling comes through that the school knows what it is about. Extensive descriptions of curriculum, pastoral care and organisation convey an air of confidence and assurance. The documents unequivocally imply that the teachers know their job and, with the cooperation of parents, can successfully educate their children. In addition to curriculum expertise, such authority is often reflected in a directness of style that lays clear the school's expectations for pupils' conduct.

This analysis of written documents could be extended much further and with profit by readers of this book. A comparison of a number of schools' material will quickly suggest many additional dimensions: is the language plain rather than elegant? crisp rather than curt? formal or informal? cheerful? hectoring? (see Green, 1975), serious, solemn or with humour? succinct or prolix? and a host of others. Although the CAP schools have certain characteristics in common, nonetheless each school has a distinctive quality of voice and on every dimension there are subtle differences of emphasis. But, however they do it, each CAP school sets out its expectations in a way that is neither condescending nor authoritarian.

5. Why?

The question is crucial: why do some schools invest so much time, energy and resources in providing written information for parents? From the wide variety of explanations advanced, three major theories may be identified: Competition, Control and Commonsense.

Competition theories view the parent-teacher communication exercise basically as competition for scarce resources, whether these are materials, cash or children. Thus booklets are referred to as 'glossies' and communication is seen principally to be about 'image building', 'a PR exercise'. The motives attributed are those of personal or institutional self-interest; a school gains a good reputation in a community and in the LEA so that, at times of falling rolls and economic recession, its survival, and the security of its staff, is assured. Usually, the unstated inference of these theories is that there is little or no match between image and reality.

Control theories view the exercise as one of control by mystification, by overloading or by distraction. Such theories are usually propagated by theorists who have little contact with teachers, children or a wide range of parents. Control by mystification implies that communication is 'blinding with science': language is used so as to obscure what are held to be fundamental realities of knowledge, social structure or social relations. Control by overloading asserts that parents have so much information pumped at them that they are incapable of making rational judgements or seeing the 'true' state of things (advocates of these theories always put inverted commas around the word, true). Control by distraction was identified by Shakespeare's Bolingbroke: 'busy giddy minds with foreign quarrels'. It argues that leaders with something to hide should focus the attention and resentment of subordinates on trivial, peripheral or external matters or groups. Thus the misled underlings will never protest about, or even recognise, what is really important to them. These theories are even more firmly based on interest theory, on false consciousness and the absence of goodwill in human conduct.

Commonsense theories arise from three beliefs: first, that the parents have a right to know what goes on in the schools that their children attend; second, that such knowledge makes for good relationships between parents and teachers; and third, that good communications will result in improvement in pupils' learning and attitudes. Further, such theories are based on the assumption that there is a fairly close match between what is described in the documents and what actually goes on in school. Unlike the two previous theories, there is the assumption that what is obvious is also true.

Why people act as they do is usually a consequence of mixed motives. It is rare indeed for human behaviour to have one single simple cause or explanation. The project has found a great deal of evidence to support commonsense theories (see, in all six case studies, the teachers' and parents' views); a certain amount to support competition theories (see particularly U, Pt. 1) and little or no evidence for control theories.

6. With what effect?

Does it work? Do the written documents do what the schools intend? What needs stressing again is that all schools see their written documents only as one of many channels of communication with parents. They insist that their effectiveness should be judged in conjunction with the visits, parents' evenings and other meetings that necessarily complement the documents.

When considering the effectiveness of teacher–parent communication three fundamental questions arise. First, do the documents result in greater parental understanding? Second, do they improve relationships between home and school? Third, do they result in improvement in pupils' learning?

On the first question, the CAP evidence is very encouraging. The newsletters and booklets are not only welcomed, but closely read by parents. Teachers' fears about parents not understanding because of language difficulties seem ill-founded. The conversational, informative style of newsletters appears to work very well: parents genuinely are kept in the picture and have few difficulties in understanding what is going on. There is a similarly encouraging finding concerning the first booklet issued by schools, typically called 'Information for New Parents'. When schools make the twenty DES recommendations (given above) the basis for their introductory booklet and present them in their own individual style, then parents can and do understand the result.

Curriculum documents issued by schools to guide option choices for the last two years of secondary education and for the sixth form present greater problems for parents. These substantial documents present complex and often unfamiliar information.

In CAP interviews, parents stressed how necessary it was to talk with their children and with teachers in order to grasp the full implications of what they read. Thus, a fairly typical comment was:

I was clear when we went to the school. We saw the Deputy Head and chatting to him we got it. Reading that [the booklet] was difficult but it was sorted out by the time we had to choose.

All the schools see discussion as vital; no school considers its documents sufficient. Curriculum documents in particular are designed to facilitate individual choice and, to this end, each school arranges and encourages meetings as an integral part of that process.

There is encouraging evidence too on the second question: are home-school relationships improved by written documents? Although an occasional parent complained of the sheer amount of information ('you could be reading *War and Peace*!') it was obvious that parents appreciated the schools' efforts to keep them informed and involved. There is little doubt that goodwill towards the schools was increased by the booklets, which informed parents of the schools' expectations and intentions, and by the newsletters, which kept up a running commentary on progress and which sought to involve the parents in activities. In the great majority of cases a climate of trust was created. Such goodwill was not the result of a public relations exercise, but also of parents coming to recognise that the image presented in the documents matched the realities of school life. Documents are one of the vital means by which teacher–parent contact is established and maintained; the knowledge parents thus acquire undoubtedly makes for good relationships. This CAP finding receives support from the 'Accountability in the Middle years of Schooling' project (East Sussex, 1979). The explanation seems fairly straightforward: people like to know what is expected, what is going on, and how they can be involved in decisions that affect their lives. The written documents help to fulfil just those functions.

The third question – does teacher–parent communication result in improvement in children's education? – is one that professional researchers usually assert to be impossible to answer. There are simply too many variables to take into account. Certainly, the project cannot produce unequivocal evidence. However, it can report that such a belief is very widely held by teachers and parents. The six schools do what they do because they believe it will result in better education for each pupil; parents think that the documents help them to help their children.

It seems very likely therefore that as parental support and encouragement is a major factor in pupils' achievement, and as parents much value being kept informed and involved by schools, then good parent–teacher communication of the type discussed in this chapter is a vital contributory element in children's learning.

5

Written reports on pupils' progress

Dave Ebbutt

This chapter examines issues surrounding written reports of pupil progress (subsequently referred to simply as reports) from two perspectives. From the point of view, first, of the teachers who write them and, second, of the parents who receive them. A detailed consideration and analysis of reports, as opposed to the process of reporting, was felt by most of the team to be outside the project's brief. However, precise details of the format of reports adopted by one CAP school are given in Rex Gibson's *Teacher–Parent Communication* (1980, pp. 125–8, p. 133).

What is clear, however, with respect to the format of reports, is that the CAP schools which have been established for some time (two were brand new) have either moved away from, or are currently in the process of rejecting, those older types of single sheet reports. The trend appears to be towards allowing more space for teachers' written comments and a consequent reduction of codified methods of presenting information. As a teacher explains:

> The idea at the beginning was to cut down the space for rude comments and merely describe the child's achievements with 3, 3, b or 4, 3, c or something. The area allowed for personal comment is relatively small – we have increased that enormously . . . (U, 18)

At least two of our schools encouraged parents to make written responses to reports. In one school, comments from parents which are critical of the report are displayed on the staff notice board and subsequently discussed at staff meetings. None of our schools used student self reports.

Change of this nature was being recommended by, Green and Marland (1970), Marland (1974) and the Association of Assistant Mistresses (1976). It is interesting to note that in one CAP school the stimulus towards such changes in format was not directly attributable to any of these, but was provided by an article in a subject association journal (Honeyford 1974) and by an article in a Sunday newspaper (McGrath 1974).

The trend towards giving more space to teachers' comments is not entirely without problems for CAP schools. One aspect of reporting which is important to teachers is the amount of time taken up writing comments. The Old Town Girls' study roughly quantifies the effort involves. Such a representation reveals clearly where in the school year the burden of reporting writing falls. Each year group on this chart comprises up to 120 pupils.

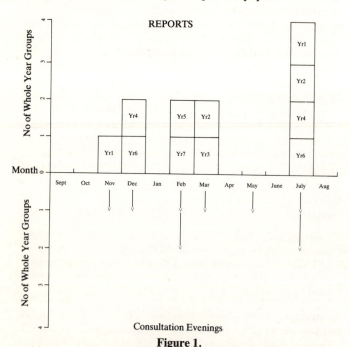

Figure 1.

The annual pattern of reports and consultation evenings in one school (adapted from OT, 1)

Consultation evenings are included in figure 1 because our studies reveal that reports are not considered sufficient in themselves either by teachers or by parents, but are rather seen as integral to the process of examination, reporting and consultation – the report often forming the basis of discussion at consultation evenings. Watts in a survey quoted by Goacher & Weindling (1978) emphasises the relationship between reports and consultation evenings.

A teacher who had assumed some responsibility for aspects of reporting on pupil progress in one of the CAP schools was concerned about the quality of comments written by teachers. The teacher felt that these should be the constituents of a quality comment which the parent audience required and deserved:

1. meaningfulness or pertinence

2. constructiveness

3. reference to some specific skill or attribute

4. advice: spiky and provocative

5. comprehensibility

He gave the following as an example of a quality comment:

X works quite hard at this subject in class, but his essays are vague and badly planned. He must get used to preparing essays before he writes them, and he must stick to the subject and not digress. His homework is obviously done hastily, and all his work is untidy.

Another teacher in the same school gave the characteristics of non-quality comment as:

a. woolly

b. pretty meaningless

c. waffly

A third teacher added:

d. platitudinous

The following example of a non-quality comment was given:

> X has made satisfactory progress in this subject during the year. There are one or two areas of weakness, but if he works at these, and puts in more effort, he should do himself justice in the forthcoming examinations. (S, 2)

Marland (op cit), addressing the same issue, which he terms 'helpful' rather than 'quality' comment, was able to note as late as 1974 some bizarre examples. He wrote:

> If you compare, say, two actual fourth form reports in art, there is little doubt which is the most helpful:
>
> > Angela works well.
>
> > Vicky's textures are good, but her proportions need care.

Bearing in mind the reporting load borne by teachers during July, as shown on the preceding chart, one cannot help wondering where the time for the consistent writing of quality comments is to come from. From teaching time? From preparation time? From time set aside for marking? From leisure time?

One of the case studies reveals two ambiguities that some teachers sense about writing reports. One teacher, when asked what the purpose of reports was, said that they were:

> Teacher: Making the school seem human to the recipients of the reports.
>
> Dave Ebbutt: Whom you see as being?
>
> T.: I'm not quite sure whether it's the parents, with the girls as interested spectators – I call them 'she', so I think it must be the parents.
>
> D.E.: But is there a little doubt in your mind that it might not be the parents? Could be a multiple audience?
>
> T.: Yes it could be, because you put things like 'Jane has done very well at improving her punctuation'; that's not entirely directed to parents is it? (OT, 2)

The ambiguity hinted at here is, I believe, a genuine one shared by many teachers. It concerns the question of the audience for the report. If teachers conceive of reports as in some way contributing to the motivation of pupils, then the problems inherent in using a single comment to serve the interests of a multiple audience – parents and pupils – are bound to surface. As I noted earlier, quality comments are characteristically for one audience only – the parents.

A perennial problem, that of the ambiguity and possible mis-interpretation of written comments, was raised by a teacher in the same school who said:

> . . . because this report situation is not ideal, one report can be said in five different ways. (OT, 2)

Other teachers recounted anecdotes about how written comments had been misinterpreted by parents, but they saw this problem as being one that could be resolved during subsequent consultation evenings. In response to the question, 'how do you feel about these consultation evenings?' another teacher said:

> I feel they are very important too. It's much better to talk to somebody because even the inflection of your voice. . . . It's very difficult to write a report which is perfect on a girl. (OT, 2)

Woods (1979) takes the analysis of the ambiguity of teacher comments much further than this chapter does. He presents a provocative sociological account which depends in its barest essentials on the notion that teachers' views, as expressed in reports, are passed through 'a filter or smokescreen' which inten-tionally obscures their real views. This, he maintains, occurs because reports are not written solely for parents, but also for colleagues. Reports are passed from teacher to teacher during the process of completion. More importantly, however, they are also written for the head or deputies who monitor all reports before adding their own comment or signature. I referred to this process in one of the case studies as 'quality control'; Woods maintains that it has wider effects. This smokescreen, in his view, contributes to miscommunication, and he illustrates his point with the following table:

Report given	Possible preferred report by teacher	Possible parental interpretation
Quite fair	Plain and undistinguished	Good
Needs to work hard Finds the subject difficult	Unintelligent and/or lacks other necessary personal qualities	The subject is difficult
Easily distracted Lacks concentration	Prefers the pointless, unproductive, dislocating mucking about with peers, to listening to my pearls of wisdom	Is misled by others in class
Well-mannered	Is no trouble (often academically weak)	Good

Although superficially persuasive I find this argument unsatisfactory in that it regards reports as an end in themselves. As our case studies show, they are generally regarded both by teachers and by parents as only part of a more complete process of examination–report–consultation. (Goacher and Weindling, op cit; and AAM op cit).

The case studies contain more information about how reports are received by parents than they do about teachers' thinking on reports. Some of this information was gathered by interviewing parents, but it was also collected from questionnaires. The tables below give the questionnaire results from four of the six schools. (Each table represents a different school.)

Several noteworthy points emerge. First it is refreshing to note the high percentages of parents who find reports from CAP schools contain about the right amount of information. But a more interesting exercise is to focus on that minority which felt there was too little information. What sort of information do these parents require? Over 90 per cent of parents in each of the schools above said that reports are written in a way that is easy to understand so that comprehensibility is not really a factor in this analysis.

Do you think the reports give:	Too much information?	Too little information?	About the right amount?	Total
Third year reports	0	10 (16%)	54 (84%)	64 (100%)
Fourth year reports	0	12 (23%)	40 (77%)	52 (100%)
Fifth year reports	0	6 (30%)	14 (70%)	20 (100%)
First year reports	1 (2%)	12 (24%)	36 (74%)	49 (100%)
Second year reports	0	14 (37%)	24 (63%)	38 (100%)
Third year reports	1 (2%)	16 (37%)	27 (61%)	44 (100%)
Fourth year reports	0	6 (38%)	10 (62%)	16 (100%)

In the fourth school a different form of questionnaire was used:

'Written reports on children give a clear indication of their progress':	Undecided	Disagree	Agree	Percentage responses
Fourth year	8%	15%	75%	98%*

*2% made no response

David Bridges, in his case study, encounters the same issue in interviews rather than in a questionnaire, and he locates a group of parents who were:

> *not getting as much information as they would really have liked about their particular child and his or her progress* (his emphasis)

He then goes on to summarise interview evidence, showing what it is about reports that these parents found unsatisfactory:

> . . .the lack of information in school reports of a kind which allowed parents to judge not only how pupils were progressing relative to their own previous standards, but how they stood in comparison with other children in their year. (RP, 2)

More interview evidence pointing to the nature of parental dis-satisfaction occurs in other case studies. Says a parent:

> . . . we get a report back which tells us an attainment level and an effort level 'above average', 'average', 'below average'. It doesn't give a parent any idea – now a parent wants to know out of 150 children, where the child actually is.

The interviewer attempted to put a counter argument:

> John Elliott: If you are 149th it's a bit difficult for the child to cope with.

> Same parent: Yes, but realism comes into it for the parents, and we want to know. Not to be assured that he's 'average' or 'above average' etc., and then find in the fifth year that his standard is not up to GCE. (U, 18)

In a different school a parent said:

> Z says they [the teachers] say, 'we always give a good report to start off'. Well that's silly. It can make *them* big headed. There was a lot there, that they could have said they didn't. It's like patting them on the head. (HO, 2)

This last extract, and indeed the implicit message in the inter-viewer's intervention above, raises yet again the point made earlier: who is the report for? Clearly there are two audiences implied for the report about Z referred to above. These comments reveal much more than a confusion over the reader audience. Underlying such comments is a fundamental misunderstanding about the purpose or function of reports. The Association of Assistant Mistresses (op cit) recommended that:

> School reports should endeavour to assess and record the pupil's general and social development and her participation in school life as well as her academic progress.

The comments above are requests for more contextual detail about the level of the learning group in which the pupil is taught, and about the level, or change in level, of the pupil within that group. Such requests are revealing, but perhaps not so surprising. Both teachers and pupils are immersed in the institution and familiar with this contextual detail, to the extent perhaps of overlooking any necessity to explain the nuances of the system to parents. It appears then that a minority of parents in CAP schools would like to see 'contextual detail' added to the criteria for quality comments.

There is a nice accountability issue here, about how much to tell. To the professional educator, contextual detail of the nature required by these parents has implications of rank ordering of pupils. In turn this raises the admittedly unproven spectre of the self-fulfilling prophecy. Should the professional teacher communicate to the lay parent that the school cannot furnish the sort of information required because it ascribes to a 'theory' which is largely unproven? If so how might such communication be achieved? Rank ordering of pupils within a mixed ability group is clearly inappropriate, and yet the advantages and disadvantages of mixed ability grouping remains a matter of debate within the profession. The same questions arise. Should the professionals communicate these issues to anxious lay parents? How best could this be achieved? The issue turns, it seems to me, on the degree to which the professionals feel accountable to lay parents, and on the nature of that accountability. This will be explored more fully later where the implications of the distinction between *giving an account* and *being held to account* are examined. Answers to the questions I have just raised will differ according to which form of accountability operates within the school.

Possibly such explanations are best imparted during the private face to face encounters of consultation evenings, as one teacher describes:

> Teacher: . . . a parent comes and says 'Look you have put this comment on my daughter's report. Why is this? Back up your statement.' Then I will expect to produce that girl's book alongside X number of other girls' books to show the comparison and explain exactly what I mean.
>
> Dave Ebbutt: Is that interference?
>
> Teacher: No. I think that's the legitimate right of a parent to wish to know more about what you have said about his child. (OT, 2)

A continuing concern of parents which we encountered in our interviews was a feeling that CSE was inferior as a qualification to GCE. Such parents found it hard to reconcile a series of glowing comments on past reports in a subject upon discovering, with some dismay, that their child in the fourth year had been embarked on a CSE course. Many of the requests for more information, which I have perhaps euphemistically referred to as a desire for contextual detail, are essentially a wish to be forewarned of this particular shock.

John Elliott, in his Uplands study, argues that working-class parents appear to be disadvantaged by the existing system of reporting:

> The lack of 'social confidence' expressed by many [of the working class parents] will make them reluctant to clarify the meaning of these reports [consultation evenings]. . . . The middle class parents may be less diffident in their approach to staff.

Be that as it may Jennifer Nias, in her case study, nicely catches the dilemma some parents feel with respect to reports:

> Many [parents] are unsure of how to measure progress ('she seems to be getting on OK, but how can we really tell?'). So they carefully study reports and many look at comments made on homework books.

There is another, minor, aspect of the 'too little information' problem, and that concerns the frequency with which reports are issued or, more accurately, the time which elapses between the receipt of two consecutive reports. In one of our schools the third year report is received in early May, whilst the report on the same pupil's fourth year achievements is not received by parents until mid July the following year: a gap of almost fifteen months (see also Goacher & Weindling, op cit).

Reports are unique in that they are the only documents which regularly come from the school addressed to parents which specifically focus on their own individual child (an exceptional case might be letters of a disciplinary nature). They are also unique amongst school–home communications for another reason. Reports are more of a corporate product, involving contributions from many teachers, whereas other school–home communications are usually written by the head, deputies or by a small group of individuals from the senior management team. As such we found that they are valued by most parents. Each year's report is compared and contrasted with previous reports, perhaps even kept as significant mementoes or benchmarks of their child's development.* Jennifer Nias gives the following account:

> The fact that the school did not send out a full report at the end of the first year, and did not explain why they had not done so, caused widespread discontent. Twenty miles away and eighteen months later, a teacher said to me '. . . that school you are working in. We've got someone on our staff who sends his child there, and he's very dissatisfied with it. He says he hasn't had a proper report for two years.' At a different social level, a loyal supporter of the school confessed to me that she'd felt 'really let down at not having a report. I've kept every report for all my children all through their school lives, and now there is one missing.'

---

* Publication of the predominantly survey-type research of the School Reports Project (NFER 1978–81) is due either in late 1981 or 1982. It will be interesting to note whether it will focus on similar issues as I have discussed here.

6

Parent–Teacher Meetings

Jennifer Nias

Without communication schools would find it impossible adequately to 'give account' of themselves and parents to hold the
school 'to account'. Prominent among the means of communication are meetings between parents and teachers. Meetings can
take many forms. All the CAP schools had a carefully worked out
programme of formal meetings which parents were invited to
attend. These were normally held at the school, and almost always
in the evening. They were of three sorts: general 'get-to-know-the-
school' meetings at which the school was actually or vicariously
(through speakers and exhibitions) on display; information meetings, normally about curriculum and teaching arrangements at
critical transfer points in pupils' school careers; consultation
meetings, for the discussion of individual pupils. In addition, there
were frequent occasions during every school year when parents
were urged to attend educational, cultural and sporting events,
organised by the school or the Parent Association. This chapter
does not consider these latter types of meetings; the first are already
very familiar to parents and teachers of children of all ages and the
second are included in Chapter Eight. Nor does it consider
individual consultations held at times other than during meetings,
even though, in every school, separate arrangements existed to
encourage and facilitate these, and teachers, especially head
teachers, gave such meetings priority over many other types of
engagement. Instead this chapter discusses the purposes of the
three main types of formal meeting, as these are perceived by
parents and teachers, and the extent to which participants feel
these functions are fulfilled.

Open meetings

'Get-to-know-the-school' meetings are known in many schools as *'open' days or evenings*. The CAP schools held 'open' parent–teacher meetings only for parents of prospective pupils. When the schools were open to parents on other occasions, it was either under the auspices of a Parent Association or in order to facilitate parental access to pupils' work and school amenities rather than to teachers. These occasions are not covered here.

At open meetings a school is consciously on show, and all the CAP schools therefore took them seriously. Those schools which were feeling the effects of falling rolls paid them particular attention. The head of one such school wrote in his governors' report:

> Recently staff have been pleased, and some even a little relieved, to learn that in the annual inter-schools competition to recruit new pupils we have attracted ten per cent more than might be regarded as a mathematical 'fair share'. (U, 9)

John Elliott interprets Open Day at Uplands in terms of competition for pupils, and Rex Gibson (1980, 6 and 11) hints that the head of Holbein School was conscious of similar pressures.

Schools threatened by falling rolls took particular pains at open meetings to make clear to parents the values, as well as the achievements, of the institution which their children might be joining. A letter to prospective parents (Gibson, 1980, 11) states:

> 7.45–8.15 . . . The Headmaster will make special mention of the school's attitude to discipline, homework and study in general.

Heads of other schools set forward their school's philosophy in terms of its 'liberal–democratic values' (U, 6) or as 'a family school' (S, 2). The head of one new school admitted that he consciously slanted his talks at feeder middle schools towards what he felt would be the main interests of the predominant local groups. As an observer said:

> He has to pretend that the school is what it isn't in order for it to become what he wants it to be. (HI, 2B1)

Open meetings are, then, in part an educational market-place in which parents come to sample the goods of teachers (and particularly headteachers). However, the latter may themselves be torn between a belief in the value of their own product and a sense that parents are shopping for different, and sometimes more traditional, wares. Nor is it always clear that headteachers' educational priorities are shared by all their staff. Thus at an open meeting the head and the team to whom he delegates part of his responsibility for 'selling' the school simultaneously perform two sets of negotiations. They must convey to parents a true sense of the school's goals and the structure by which they seek to attain these without alienating potential clients (i.e. they have to decide both what to say, and what not to say). At the same time, they have to present a coherent picture of the school without running such a tightly-structured meeting that parents go away with the feeling that teachers are closed to the questions and comments of parents. It is small wonder that despite teachers' attempts to lay their values 'on the line', some parents in CAP schools felt that their queries at meetings had been 'glossed over'. For example:

> Mrs Judd: We have attended every open evening concerning our children. I was up for my daughter's in her first year . . . somebody said 'well what is basic studies,' and it was very glossed over. (U, 15)

> Mrs C.: There were one or two questions asked that evening that . . . were glossed over a little bit. (RP, III 5)

Yet parents seemed not to make up their minds solely, or even chiefly, on the basis of open meetings. Instead, they relied heavily upon social and occupational grapevines and upon their own impressions of current pupils' behaviour and attainment. This applies to both new CAP schools and established ones.

Indeed some teachers claimed that parents came to meetings to seek confirmation of judgements already made, rather than to exercise choice:

> I think they come to the school out of interest but I believe that the majority have made up their minds one way or the other beforehand and merely wish to confirm to themselves that they have made the right choice. (U, 6)

No matter what parents' motives for attending are, teachers face particular difficulties in running a meeting at which the school tries simultaneously to convey an accurate picture of its functioning and is genuinely open to prospective parents. Evening meetings do not give a proper sense of what the school is normally like, even when arrangements have been made for pupils to be seen at work in particular curriculum areas. Yet open mornings (or days) exclude working parents, especially those paid by the day or hour. Moreover, open days present teachers with a dilemma: if they free themselves to discuss their work with parents, they look as if they are not 'teaching', whereas, if they are 'teaching' parents may not wish to disturb them. In addition, neither heads nor teachers always made it clear to parents whether or not they were free to enter classrooms or should simply observe from outside. Even when parents had been given a 'short common briefing' neither parents nor teachers seemed certain of the behaviour expected of them. In general, there appeared to be a greater chance of parents taking an active interest in the details of school life when groups on guided tours were small (8–10), rather than large (over 12), and had pupil, rather than teacher, guides. One particularly successful occasion, at Highstones School, incorporated Open Evening into a Community Arts Week so that parents saw not only pupils but also local craftspeople at work. Though these activities may not have given parents a very accurate view of the school's daily life they successfully blurred the boundary between the institution and the outside world and made it easier for diffident parents to effect an initial entry into the school.

The way in which meetings are arranged and run is another means by which parents learn the school's values. In most of the CAP schools the main entrance was difficult to find (especially after dark) and visitors were met by closed doors. Parents and others appreciated the provision of maps and signs and were favourably impressed when there was someone to greet them, preferably by name, at the main entrance to the school or meeting. The relative value attached by the school to accessibility and availability was emphasised by coffee arrangements, the length and style of speeches, and the nature of the seating. Spatial arrangements generally were important, partly because of their associations (researchers saw rooms set out for open meetings which reminded them of living rooms, political meetings and craft fairs) and partly because of the interactions they encouraged and discouraged. For example, in one school, the headteacher's deliberate attempt to foster dialogue between himself and several of the parents was foiled by the seating arrangements which placed parents on either side of a room divider, unable to see one another and facing a row of senior teachers seated behind an imposing table (HI, 2B4). In all the schools, the nature and quality of documents, slides and signs were an indication of teachers' efficiency and their attitudes to meetings, and suggested how concerned they were to communicate in a clear and orderly fashion.

Over and above these organisational details, two more intimate factors gave visitors a powerful sense of the school's values. These were the self-presentation of the head and teachers (i.e. dress, appearance and style of speech) and their choice of setting (e.g. décor, flower arrangements, wall displays). This is not to say that one school's or teacher's choice is 'right' and another's is 'wrong' (e.g. dress which seems to one parent reassuringly workaday may appear 'sloppy' to another; the flowers on the speaker's table may tell one parent about the school's concern for aesthetic values and seem 'sissy' to another). Rather it is to suggest that many parents attended to details such as these and picked up from them a strong impression of where teachers' priorities lay. As one parent said, praising the openness of the school:

> I like the way the teachers dress. It's not like they were better than us. (HI, 2A2)

Some heads pay more attention than others to details of this kind. John Elliott suggests that the difficulty he experienced in entering Uplands on his first visit may reflect 'a total absence of any desire to control visitors' impressions of the school', whereas Dave Ebbutt describes a meeting at which 'the performance [of the head and "the front line of the chorus"] was most carefully managed'. (S, 2)

It would be wrong to assume that the image which a school presents of itself is always deliberately contrived. For instance:

> I don't think these [displays, plants in the foyer, pictures] are there to impress parents . . . because, partly, our image is good enough not to need manipulating. (S, 2)

Yet parents do learn more about a school at an open meeting than teachers tell them. This is not to claim that the details of organisation and self-presentation through which a school's ethos is created are therefore sustained solely for show. However, they matter: in questions of value and belief, actions speak more loudly than words.

Information meetings

By comparison, these appear at first glance to be less complex affairs. They have limited objectives and the extent to which these are attained can be judged by the level of understanding subsequently shown by parents or pupils. Indeed, the success of information meetings at all the schools can be judged by the typical parental comment:

> They tell you all that you want to know and sometimes more than you want to know. (HI, 2A2)

Yet in practice these meetings were no easier to run well than were the open meetings. Parents could not always see or hear clearly, speakers – particularly headteachers – frequently overestimated their attention-span and/or their capacity to apprehend details presented aurally, and were themselves sometimes muddled or boring. When, as frequently happens, an information evening precedes a decision which has to be made concerning a child's subsequent school career (e.g. curriculum options; sixth form opportunities; career choices), the school often puts the information into a booklet which is issued to parents. CAP schools did not always make clear to parents whether the meeting was intended to be a substitute for or a supplement to such a booklet. This was particularly the case when documents were issued at, rather than before, a meeting. Many of these difficulties are summed up in the following extract:

> Mrs S.: It didn't mean an awful lot to me. I came away thinking, 'It's a bit of a waste for a couple of hours.' I think it confused me really.
>
> David Bridges: In what respect?

Mrs S.: I felt it was more straightforward in the forms. You can either do this or this. If it would have only been that one evening, I don't think I would have been a lot wiser.

David Bridges: Why was that? Was he trying to cover too much?

Mrs S.: Possibly. He could have made it more simple. Many parents get so bored of sitting at meeting after meeting, having to listen to a lot of silly comments which are quite irrelevant to the evening anyway. (RP, III5)

Meetings also tended to be run in ways which hindered parents from filling in the gaps in their understanding by asking questions. Forms of organisation and layout which ensured that information was conveyed clearly by their very success discouraged parents from discussion and from challenging the speakers. Many parents, and especially those who were afraid of 'making fools of themselves', found it hard to speak out at a large public gathering, could not formulate their questions in such a way as to elicit the information they desired, or were unaccustomed to the conventions of a formally-chaired meeting. These points are further elaborated in Chapters Seven and Eight. Though most schools made it possible for parents to meet teachers informally after the meeting, not all parents found this satisfactory. They could not always decide who was not a teacher, or identify a specific one, and by the time they had done this he or she had sometimes left. More significant, some parents were more assertive than others in claiming, and then keeping, the attention of key teachers. Since these meetings were not designated by the school as consultation evenings, it was often left to individual teachers to decide whether or not they attended. Indeed, teachers themselves were not always clear as to whether a particular meeting was seen by the head as primarily informative or consultative.

Thus, in the typical school sequence – booklet and information meeting, parent consultation at home with pupil, parent–teacher consultation meeting, decision (made jointly by pupil, parent and teacher) – some parents fell at the first fence. If, as tended to happen at both the new schools, they came away from the information meeting feeling confused, daunted or frustrated, then the pupil was often left to complete the decision-making sequence on his or her own. I noted, for example, after an information meeting on curriculum options, that:

> . . . several parents said, in the words of one, 'I don't really know why they've done it. . . . I don't understand it.' Others, . . . despite all the school's efforts, left fourth year choices entirely to their children, because they did not feel competent to advise them. (HI, 2B4)

By contrast, at Uplands school which was both longer-established and served an urban area, most parents felt more fully involved in their children's choices.

In short, notwithstanding their prodigious efforts, none of the CAP schools succeeded in running information meetings which met the needs of all their parents, and especially of those who themselves felt ill-at-ease in school. Some schools were more successful than others, in part because they had had longer in which to 'foster high expectations . . . of partnership' (U, 19) but all left some parents passively acquiescent, anxious or bewildered.

Another aspect of these meetings which parents found unsatisfactory was that they frequently received ambiguous information about their own expected roles. Sometimes parents were assured that the school wished to take them into educational partnership, but were given no opportunity to air fundamental disquiets (e.g. over the school's curriculum policy). At others the verbal or non-verbal messages they picked up at the meeting prepared them to ask questions of individual teachers, but the organisation denied them the opportunity to do this. As one worried parent declared:

> He did say that you could speak to the teachers afterward but . . . the science master . . . wasn't there that evening anyhow. So we couldn't talk to him. So really that was a bit of a waste of time. (RP, III5)

Many would have liked to have been told in advance whether or not it would be helpful if they brought their child with them, and to have been given clearer guidance as to the latter's part in any subsequent discussion.

Consultation meetings

Teachers also went to a great deal of trouble over these meetings, aware that they provided a unique opportunity for them to express their sense of answerability to parents. These meetings were of two kinds: pastoral and academic. Some schools left it to house or form tutors and/or parents to initiate *pastoral meetings* on the basis of individual need. Others included them in their annual cycle of meetings. When regular meetings existed, parents usually used them to check that their child was 'getting on alright'. For example:

> The first meeting was just to see if he was really fitting in to the school. You talk about how he's getting on with the other teachers later on. (HI, 3A)

Some, however, tended not to distinguish between these and academic consultations and expected the tutor to have more detailed knowledge than he did. For their part, many tutors perceived consultation meetings as a necessary evil, realising the importance of providing child and parent with the evidence of stable, personalised care but, because much of their knowledge of the child came through other teachers, finding it hard to say anything which did not sound routine and remote. Thus, as the quotation below suggests, those parents who did not fully understand the role of the form or house tutor sometimes came away from meetings dissatisfied with the latter's knowledge of a particular academic problem or with his apparent capacity to put it right:

> Sometimes they don't realise who your child is. They search through lists and . . . they think there is only one thing you need – the child's tutor – and unless you particularly ask for an interview . . . there is never any call forward from a member of staff. (U, 17)

Academic consultation meetings were a regular feature of the annual calendar of all the CAP schools. Chronologically they generally followed some form of reporting to parents and were often designed to help pupils make appropriate decisions at significant points in their school careers. Parents and teachers held a common view of their central purpose, but each also brought to them perspectives not shared by the other. As a result, despite the hard work, enthusiasm and goodwill of teachers, and the relative simplicity of both the structure and the functions of meetings, these evenings were often occasions of considerable tension for parents and teachers.

Neither had any doubt about their value. For example:

Parent: The best form of communication there is. There's no substitute for talking to a teacher, is there?

Teacher: I think a letter . . . from teachers to parents isn't often very successful . . . Talking is so much better. (HI, 3A)

Parent: Couldn't do without them. You meet other parents too. It's a night out for both of us. The teachers are always very helpful. (HO, 2)

Both sides were appreciative of what their schools had achieved. Many teachers tried hard to make themselves approachable, and were rewarded by feeling that their schools had gone a long way towards breaking down the traditional barriers between home and school. Supporting evidence is too plentiful to cite in full, but typical comments were:

Teacher: At least parents are welcome here, whereas [at my previous school] if they got over the front step they were lucky. (HI, 2B6)

Parent: You can talk to them. It's a friendly school, clean. I like going there. You never feel not wanted and they make you welcome. (HO, 2)

Yet, notwithstanding, problems persisted. Teachers were very willing to supply parents with all the information the latter wanted and to give them full details of their children's progress. They were also ready to question parents when they felt they needed more information about a particular pupil. Indeed, some teachers encouraged parents to talk, welcoming the chance to set the child in his family context:

How do you get to know about the child and his problems, and the parents' aspirations, if you have nothing coming back from them? It's useless just giving all the information from your side. . . . Work with them, not at them or against them. (HI, 2B6)

Yet individual meetings were short (a fact to which I shall return later) and to many parents it seemed as if teachers claimed the right to decide how the allotted five minutes or so would be spent. Sometimes they resented this, hinting that their ability to contribute to a joint educational process had not been recognised:

> The overall point I feel on that is, 'Are the teachers making full use of parents?'. . . I am sure there are lots of ways we can help the teachers. (U, 17)

Similarly, a few parents came to meetings in order tacitly to express their satisfaction with the school:

> We think the school is doing a good job – we know we ought to go and support [it]. . . . (HO, 2)

Yet few teachers realised that parents' readiness to present a personal viewpoint was an indication not of criticism but of trust, and that their attendance might be interpreted as a gesture of goodwill.

Similarly, though both parents and teachers valued consultation meetings, differences in emphasis persisted. Teachers were ready, and sometimes eager, to give further information; parents occasionally wanted to air grievances (e.g. over homework policies) or give opinions (e.g. on the use of work sheets). There were teachers in every school who felt that these kinds of comments were a reflection upon their competence or an attack upon their professional autonomy, not realising that parents might be seeking reassurance or volunteering worthwhile lay opinions.

In addition, parents used consultation meetings for their own ends. Meeting individuals enabled them to personalise the teachers and thus subsequently to make subjective interpretations of comments in reports and letters, to share their children's experiences of school and to contribute to their own continuing evaluation of it. A typical parent comment shows some of this:

> It's an excellent chance to meet the teachers. We learn about them from X – it's funny to actually talk with them. Very helpful. Sometimes they are like what you think, but sometimes . . . (laughs). (HO, 2)

The need to attend a meeting gave some a reason for coming to school which they might otherwise have lacked, and some were glad to be able to share personal worries (not necessarily about a pupil) with a teacher. A few also enjoyed the evening as a social occasion.

Thus both parents and teachers come to consultation evenings with their own agendas. The teacher's is the simpler of the two: to get to know the child's parents in so far as this will help him to teach more effectively, and to offer the parent information and advice about a specific problem or decision. The parent's may be complex: to hear what the teacher thinks about his child, but also to volunteer help and information, to ask questions about school policies, to get to know the teacher, to find out about the school, to air complaints, to enlist the teacher's sympathy and support, to demonstrate confidence in the school, to see and be seen. Yet, by convention and by practice in the CAP schools, the lion's share of the short meetings is devoted to the teacher's agenda. It is not surprising that consultation meetings remained for some parents occasions of stress.

The way in which meetings were run did not help to reduce this tension. In the first place, as with information evenings, unambiguous instructions were not always sent to parents and pupils beforehand, giving the school's view of the purpose and the procedures of the meetings and indicating whether the presence of pupils would be helpful or desirable. Secondly, parents appreciated being put at their ease. Among the points observers or parents raised as significant were:

clear signs indicating the entrance to the school, the rooms in use and the names and roles of teachers

a 'reception party' at main entrances

a clock in chief rooms

coffee easily available, with pupils to help in serving it

informal seating arrangements in waiting areas

teachers whose manner, appearance and dress made them seem accessible rather than authoritarian

enough privacy to encourage openness by both participants.

Some parents and some teachers also felt that even when all these were achieved a number of parents would never be fully at ease on school territory and in consequence they advocated teacher visits to pupils' homes.

Thirdly, parents, especially those with many other claims on their time, needed to feel that meetings were worthwhile. They appreciated teachers who were willing not only to solicit and listen to their views but also to be 'straight' with them (i.e. to give them the bad news as well as the good.) They also wanted efficient arrangements of time and space which reduced the hours spent waiting in overcrowded, uncomfortable conditions and minimised the sense of being rushed during a consultation. Some parents coming to their first meetings in secondary or upper schools had grown accustomed to seeing pupils' work on display and several said that waiting to see teachers would have been less irksome if they could have studied such work while they waited. Above all, parents wanted reassurance that teachers knew and cared about their children as individuals, and that they themselves were valued as highly as other people seemed to be.

Parents' level of satisfaction with consultation evenings depended on two interacting sets of variables. Over the first of these (i.e. their own attitudes, to some extent the nature of their interaction with parents and the organisational setting of meetings) teachers have some control. The intractable problem in all schools was time. Whatever the arrangements, some parents ended up waiting, sometimes for as long as three hours, for a consultation with an individual teacher which seldom lasted more than ten minutes and often less than five; and some parents always felt that teachers' time had been unfairly divided. The only solution appeared to be more meetings, but as it was, the existing ones generally lasted for three to four hours, and already consumed, for some teachers, the equivalent of one evening per fortnight.

Teachers do not, however, have much direct influence over the attitudes and behaviour of parents. No matter how hard they worked and no matter what arrangements they tried, there were always some parents who did not know or understand the procedures at meetings or who ignored them. There were others who wanted to turn individual consultations into general educational discussions. The first problem probably responds only, if at all, to the patient education of parents. The second reflects a need which is further explored in Chapter Eight. Briefly, there are some parents who see themselves as the professional equals of teachers. They would like to be able to criticise teachers directly, to discuss educational principles and strategies and to put their own viewpoint to them, but there is no forum in which they feel comfortable in doing so, and in any case most are not convinced that their opinions would be heeded. It is not therefore surprising that they sometimes seize upon the opportunity offered in a one-to-one interview with an apparently receptive teacher. Thus the staff find themselves in a dilemma. The constraints of their position mean that they can become fully accountable to a few parents only by appearing to neglect the rest, a stance which encourages withdrawal and alienation on the part of the latter. Indeed, the existence of parents who do not attend consultation meetings may reflect this problem.

To sum up, then: all three types of parent–teacher meetings were taken very seriously in all the CAP schools as an expression of teachers' felt need to be both answerable and accountable. Parents too believed these meetings to be of crucial importance to communication, and thus to relationships between themselves and teachers. Yet despite a high degree of goodwill on both sides, meetings often left participants feeling confused and frustrated. Although they generally reassured parents as to teachers' authority, competence and concern for individuals, they did not give them the feeling that they were perceived by teachers as partners in their children's education. In part this was due to the complexity of parents' agendas, in part to teachers' attitudes. In addition, organisational arrangements and parents' response to these were often to blame.

7

'It's the ones who never turn up that you really want to see': the 'problem' of the non-attending parent

David Bridges

To a group of schools which take seriously the business of communication with parents, those parents who are apparently unwilling, unable or reluctant to engage in this communication represent something of a problem or failure. Not surprisingly therefore a number of the CAP schools asked us to explore this problem for them and help to explain the case of the non-communicating or non-attending parents.

Before going on to see what we have to offer towards such explanation, let me comment briefly on the nature of the 'problem' itself. To begin with, is it a problem? or why is it a problem? or what assumptions about the purpose or concerns underlying the school's commitment to strong lines of communication with parents are implied by defining the 'non-communicating parent' as a problem? The point is that if we simply see the information that the school provides as something to which the parent is entitled, then a parent's decision (if that is what it is) not to involve himself in the affairs of the school need not concern the school – the school will have acquitted itself of its own obligation. Alternatively, if the school sees the process of mutual communication as integral to the mutually supporting work of parents and school in the education of the child, then the school might feel that the non-communicating parent is not fulfilling his or her share of the joint obligation. Or, thirdly, the school might worry that the non-communication was somehow a reflection of its own failure to make itself accessible to parents who were perhaps inhibited practically or psychologically from communicating with the school.

The attitude of the staff of the school I was most directly concerned with, Robert Peel, was I think somewhere between the last two mentioned: a mixture of a feeling that parents owed it to their children to be in close communication with their teachers, combined with a desire to help those parents who for one reason or another found communication with the school difficult. Jennifer Nias' comment on Highstones suggests that she interprets that school's attitude in much the same terms:

> For those teachers who accept, as part of their moral account-ability to parents, the responsibility for helping them to be effective partners in their children's education, the school's problem is *how to reach them.* (her emphasis)

Increasingly perhaps these finer sentiments relating to duties, rights and responsibilities are supported by more prudential considerations. In contexts in which schools are effectively competing for pupils in a contracting market, or where schools are anxiously trying to establish a new reputation or change an old one (we had examples of all of these), the school's capacity to communicate its own view of itself to its parent 'clients' is crucial. The schools we worked with were especially alive to what they regarded as the misrepresentation of what they did or stood for through the informal network of communication and especially keen to provide their own accounts through the channels they had at their disposal.

> I think the more you inform them about what's going on the less likely gossip, rumours and misunderstandings will be to arise. (HI, 2B3)

Parents' non-participation in such channels had, among other consequences, the effect of weakening the school's capacity to present its own picture of its work and character.

Beyond this there was some, though never precisely articulated, awareness that the institution of compulsory schooling can be undermined if parents give it anything less than energetic and visible support. Indeed, as one education welfare officer explained, persistent non-attending pupils tend to absent themselves from schools with the connivance and support of parents who share their childrens' reluctance to submit themselves to its demands.

Some of the reasons CAP parents give for their reluctance to attend one kind of event or occasion are not necessarily generalisable to others. In a longer and more complex chapter I might have tried to discuss different kinds of occasions in turn. But we often elicited from parents fairly general explanations as to why they did or did not attend school functions and they do not always stand up to detailed analysis in relation to specific events. I shall therefore leave it to the reader to consider or explore which explanation would most probably apply to which kind of non-involvement.

1. Practical difficulties

A number of parents explained that their non-attendance at evening events reflected no lack of interest but rather some practical difficulties in getting there. They referred to the lack of public transport, not having a car, evening shift work, family ties and sheer exhaustion by that time of the evening.

> They might think we don't care because we don't go. We do care, but when you are out working all day and X [spouse] is on shifts you can't always get there and you feel so tired. (HO, 2)

Jennifer Nias reported that in response to her enquiries of non-attending parents at Highstones:

> Most replied and, overwhelmingly, they attributed their absences to lack of either transport or a baby sitter. As one parent put it 'If I'm asked to work extra, that's four hours overtime, say, and I feel, well I can do that for my family.' (HI, 2A4)

One of my own interviews was with a mother who on her own account had not been to a school event for a long time. This was a person who was trying to bring up a family on her own, working a full day, returning home to deal with household chores and preoccupied with other domestic worries. It is perhaps hardly surprising if at the end of the day she is left with relatively little energy or desire to face a parents' evening at school – especially if this is itself, as I shall go on to suggest, anxiety-inducing.

Some of the teachers we spoke to recognised that these practical difficulties can operate to the disadvantage of those already disadvantaged in terms of working hours and wealth. One teacher saw this as a problem associated with giving parents access to classrooms during the school day.

> In a way I think sometimes it's a little bit divisive in society to have your school open during the day for that sort of thing, because it tends to be those that have a kind of posh job who can negotiate some time off to come, whereas the ordinary working man really can't find the time to come, or it's the mum who doesn't need to work. (U, 15)

What we also observed was that in areas where there was a lot of night shift working it could be the same kind of people who were disadvantaged in terms of access to evening functions.

Without for one moment denying that parents, and some parents more than others, experienced practical problems which made it difficult for them to attend school events, it is worth noting that these did not always make it impossible. What they did was to face parents with a set of priorities and a decision which was not always made in favour of attendance at school.

2. Deference to teachers

We collected a good deal of evidence to the effect that parents were by and large perfectly happy to leave questions of broad educational policy to the teachers. The following comment is characteristic:

> I don't really know enough about education basically to feel that I have any right to comment on it. I think that if the school – that's their part of the thing. They do obviously know the right curriculum to set the children for what they are going to do. I don't think that parents really can comment on that. (RP, III6)

This was supported for some parents by their satisfaction with what the schools were doing:

> We've been to no end of meetings with [the Head] – he's a very nice chap – no doubt about it – but he goes on and

on – and in the end you feel you know it and can't hear it over again. We could be more involved if we had time and were nearer. The school gives us plenty of opportunity to be involved but though one of us goes to [Y's reports] meetings we don't go to the others. They know best anyway and we are very satisfied.

I leave it to X [spouse]. And X doesn't always go – but we like to know what's happening and we feel the school is doing a good job generally. You just can't go to everything. (HO, 2)

Now the point of all this in relation to the parent who, for example, does not attend an evening meeting on the curriculum, the teaching of maths or some other matter of educational policy, is that such a parent may simply regard these questions as ones best left to the teachers. Consequently he (or even more probably she) does not see much point in getting involved with occasions of this kind.

John Elliott illustrates this same point in the context of Upland PTA Committee discussions. He quotes one parent as explaining:

I think in the last few months that only one point came up in the committee; that was about the sick children – and I discussed that – and that's the only thing – because there is a big gap really, they think it's not their business. Members are under the impression that the duty of the parents' committee is to raise money for a lot of things. (U, 15)

Parents' deference to teachers' expertise was if anything fed by the occasional evenings which were held on e.g. maths in the curriculum. (It is interesting to conjecture, in the absence of any evidence, whether parents would show the same deference to an evening on Home Economics or Motor Vehicle Maintenance.) Such evenings were very largely organised in a way which set up teachers as the source of information, the repository of educational wisdom, the people who could explain what parents did not understand and answer their questions. If teachers managed to avoid using language that parents did not understand then it was plainly only at the price of careful explanation. Even so a good number of parents would leave confirmed in their sense of their own inability to understand 'educational' arguments.

The thing was, if there was something you didn't understand you didn't really like to attract him and ask him to explain. I think had you done that it would have taken another hour. (RP, III5)

In some cases parents' deference to teachers is cheerful, based upon satisfaction with the school and a ready acknowledgement of the teachers' superior expertise; sometimes it is indifferent, based on apathy; in other cases it is grudging and feeds parents' cynicism in relation to the whole character of communication between the school and themselves.

3. Cynicism

A number of parents whom we interviewed, perhaps those with more personal confidence, might have taken part in more formal school–parent discussion had they not become cynical about the value of such discussion.

In her study of Highstones, Jennifer Nias suggests that 'a reluctance on the part of parents to participate more vigorously, and even critically, in their children's schooling may reflect upon their previous experience of local democracy.' She collected statements from a number of parents of which the following are representative:

You see, I think that schools do what they want to do anyway, regardless of what parents think. That's why I don't bother [with school], because I think that. Regardless of what we think, they'd do as they want anyway.

The teachers might listen [to parents] but not do anything . . . they all stick together. (HI, 3A11)

It was in fact a dinner lady who observed:

One reason why parents don't get involved is because they know they can't alter the general policy of the school. They know they couldn't make an impact on the big things (like the changes in school dinner).

Another parent added:

> It's not because parents aren't interested. It's because they don't have a choice. If they did, they'd take more trouble to find out what the school is really like. (HI, 3A11)

John Elliott has I think something similar in mind, though he talks in terms of 'scepticism' rather than 'cynicism'.

> Is it conceivable that some parents may not turn out to educational evenings not out of indifference or deference; but rather because they are sceptical about the school's capacity to have its practices questioned? . . . Parents seemed to be sensitive to what one at least called 'glossing over' responses to their questions. The phrase describes a response which fails to take into account the issues and doubts which motivate a parent's questions. It is interesting that, although they may ask teachers questions, parents do not always see themselves doing so from a position of ignorance. In 'asking a question' they are often tacitly 'questioning', and the teachers' responses are judged in terms of how they deal with this tacit content. (U, 15)

These comments throw revealing light on the nature of 'the problem of the non communicating parent'. It is I believe only a minority of teachers who will be greatly concerned if parents are reluctant to offer their own opinions on a regular basis. The wider concern is that parents should be prepared to place themselves regularly in a position to receive and attend to the things that teachers want them to hear. As John Elliott argues:

> There is a kind of approachability which the expert may possess in relation to the lay person who is perceived to be in need of enlightenment. The experts are sympathetic to the concerns of the laymen and listen to their questions, but they are the ones who 'know best'. They see their role in terms of enlightening others but not being enlightened by others. Their 'knowledge' is not open to question. The communications of the 'approachable' expert, although responsive to lay persons' questions, are paternalistic. The exchange is not one of dialogue. (U, 15)

It will not be surprising, therefore, where communication is emphatically in one direction, that parents who do feel that they have something to contribute to discussion become disenchanted and in the end 'apathetic'.

4. Dominant parents

It is not only the dynamics of teacher–parent relationships which can discourage parents from participating in school meetings and other events. I have already begun to depict something of the different level of confidence in dealing with educational affairs that parents have. This in itself can add to the sense which some parents have of their own inadequacy in school and exclusion from the main hub of activity. Thus Jennifer Nias suggested on the basis of her study of Highstones that:

> Many parents feel inadequate when faced with curriculum and examination innovations, and this insecurity is compounded for some by educational differences between them. Many, especially in the isolated villages, themselves attended all-age village schools, or secondary moderns. They lack confidence when faced with other parents, the ones whom from their own childhood experience they described to me as 'the grammar school snobs'. (HI, 2A4)

She illustrates one parent's acute sense of his own educational inadequacy.

> We could have our say at meetings, but you don't know if they'd listen, and anyway I can't speak out at meetings, because I am not educated. The ones who're educated go to the meetings, and do all the talking, and it'd sound funny to them if we spoke. . . . Well, it's my Suffolk accent, I don't feel I can express myself properly. . . . At parents' evenings, the forceful and educated ones push in; we might as well go home. (HI, 2A4)

Some parents expressed their sense of disqualification from active participation in school affairs in explicitly class terms:

> I'd quite like to be a parent governor but they don't want working class people – they wouldn't be interested in me. (HI, 3A11)

Some parents' ability to monopolise teachers' attention encouraged others to feel that the teachers were discriminating between those they wanted to talk to and those they did not:

> You *are* welcome . . . but you get the feeling, I don't know how to put it, that some are more welcome than others.

One consequence of this was distrust of any moves to give parent representatives more power in the school and a lack of confidence in the ability of one set of parents (e.g. parent governors) to represent the interests of others. Another consequence was to discourage less confident parents from participating in school events and institutions which would be dominated by the more confident, educated and articulate parents.

5. Alien Social Events

It is not only formal meetings and discussions about educational issues which discomfort the less confident parents. Even the kind of social evening devised particularly to allow a relaxed and informal meeting of parents and teachers can inhibit the participation of at least a certain section of parents. In any case not all parents are socially gregarious. As one parent explained, in commenting on a school newsletter:

> It paints a picture of a very active school from the point of view of parental involvement that makes us feel somewhat guilty – because we are not really the kind of people who are wanting to be involved socially. (U, 14)

Those of a generally more gregarious disposition may however be put off by the particular form of social event put on offer – especially if it is perceived as one located within a different social culture from that of the parents concerned:

> Mother: . . . there is nothing there. Even for the parents – you know – like dances and things for the parents. Not many – just once in a while, like Christmas time.
>
> Child: People would enjoy that sort of thing. It's one thing where all the teachers and parents can really get together and get to know each other. I think it would be a really great idea.

Mother: Yes the parents would get to know the teachers more. Have an evening out with the teachers just to be one – do you know what I mean?

John Elliott: There's not many of those at all?

Mother: No, only near Christmas.

John Elliott: There is one in a few weeks, at the end of term – cheese and wine.

Mother: [looking doubtful] Yes.

John Elliott: You don't think that cheese and wine is your sort of thing?

Child: Not the sort of thing that Mum would go to.

Mother: No, not really. A group or band or something like that.

John Elliott: A dance?

Mother: Yes. (U, 14)

But if, as John Elliott remarks, a Wine and Cheese Evening had little appeal to a family from the Caribbean, the Calypso Evening which also featured on the programme was just as out of key with the real enthusiasms of a working class West Indian family.

Perhaps it is an impossible task to devise social events at which all sections of the school community can feel equally at ease. However, if the PTA is dominated by one particular social/cultural group they may have little alternative but to risk the charge either of preferring the kind of events favoured by their own social set or of patronising other social groups.

6. Dread of School

I have already made many references to the anxiety which parents feel about attending certain school events. This was a recurring theme in our interviews with parents who had not attended school events or had much to do with the schools, especially among parents who had little or no contact with the school at all. Jennifer Nias reported:

Only two sets of parents claimed never to have been inside the school, and in one of these, both mother and father bluntly

said, 'I hate schools. . . .' Later each told a story of educational unhappiness, boredom and failure which would
provide a reason, if not an excuse, for their confessed indif-
ference to their children's schooling. (HI, 2A4)

I concluded on the basis of interviews with parents at Robert Peel
that for a parent whose own memories of school are unpleasant –
and especially one who learned to live in fear of teachers – the
anxieties and inhibitions attached to re-entering the portals of a
school can be quite overwhelming. Some teachers at least seemed
sensitive to this:

> I think some of them are afraid. Particularly those that have
> memories of their school days which aren't very pleasant.
> Some of them I think are afraid because they know their child is
> failing and they don't want to be told so. (U, unpublished
> interview)

> When I get a parent on the 'phone, it was a very difficult
> situation – it has only happened . . . once – and I suddenly
> realised how nervous that parent was by the way they were
> behaving. I don't think we pay it enough attention perhaps.
> (HI, 2A4)

Parents' anxieties can be heightened when it comes to an interview
with a teacher about a child who is not performing well, mis-
behaving, not doing homework, or truanting (perhaps with the
connivance of the parent). The parents' expectation of the interview with the teacher may well be one of bleak prognosis and
complaint together with some implicit criticism of the parent for
failing to exercise proper responsibility. 'It's the ones who never
come whom you really want to see', say the teachers – and 'the
ones who never come' are alert to the note of recrimination.

Humiliation (or anticipated humiliation) at the hands of the
teacher can be reinforced by the exhibitions of pride of the parents
of more successful children. As one governor observed:

> Parents can be very hurtful when they are discussing the
> progress of their children. Every parent I think boasts or likes
> to boast, and that can be very hurtful to other parents. I have
> noticed this on open days, that the parents of the best children
> always manage to stay in the classroom examining the work

much, much longer than parents of a child that works much harder but hasn't done so well. (HI, 2A4)

The extreme case of the non-communicating, non-attending parent almost amounts to 'parental truancy' – and we may usefully seek an understanding of this in the same sort of terms as pupils' truancy (with which I suspect it is commonly associated). In the course of our interviews we were offered a number of suggestions as to how this problem might be tackled.

One suggestion was to change the venue for the meeting between parents and teachers. Apart from anything else parents disliked the lack of privacy at meetings.

I don't go as often as I should . . . you can communicate better by seeing someone on your own rather than going to an evening. I don't like big crowds. We all sit looking at each other. (U, 15)

Parents commented that meetings with individual teachers took place on the teachers' own 'territory' – a fact which some parents mentioned as an obstacle to the free expression of their views. As one said:

There ought to be a place where you could talk to a teacher that isn't his place. (HI, 2A3)

Parents were often warmly appreciative of the conversations which they had with members of the CAP team in their (the parents') own homes. One commented approvingly on the practice of a friend of hers, a teacher, who visits the parents of her children once or twice during the course of a year in their own homes.

A second and rather interesting response to parental anxiety about coming to school was indicated in a wide variety of comments which pointed to the importance of having someone to support you on such visits.

You don't go because you don't want to make a fool of yourself. . . . It would be easier to go to some things if you had someone to go with. (HI, 2A4)

Our studies showed instances of people reluctant to go to school without the company of a *husband*, 'My husband is on night shift and I feel left out going on my own' (U, 15); a *neighbour* (as Jennifer Nias explained, in the scattered housing which made up her school's catchment area there may be only one child of a given age group in a single hamlet or group of houses); or a person of the same *colour* or *ethnic group*:

> I used to attend every meeting. Sometimes its me alone. I don't know other parents attending. It embarrasses you. It makes you feel 'why don't coloured people turn out like the English do?' (U, 15)

It may even be a *child* who can provide the support:

> One thing I realised on these visits to 'non-attending' parents' houses was the closeness of the mother-daughter relationship (the latter often sitting through the conversation and chipping in). I was reminded of a sixth former's objection to children not being able to attend evenings with their parents below the fifth year. If this taboo was not enforced it might give these mothers the social support they needed to attend. (U, 15)

In the extreme case perhaps a parent needs the professional support of a *social worker*. One school's education welfare officer in trying to help parents of school refusers sometimes found it useful to offer to accompany them to school, giving them not only free transport but support in the interview with the headteacher (RP, II2). Perhaps similar support could help to overcome the anxieties of parents who were themselves in a sense school refusers.

It was a parent, not a teacher, who expressed the opinion:

> I think that those parents who are interested in their children's education will approach any school whatever it is like – and those that aren't won't. (RP, II2)

Our evidence suggests this is an over harsh judgement which underestimates the psychological complexity of parents' relations with teachers and ignores the ways in which the social and cultural character of those relations and their context can operate to the advantage of some parents and the disadvantage of others.

8

Parent associations

Jennifer Nias

Parent associations are a mixed blessing for parents and teachers. They are often the only collective link between teachers and parents and the only organised way in which parents can become informally involved with school affairs. All the CAP schools had one. Heads and teachers welcomed the financial, material and moral support which the associations gave to their work, and used meetings to describe and justify their activities in ways which were not possible at routine parents' evenings. Yet they resisted any notion that associations, lacking legal powers and responsibilities, should behave as if they had a right to hold schools to account.

For their part, many parents regarded their association, despite its lack of legal status, as an important part of the school's procedures for giving account and some as a means of holding it to account. Their motives for involvement were complex. Some wanted more information about the school and the staff, others hoped to obtain better facilities for pupils. Most sought to support the teachers, whereas a few turned to it in the hope of finding a means of exerting individual and collective influence upon educational policies. The title of a recent article, 'What to do when a head doesn't want a PTA', (Taylor 1979) suggests that teachers may find associations threatening. Yet the local influence of associations represented powerful potential backing for, rather than a threat to, CAP schools. Thus teachers who fear parental involvement in associations may be confusing accountability with answerability.

On the other hand, the very existence of an association may, in certain catchment areas, alienate parents from collective involvement in the school and thus reduce the likelihood of organised community support for it. The way in which associations in CAP schools were constituted and run tended to emphasise the gap between the minority who were actively involved in committee membership and the majority who were not, thus alienating the latter from association activities. Yet these activities were one way in which parents could show support for the school, express a sense of shared responsibility for the education of pupils and demonstrate that accountability was a two-way process. There is a paradox in the fact that the only organisation which potentially allows expression of teachers' accountability to the full parental body and of parents' accountability to the whole school tends to reduce its own potency by its very existence.

In the CAP schools parent associations had different names. To the observer, these names suggested differences in membership, though in fact all parents were automatically, and without subscription, members of their association whatever its title. Parent–teacher associations explicitly seek to involve representatives of both groups in active membership and usually, by custom or constitution, give the head or deputy the position of committee member, if not actually chairman. Parent associations often involve teachers only as advisers. School associations and Friends of the School are open to parents of past and present pupils, teachers, governors and members of the community. Committees may include representatives of all these groups.

Associations were also run with differing degrees of administrative independence from the school. For example, in one school the Parent Association Newsletter at the start of the school year said:

> The P.A. Committee are your representatives at the school; if there is anything that you want to discuss or know in connection with the school (and you don't want to bother the teaching or secretarial staff) get in touch with one of us – there is a complete list over-leaf. If we cannot help you immediately we will do our best to find out what you want to know, or help to discuss your problem, or point, with the right person. (OT, 3)

In others, news of PTA activities were circulated to the parents only as part of the school newsletter, and members of staff who were not committee members sent out letters under the school association letterhead.

A further difference between associations lay in the extent and nature of formal and informal links with the governors. At one extreme certain parent governors who were also association committee members deliberately, as a matter of principle, kept the two roles completely separate, never mentioning in one arena discussions from the other. At the other, PA activities appeared as agenda items at governors' meetings, parent governors spoke as representatives of the PA at these meetings and were sponsored for election as governors through the PA. In between were schools where parent governors formally, as elected or co-opted members, reported to PTA or school association meetings.

Another significant constitutional difference was the parent constituency represented on or by the committee. In Uplands School, there was a committee for each year-group, which resulted in a greater degree of responsiveness and flexibility than is usually possible for the committees of large secondary schools. Robert Peel School ensured that groups of villages had two or three representatives so that the whole catchment area was covered by a network of communication and shared interest. At Highstones School, where this did not happen, I found an exaggerated tendency for unrepresented villages to disassociate themselves from committee activities.

There is no evidence to suggest that these variations in formal structure indicated significant differences in status or aim. Whatever their title and constitution the associations accepted a responsibility to raise funds for the school and organise social events for their members. In addition, some associations supported the school in less material ways and others organised meetings at which parents could learn more about the policies and work of the school.

The fund-raising function of the association is its least problematic one. Teachers in the CAP schools generally felt that they could not manage financially without the PA. Most parents and governors accepted the need for an association which would supplement local authority provision. Moreover, there was general agreement that parents who wished to help the school could show an interest in its facilities and work towards the improvement of these without infringing the professional autonomy of teachers. According to this view, parent members of the association could, and should, show their support for the school by raising money for it. In most cases it was also considered legitimate for them to offer practical assistance (e.g. garden landscaping; helping to build a garage for the mini-bus or a medical room). There were occasions, however, when local trade unions objected to this kind of parental activity.

In most schools it was open to anyone to suggest projects for which association funds or parent labour might be used. In one school, the PA Newsletter urged: 'If you have heard your daughter bemoaning the lack of certain facilities or equipment at school, get in touch with a Committee member and talk about it' (OT, 3). Here and elsewhere suggestions also came from pupils (sometimes through the School Council), governors (reporting to the committee through a parent governor) or teachers.

The fund-raising function of the association is customarily, but not constitutionally, linked with its social role, since social events are often held to be the quickest and most acceptable way of raising substantial sums of money. Paradoxically, these are often the events which receive the least support from parents and teachers. To be sure, the CAP team found that in predominantly urban, middle-class areas association activities such as Old Tyme Dances were well-supported and lucrative. Yet in other areas parents spoke slightingly of both the committee's choice of activities and their conduct of them. Typical comments were:

> I no longer support the Parent Association because basically I don't like barbecues, or cheese-and-wine functions. (OT, 4)

> Mr Maclaren: We are not motivated in terms of social contact with other parents and Barn Dances . . . if it's going to be a social get-together, then we don't see any need for it. (U, 14)

In addition, the social programmes arranged by the committees were held by many parents to reflect white, middle-class tastes. They were felt to be culturally inappropriate (e.g. Antique Auctions for working class parents), socially difficult (e.g. dances for widows or single parents), and too expensive (especially in rural areas where transport might more than double the cost of a ticket) (U, 14; OT, 4; HI, 2A4). As a result, few parents participated in their association's full social calendar and many events were poorly supported. A teacher commented:

You see if you have got a year Committee who are interested in
fund-raising and really involved in the school, the chances are
they are middle class people anyway. . . . I personally hadn't
considered the fact that the school social events are frequently
orientated towards the more middle class parents. (U, 15)

Moreover, in certain areas the existence of the association
committee actually discouraged parents from participating. Frequently parents did not distinguish between the association and its
committee and boycotted all association activities because they
felt excluded from the committee, which in several schools was
seen as a closed shop. There seemed to be a widely-held parent
view, explored in greater detail in Chapter Seven, that the PTA
committee is 'one little bunch and outside that bunch you're an
outsider' (HI, 2A4). Thus parents already discouraged by the
association's social programme may be further alienated by their
view of its committee. Such prejudice, may be particularly hard to
dispel in secondary schools, especially in rural and working-class
areas, where many parents claim already to have suffered embar-
rassment and even humiliation in their contacts with committee
members in infant and junior schools.

Parent members of committees in the CAP schools were not
insensitive to this problem. As one said:

Everyone has their own social level at which they feel confident . . . with a lot of parents who don't join in things, it's not
apathy, it's finding a way that they can get involved at their own
level. (HI, 2A4)

Yet this awareness can apparently do little, in the short term, to
provide constructive solutions. One PTA committee became
aware through the project of how they were viewed by other
parents. As a result they tried extremely hard for the rest of the
school year to 'build bridges' (as the secretary put it). They
diversified their programme, wrote personal letters to parents and
delivered them by hand, made contact with them in their homes –
but all to no avail. Despite the high regard in which the school is held
locally, social functions continued to be poorly attended or even
boycotted. Yet a sponsored spell raised on average £3.00 per child
in three weeks; parents who were unwilling to attend barbecues
and dances were nevertheless prepared to spend money in support

of their children's education. Clearly, it is not easy for committee members, who wish to change the policies of the association in an attempt to secure wider attendance at social functions, to do so.

Although social events tend usually to be for fund raising, they are normally separated in the stated aims of the association. Many associations exist, at least on paper, in order to improve relationships between staff and parents (and, sometimes, others associated with the school). Yet among both parents and teachers there is some ambivalence towards informal contact outside school. The CAP team found that some parents felt that they were already over-committed. By the time they had worked, run a home and supported their children at parents' evenings they had time and inclination only for their own friends and leisure pursuits. Others, however, wanted to get to know teachers as people, to see them pushing a pram, to know they played cricket, used the local market, chainstore or pub. Casual encounters either made it easier for them subsequently to talk to teachers in school, or meant that, in the event of a complaint or query, they knew someone to approach. Yet even these parents were unconvinced of the value of associations. As one parent said, 'PTAs never work. It's always us – and – them with teachers' (HI,24A). Another felt that 'teachers are not like ordinary people. The problem is that they only talk to teachers. They even marry other teachers'. (HI, 3A)

For their part, teachers tended to feel that attendance at association social functions was another demand on evenings or weekends already crowded with parents' meetings and professional commitments. Moreover, many of the teachers were anxious to safeguard the private existence which some parents wished to make public (e.g. they preferred to live out of the school catchment area). Hence, staff attendance at association social events was often reluctant and sometimes explicitly undertaken only for fund-raising reasons.

When personal relationships were established through association activities, it appears most frequently to have been because of 'shared coping' rather than by attendance at social events. Observations at Highstones and Robert Peel suggested that teachers and parents got to know one another not by dancing together, but by jointly manning the bar at the dance, not by walking together round the Summer Fayre, but by cutting sandwiches and washing up cups for the teas. Indeed, one parent put his experience plainly:

> The only time I ever got over [the social gap] was when we were building that swimming pool. And it was when you went along all sweaty to the local, that's when you really began to get to know them. (HI, 2A3)

Yet, as I have suggested, there can be a conflict of interest in such shared undertakings between a parent's trade union and association loyalties; and between the desire, expressed by some teachers and some parents, to increase informal contacts between them and the feeling, expressed by a few teachers and parents, that it was a dangerous precedent to allow volunteer labour to fill the gaps in educational provision left by financial cuts.

In some schools, associations also have an explicitly educational function. They organise meetings at which school policies are described and discussed, parts of the curriculum are explained and justified, questions from parents are answered by teachers, or parents are given the opportunity to attend a 'typical' lesson in one or more subject areas. Parents in the CAP schools were anxious to learn as much as possible about 'what actually goes on in classrooms', as accounts of meetings in Robert Peel, Old Town and Uplands show. Those who attended such events generally felt they had been useful and successful, and would have liked more of them.

Yet, given parents' apparently insatiable appetite for information about their children's education, how can one account for the fact that only a few of them attended association educational meetings? In part, lack of attendance may be attributed to the same causes that made it difficult for parents to attend other school meetings (see Chapter Seven). It is possible, however, that teachers' understandings of the purposes of these meetings, and, as a result, the way in which they were conducted, also had an inhibiting effect upon parents.

In general, the teachers seemed to see them as part of a wider school policy of 'giving account' to parents, of keeping them fully informed. Although the precise conduct of the meetings varied, it was generally consistent with this interpretation. Usually the seating was arranged so that questions were directed from the parents to a small group of teachers, sitting separately, who replied

as 'experts'. Where documentation was used it was 'professionally' produced, and made considerable reading demands on the
parents. Observers noted that teachers often subtly discouraged
comments or queries from parents which called in question the
practices of the school. Yet they were fully committed to 'parents'
right to know' and welcomed this chance to explain and explicate
their teaching.

For their part, parents with questions or misgivings about school
policies encountered several difficulties at educational meetings.
These are explained in greater detail in Chapter Seven and briefly
listed here. In the first place, most parents were deferential toward
teachers' knowledge of education and were content to leave
teaching in their hands. Secondly, teachers shared parents' views
on the inviolability of the professional's 'expert knowledge' and
tacitly discouraged parents from calling it in question. As one
parent said:

[These meetings] are a waste of time. Teachers don't listen.
(HI, 3A)

Thirdly, the form and structure of the meetings was consistent with
white, middle-class conventions, but made parents from other
social groups feel ill-at-ease. Finally, in all schools, but especially in
the rural areas, there were parents who were concerned about the
future of their children but felt handicapped by their own education
from attending or speaking out at meetings.

Despite the relatively unchallenged position of teachers as
experts most schools seemed to have at least a minority of parents
who felt that they were equipped to enter into public dialogue with
the staff. In each school there was also a small number of parents
who wanted a greater say in school policy (e.g. on discipline,
curriculum options). Indeed at Uplands this group seemed to be
fairly substantial. Although both sets of parents were discouraged
by the form and conventions of educational evenings from claiming
professional equality with teachers, they had no other body
through which to attempt to express their views. The majority of
parents felt remote from the governors and expressed ignorance of
their functions; in any case, no school had more than two parent
governors. In default of any alternative, parent-activists turned to

the association because it offered them collective force. As one said:

> I'd like to feel that if there were enough parents who disagreed [with the school's policy on an issue], at least we'd be noticed. (HI, 2A3)

Yet they were not satisfied with the degree of influence that involvement gave them. There was widespread scepticism about the power of formal meetings and groups, and, in several schools, Project members heard parents complain of feeling ineffectual. Indeed, in one school, a parent had rejected active membership of the PTA precisely because of his experience in another school of the association's lack of influence.

> I went to a PTA meeting [there] and the headmaster opened by saying that he was an ex-officio chairman; and he would welcome any suggestions on how to raise funds, but if anyone wanted to talk about what to do with the funds or the curriculum or anything funny like that, we had better mind our own business because he would sort all that out. . . . That destroyed my enthusiasm for the PTA. (HI, 2A3)

Powerless though many association members felt, active membership, especially of the committee, had one advantage – it gave access to information which parents suspected might otherwise have been filtered many times before it reached them. This sense of 'being in the know' was particularly noticeable in schools where governors reported direct to the association committee.

> Mrs. R.: I suppose in the PTA meeting we get more information than perhaps comes out generally . . . we do have a parent governor who comes and reports about the meeting. In other PTAs I've been on the governors' meeting is a closed shop. . . . (RP, II2)

Unfortunately, the notion that committee members had privileged access to information reinforced the suspicion of parents outside the committee that the latter were an élite whose loyalty to the staff might be stronger than their commitment to other parents.

> Mrs. J.: I'm not a great believer in PTAs actually because in the end you get an élitist little group who are close to the ear of the Headmaster, and everybody else is very much out of it. (RP, II2)

In other words, there is a danger that action which seems to a few parents to be a legitimate search for ways of acquiring information and exercising control may make the school seem less accountable in the eyes of the majority.

Teachers themselves increased parents' sense of ineffectuality by stressing the fund-raising function of the association and sometimes by opposing its assumption of any other role. As one parent said:

> I think in the last few months that only one point came up in the Committee, that was about the sick children. . Members are under the impression that the duty of the Parents' Committee is to raise money for a lot of things. (U, 15)

In another school, teachers were very hostile to the view that parents should discuss educational matters at PTA meetings unless these had been arranged on the school's initiative. Association meetings were not, it was said, 'a place where parents should discuss school problems', or, 'a forum for airing grievances' (HI, 2B4).

Parents in all schools were left wondering where they could voice legitimate criticisms. As one said:

> I recently discovered how powerless you can feel as a parent. How difficult it is to fight the system. . . . And for parents who are not middle class, articulate and downright stubborn or obstinate, they can't help but feel very powerless with regard to the school. (U, 15)

Both teachers and parents also knew how difficult it was to separate questions about the content and practice of education from those of personality and professional competence, and this further inhibited discussion at educational meetings.

In all of this a paradox seems to exist. The heads and teachers of all CAP schools justly prided themselves on their accessibility. To them, accountability was in part a question of opening up the school and reducing the anxiety of parents in dealing with teachers. This policy of direct and easy access to individual teachers contributed strongly to the expressed satisfaction of most parents. Yet it reduces the likelihood that associations will develop as formally-constituted organisations with an interest in general educational policies. Thus, by maximising their accountability to individual parents, schools may be inhibiting the growth of organised parental interest in the education of everybody's children.

There were also those who wanted to help their schools but felt that the initiatives open to them in primary schools were now closed. As one said:

> When your children are younger, you can help . . . but when they get older they don't want you up at the school. (HI, 2A3)

Some felt that the PA offered an alternative. For example, the PA at Old Town initiated and organised the purchase of a teletype and micro-computer. Other typical comments were:

> We don't know what we can do to help. . . . We don't want to push ourselves forward but I thought maybe if I joined the PTA I could do something. (HI, A3)

> Parent: We would be interested in parental involvement. We would be interested in the business of cash raising if that is necessary – it seems to us that it should be unnecessary, but since it is necessary within the system now – we've got to back up the local education grants and funding. (U, 15)

In short, by confining associations to a passive role in all other areas than fund-raising, and by encouraging parents to see the school as accountable to them only through their individual children, teachers may be depriving themselves of the potential backing of organised parental support.

Moreover, governing bodies are politically controlled; parent and school associations are not. At a time of falling rolls and financial cuts, schools can ill-afford to ignore this fact. To be sure, some committees in CAP schools seemed to run in tandem with the governors, and while this generally worked to the overall good of the school because of the apparent existence of consensus, committee independence might be threatened if conflict were to develop over school goals or the means of achieving them. Further, the composition and conduct of many committees gave the parents the impression that they represented only a narrow, sectional interest. It could therefore be argued that, as presently constituted, they are in the broadest sense political bodies. Yet membership of the association in CAP schools was open to all parents, and the occupation of parents on some of the committees refuted the 'white, middle-class' stereotype which was attached to them.

Further, there are very few formal procedures in the English educational system to enable the school to account to parents as a whole. Reports deal with individuals, school parents' meetings are normally arranged to deal with specific topics affecting groups of pupils, newsletters and other written communications are not easily susceptible to reply. The school can and sometimes effectively does communicate with the community as a whole through the press, but newspapers are unreliable and use of them denies parents and teachers the opportunity of face-to-face discussion. Governors, even parent governors, seem remote, inaccessible and difficult to influence. Associations alone of existing alternatives have the potential for developing procedures which would enable a school to give account of itself to the whole parental body, or community, and to hear the views of its members. Yet, if CAP schools are typical this potential is either largely ignored or channelled into fund-raising activities.

From this brief survey it is possible to draw a number of tentative conclusions:

1) The fund-raising and practical-assistance functions of associations are widely regarded as uncontroversial, except by those who fear that fund-raising and parent-labour may come to represent 'tax supplements'. Parents and teachers share the view that, in a practical sense, accountability is a two-way process. However, some schools find it self-defeating to combine social activities with fund-raising. The nature of the social programme, and the fact that it is seen to be organised by a committee whom many parents regard as socially exclusive, contribute to poor attendance and limited financial support, especially in rural and working-class areas.

2) Association committees, often stereotyped as exclusive 'in-groups', are not generally perceived as representative of the majority of parents and may appear to have privileged access to the head or governors. As a result other parents may be alienated from the association. Increased accountability by the head and the senior teachers to a small group of parents may thus reduce the school's overall capacity to give effective account of itself.

3) It is worth paying attention to the constitutional details of the association (e.g. name: 'Parent–Teacher Association' holds exclusive, socially-threatening connotations for many parents of secondary school children; size: associations which are sub-divided into smaller units and are supported by local networks are potentially more responsive than larger, more unitary ones; membership: if it is automatic, it cannot be exclusive).

4) Many of the parents who would welcome informal social contact with teachers lack self-confidence in dealing with schools. Yet, informal relationships between parents and teachers develop more satisfactorily through shared work undertaken by the association than through shared social activities. In other words, teachers' capacity to give account of themselves may be adversely affected if either teachers or parents adhere too closely to self-imposed definitions of their respective roles.

5) Many parents who do not wish to be involved in the association's social activities are anxious to support and help the school, often as a way of expressing their sense of shared responsibility for the education of their children. More parents might become involved in more activities if different types of activity were differentiated from one another in publicity material; if it were made clear to parents that involvement in one activity could be sustained independently of the others; and if fund-raising activities made more appeal to those with little to give.

6) Associations or association meetings over which teachers retain strong influence or control may help schools to 'give account' of their policies more effectively, but are unlikely

to stimulate dialogue between parents and teachers. Some parents, especially those who wish to hold the school 'to account', may find this very frustrating, particularly at educational meetings.

7) Headteachers and teachers who are accessible to individual parents may encourage dialogue with them, but in doing so may reduce the potency of organised criticism and support from the association. They may in fact make it less likely that they will be 'held to account' by parents in general.

8) Parent associations are the only formally-constituted body, other than the governors, through which parents can criticise the school, help and support it, and take educational initiatives on its behalf. Unlike the governors, association officers are not politically appointed and have no legal responsibility for the school. This generally gives the association a freedom of action which, in some instances, the former lack. In turn this creates the conditions for three-sided debate and negotiation, a situation in which the political skill of the head assumes great importance.

9

Teachers and 'the world of work'

David Bridges

The CAP case studies were conducted during a period of mounting unemployment and in a context in which successive official publications* had criticised secondary schools for failing to respond sufficiently to the needs of the commercial and industrial section of society or to present to their pupils a sufficiently positive picture of the importance of industry and commerce to national life. The 'Great Debate' on education was not long past and one official publication after another had taken up the refrain of closer relationships between schools and 'the world of work':

> The Secretaries of State believe that all authorities should regard the setting up of adequate liaison arrangements between schools and industry as a major educational responsibility. They commend three particular matters to authorities for further action: careers education, work experience and understanding the national importance of industry. It remains a matter for concern that . . . many pupils are not being taught how industry creates national wealth and the ways in which we depend upon industry for our standards of living. (DES and the Welsh Office, 1979: 6)

Not surprisingly therefore a number of schools we were working with included among the concerns they wanted us to explore their relations with local employers. More specifically they were concerned to study the kind of picture of the school which had been

*For a fuller account of the 'official' pressure in support of greater responsiveness by schools to the 'needs of industrial society' see Beck 1981.

communicated to local employers; employers' satisfaction or dissatisfaction with the amount and kind of information they received; employers' interest in closer contact with the school; employers' responses to what they knew of the school and its curriculum; and their ideas about different ways in which they and the schools might develop their mutual understanding and cooperation. The CAP team accepted these questions as relevant to the study of the school's 'accountability' to employers.*

This led us into visiting and interviewing local employers (mainly those involved in manufacturing and processing industries). We also interviewed teachers, headteachers, and parents. One school in particular was concerned to explore this area, and in this instance a substantial section of the case study on 'The school and local employers' provided the basis for a special evening meeting between school staff members and some fifteen local employers. Transcripts from this discussion as well as interviews conducted by the CAP team provided the raw material from which the following observations and examples are derived.

What picture emerged from these studies of relations between schools and local employers, and what implications does it have for schools' accountability to local employers?

First, and as an important preliminary to the conflict which I shall present, it needs to be emphasised that the schools we worked with enjoyed almost universally excellent relations with local employers. Employers spoke approvingly of them, often presenting

---

* It has been interesting to note subsequently the extent to which the Schools Council Industry Project concerned specifically 'to introduce into the education of young people from the age of 14 an awareness and understanding of industry and its contribution to social, economic and cultural well-being' has itself been drawn into accountability issues. At an early stage the Planning Group agreed that 'the accomplishment of this aim will depend upon the development of a sense of partnership, at both national and local levels, between participants from education and industry, so that both are better informed about each other's work and are fully involved in creating a good relationship'. Important sections of the interim report by the Project Director are devoted to the way those in different LEAs responded to the Project's expectation of local consultation including illuminating comment on the role (or lack of it) of school governors in the process.

The Interim Report (from which the above quotations are taken), *The Schools Council Industry Project* (July 1979), is available free from the Schools Council.

them as exceptions to national trends. The examples they gave of what they took to be bad practice were almost all from other schools than those we were examining. Local employers gave the schools all sorts of tangible practical support from fruitful work experience opportunities to money for the school library and sausages at cost price for the summer fair.

Besides this it was clear that there were certain areas of school work in which schools and employers shared a concern for development and improvement – in the provision of work experience, better careers advice, clearer identification of and better teaching of the 'transitionary skills' which would help pupils take the step from school to work: competence in filling up application forms; skill in presenting oneself effectively in interviews; and understanding things like contracts of employment, health and safety regulations, conditions of employment, income tax, national insurance. In all these areas schools recognised that there was now scope for continuing improvement of which local employers would in general approve. Indeed, the schools were interested in the project partly because of their concern to develop the means of communication which would make this improvement possible.

The context is thus on the whole one of amiable relationships between schools which are not oblivious of the need to be thinking of and equipping children for the transition to work and employers who have fairly high regard for the CAP schools.

Nevertheless our interviews and case studies seem to me to indicate certain fairly fundamental differences. I shall present these rather crudely as differences of perspective between teachers on the one hand and employers on the other, though I hasten to acknowledge that the picture was not that simple and that significant differences are to be found in both camps. On the whole both teachers and employers preferred to blur the contrasts, not least because of the enormous fund of goodwill and the strong interest in closer cooperation which teachers, in particular, did not want to upset by bringing serious differences of aspiration or ideology too near to the surface. I have chosen to sharpen these differences because I believe they are educationally significant even if they are politically uncomfortable.

1. The gap between the aspirations which teachers have for the future careers of their pupils and the job opportunities currently provided by employers

> I suppose it's summed up in the parrot cry 'If you don't do well, you'll end up in a factory', which you can hear in schools all over the country. (Teacher, RP, II4:4)

The teachers on the one hand have pupils in their charge to whom they (very properly?) feel a certain kind of loyalty and for whom they have high ambitions. They make it their business to develop as far as they can their intellect, imagination, independence of mind, sensitivity and skills. They want for their pupils employment and conditions of work which will encourage the full and continued development of these qualities. But, as one teacher expressed it:

> Industry isn't concerned with people developing personally, is it? It's concerned, admittedly reasonably enough in some ways, with them as producers. That's very partial. If you think of the whole idea of the common curriculum which we've established here, that's about all round development and not allowing people to go off and be only partially developed. (RP, II 4:4)

The trouble is, even if employers value continuing personal development, such development is not their *raison d'être*.

> We, in industry, are in the business to make a profit; that's how we live; that's the mode of operation. Whereas the philosophy of the teacher is something totally different. . . . Our objectives are, I believe, very different from your own. (Director of small engineering firm, Robert Peel seminar, p. 15)

Many employers acknowledged that a considerable proportion of the jobs which they could actually provide offered nothing like the opportunities for continuing personal development which teachers valued so highly.

> Some of the jobs are extremely boring even within a quarter of an hour. And to go and talk and work with them is to be aware of what they do. It reminds me how important it is just to talk to

people as I walk round because it gives them something else to think about, and they like to talk to somebody. (RP, II 4:4)

What this employer might have added was that many of the jobs in his factory were not only boring and repetitive but also done in conditions of such noise and dust that they effectively prevented all social communication between one employee and another during working hours.

One employer told this story of a young man who was taken on to do a wholly unskilled assembly job.

He was very good, but he got worse and worse, and I said to him 'Look you have got to do twenty an hour'. I said to him 'do twenty and come and see me and tell me when you have finished.' He came back. He did those in forty-five minutes. I said to him 'I am not asking you to do a lot am I?' I said to him, 'Keep track of yourself, make a note of how many you have done, then if you fall behind, go a bit quicker the next time and you will pick up'. Well the 200 that he was supposed to do 20 an hour to take him 10 hours, took him 28 hours and he complained and moaned, 'I don't want to do this I want to do car alarms'. I said 'You can't do those until we have finished this'. 'You can't just get halfway through a job, and stop and say right I am fed up'. I said, 'Life is not like that in our business, you have got to start a job and you have got to stick at it, however boring it is. If it is boring the thing is to do it as quickly as you possibly can, not to draw it out. You are like all these kids, that moan about being at school, you don't learn anything, and you are there another couple of years trying to get exams. All the clever ones learn something and get out when they are 16 because they don't like school.

In the end I told him that he just wasn't cut out for the job. (Elliott interview F, pp. 6, 7)

Several employers dealing with repetitive unskilled work had almost given up trying to get youngsters from school to stick at it:

Some of our people do a job called twisting and tinning – boring and repetitive. You would never get a youngster to stick at that job – it's mainly the older woman . . . (RP, II 4:4)

They are very keen to solder and after a time they can solder fairly proficiently. But you give them some job to do all day long, every day for a couple of weeks, after the first three days they don't want to know. Whereas you get a middle-aged woman doing it, she will sit there all day long and do it. A middle-aged lady will sit at a bench all day long, particularly if you can get a couple of them, and they can chat. But you get a kid from school, it's the application they lack, they learn the skills, but after they have learnt the skill they don't want to know about keeping on doing the same job. (Elliott interview F, p. 5).

Not surprisingly, perhaps, teachers are generally unimpressed by these as future jobs let alone future careers for their pupils. They do indeed, as some employers suspect, discourage pupils from going into work of this kind and even represent it as a threat to be used against the idle. One teacher resisted firmly the suggestion that there was anything improper in schools encouraging pupils to look critically at some of the jobs on offer:

From some of the comments that are made from time to time we do get the impression (perhaps wrongly) that in the eyes of some people we are being almost disruptive in schools because we are encouraging people to be dissatisfied with the kind of hum-drum job. Now obviously that is a view that we couldn't accept. (Robert Peel discussion, p. 11)

However, teachers may create different problems for their pupils by encouraging them to aspire to jobs which simply are not available. A personnel officer for a telecommunications company explained:

Another thing, one year their careers master – I don't know if he is still there – was saying you don't want to go into factories, you don't want to go into shops. Go for the clerical jobs. Now anybody with a grain of sense would know that there was at that time virtually no clerical work round here. So it meant that all these youngsters leaving school – a very high proportion of them – had this blasé idea of how fantastic clerical work is. In actual fact it's very boring – and the poor little devils were having to commute to Cambridge because there was no work round here. And also, of course, they are not really suitable for office work, a lot of them, and they were being turned down. And that can be soul-destroying for a youngster to keep being turned down, over and over again. (RP, II 4:4)

But, as the managing director of one manufacturing company observed, the social consequences of taking into employment young people who are going to be working at a level below their real capacity and aspiration can be worrying in a different way.

> It worries me no end because I think whatever politically we finish up with we just finish up with people who are dissatisfied. They can either be dissatisfied in a free society or they can be dissatisfied in an oppressive society, but they are going to be dissatisfied. That may lead to a more oppressive society politically – through their dissatisfaction – it turns into a so-called communist country. But in the end all you've got is the same dissatisfaction but they are more oppressed. So what can I do other than work to try to keep the people here happy and interested, aware of what they can contribute in general? (RP, II 4:4)

There seemed to me to be three common features of employers' views about employing young people in what they saw as a large number of boring and repetitive jobs:

(i) *These are the jobs that exist and someone's going to have to do them.*

> Some of those jobs are always going to exist and I think it is perhaps a negative attitude to think that the youngsters don't want it and therefore we won't encourage them. Somebody will have to encourage them to do those jobs in any case. (Robert Peel seminar transcript, p. 12)

(ii) *Not all young people can expect to find intrinsic interest or satisfaction in the jobs they are doing. They are going to have to see it as a means to an end rather than an end in itself and find their satisfaction elsewhere.*

> What we try to do is to instil a commercial awareness into them. We say 'well you have got to make those to earn your wage packet on Friday'. You keep drumming this in and after a time they begin to realise it. They say 'well we have got to do 200 of those this week to get a salary' – after a time they get the message. (John Elliott transcript F, p. 5)

(iii)   *There are simply different types of people who are more or less naturally suited to different types of employment, including the most routine, repetitive and apparently boring.*

> There are people who are going to be happy for the whole of their working life, doing a very mundane job. They just don't want to get out of the warmth of the flock, you know. They see that as too much responsibility for them. You can usually recognise them from the sort of backgrounds they come from and you can see them very early on in their career in industry. You know, I think it's sorting out those sort of people, the different sorts of people that you have got to cater for, that is the big problem. (Robert Peel seminar, p. 12)

Few if any of the teachers we spoke to could really accept the standpoint represented in these propositions. First, perhaps stubbornly and unrealistically, they would be reluctant to accept that the only future available for one of the pupils they had responsibility for and had come to care for was in a dull repetitive job with little or no career prospect. They insist on having higher aspirations for their pupils than the job market will perhaps realistically support.

Secondly, perhaps naively or perhaps as part of the proper exercise of their responsibility, the teachers we interviewed did seek to engage children in activities which are intrinsically worthwhile and satisfying (which is not to say that they had to be continuously gratifying or pleasurable). The employers themselves frequently spoke of the excitement, interest and satisfaction which they themselves found in their own work. Teachers on the whole persist in the hope that their pupils too will find such satisfaction.

Thirdly, and perhaps most significantly, there is a particular tension between the employers' requirement for a labour force with a clearly sorted, pyramid-like structure of ability, and the commitment of many schools to the egalitarian principles of comprehensive education. This is especially the case where such principles are extended into providing a broad common curriculum for all children and mixed ability grouping and postponing as far as possible until after school the kind of competition which leads to the clear differentiation of children on some kind of criteria of ability. In other words many teachers have sought quite deliberately (though not always successfully) to disassociate education from the business of sorting out children to match a given hierarchy of work opportunity.*

I have been concerned almost exclusively so far with the tensions between aspirations of teachers and expectations of employers in relation to broadly the lower 50 per cent to 80 per cent of the ability range (depending very much on local job opportunities). We found *less* discrepancy in expectations in relation to the top 10 per cent or 20 per cent of the ability range – but, as we shall see, there are differences here too.

2. The gap between teachers' and employers' views of the sort of attitudes which they wish children to develop

> They don't really expect us to breed a load of automatons, do they? (RP, 4)

Employers were commonly more disturbed by the inappropriate 'attitudes' that young people seemed to bring to their work than by their inadequate skill, though very often they had difficulty in articulating precisely what it was they were looking for. Sometimes they would express a view that teachers would have little difficulty in sharing . . .

> The kind of employees that we want are intelligent, flexible, resourceful people who can explain themselves clearly, think about what they are doing and adapt to it. (HI, 2B7D)

. . . but usually in such cases they would turn out to be talking about trainee managers or appointments of this kind.

More commonly the complaint of those seeking employees among the average and below-average sector of the ability range focussed on their lack of application, their attitudes towards authority and the qualities of 'adaptability and enthusiasm' which

---

* For a radical and challenging discussion of issues raised in this section see Edgley 1977.

employers seemed to be looking for in vain in many of their young employees.*

(i) Application

They do tend to find it very difficult to sustain the effort. That's one of the things that I feel about school in the latter years. I understand it in Junior Schools where they say kids come out of school with rather a . . . you know, you do something for forty-five minutes and then get up, wander around, and go off somewhere else, and do something totally different. I think this is one of the biggest hurdles that they have to get over. You know, that you have got to sit in the same place, and do virtually the same thing all day long, in a lot of those jobs you know . . . (Elliott interview F, p. 4)

We return here to the boring, repetitive nature of some of the work which employees are expected to do. It clearly requires a different kind of routine to that experienced in school. But how and to what extent should schools prepare them for it?

While valuing application and 'stickability' teachers cannot easily bring themselves to see it as their responsibility to train pupils to attend for hours on end to acknowledgedly repetitive work. On the contrary they see educational stimulus as arising out of a variety of activities during a day. This is how one teacher with responsibility for careers education expressed her frustration to a group of employers:

Now at 16 the children are leaving a school where they have had – all right they might not find maths interesting – but they

* There have of course been numerous independent statements of the attitudes which employers are looking for in young people. The ones which I have picked out are the ones which recur in our case studies. C.f. for example Sir John Methven's assessment made in a speech in October 1976 when he was Director General of the CBI:

Apart from the scholastic requirements . . . employers are also looking more closely for evidence of such personal qualities as self-discipline and self-reliance, loyalty and enthusiasm, right attitudes to work, ability to communicate and work as a team, a critical and thinking approach to problems, willingness to accept change . . .

(edited and reprinted as 'What Industry Wants', *Times Educational Supplement,* 29th October 1976).

have a change of lesson every so often in a day; they have perhaps a club they go to in the week; they have sports, school visits, outings and so on. How do we say to them, 'All that is going to change – imagine that you are in this room waiting at the end of this line for a piece of paper or whatever it is that comes along?' I mean we can't do that, in all fairness I could ask you what are *you* doing to help the children when they come in to adjust to this monotony that some of them are going into? (Robert Peel seminar, p. 12)

(ii) Attitudes towards authority

A number of employers expressed unease about young people's attitudes to authority. As one employer observed:

It's a hell of a shock for them when they suddenly come to work and they find that they have for instance a foreman telling them what to do. For some of them that's quite amazing, somebody to tell them what to do. And he is not inviting you to argue. If you argue, he just looks at you and says, 'Well don't bother to argue, just do it.' And that is in the end the only way we can run an organisation. . . .

They need to have a basic understanding that when they work in a structured part of society, which going to work is all about, in that particular area of activity they have to do what someone with authority tells them to do. (RP, II4:2)

Some of the teachers of science and of practical subjects I spoke to had every sympathy with this attitude, particularly in circumstances where there were dangerous machinery or chemicals about. But one English teacher took a stance which I believe represents more liberal minded opinion among teachers of the humanities. I began by putting to him the employer's opinion which I have quoted in the paragraph above and suggested:

David Bridges: There seems to be here some sort of tension between a school concerned to develop critical, autonomous pupils and a firm concerned to get ready obedience to somebody in authority. I don't know whether that directly bears on English teaching . . .?

Teacher: Well, I suppose it does. Most English teachers as I'm sure you know base their work on literature. It's all about people and relationships, and I would have thought that, certainly, I would not want anyone to be unquestioningly obedient. I would hate that. Really, the word 'why' is very important. That seems to me a poor way of looking at people. I can see why they do it but I don't think in any way we should – they don't really expect us to breed a lot of automatons, do they? . . .

I think it is really a matter of how the experienced person puts his case. I think people have a right to have a case put to them. To say 'because I say so' seems to deny all that we are doing in school. . . . I think acquiescence – just plain, dull, acquiescence – is an awful thing. . . . I'm a bit thrown by that statement. It seems such a rotten way of regarding people. (RP, II4:4)

Employers are not themselves oblivious of the tension:

There is a contradiction there to some extent. We can't encourage a child to have an enquiring mind at school and to be looking for reasons and learning, and then to expect them to switch that off and accept unquestioningly the discipline. In some way industry has got to be educated to accept that kids have got an individuality and a questioning attitude. On the other hand you do get some children who have just switched off to any form of discipline and their attitude is just anarchic. (RP, II4:4)

(iii) Adaptability

This was a quality which employers were constantly referring to without ever satisfactorily explaining. I came to suspect that it often meant in practice that a young person was able to cope relatively easily with the change from school to work, that he knuckled down (knuckled under?) fairly readily and was amenable to the changing demands that an employer might put on him.

Interpreted in this way, adaptability is a sort of composite quality involving the desired attitude to getting down to work and to those in authority. It is, however, somewhat ambiguous between the sort of qualities which educators might admire and seek to develop (life coping skills, varied and creative response to different circumstances, etc.?) and others that many of them regarded as the very antithesis of education (docile subservience to the will of others?)

3. The gap between teachers' and employers' priorities in the curriculum and within the teaching of particular subjects

> What I'm worried about is that possibly sometimes there is a bit too much concentration on the academic skills to the detriment of the practical skills, to life coping skills. (Employers, RP, II4:4)

(i) Basic skills and intellectual disciplines

Some employers argued from the kind of judgement I have already illustrated – that teachers had unrealistic ambitions for their pupils – to the view that they were also giving inappropriate emphasis to the 'academic' aspects of knowledge at the expense of basic intellectual and 'life-coping' skills.

> There are vast groups of children who are never going to be academic. . . . We have got to accept that on the learning rate and intelligence rate half the population is below average. It is going to take them a lot more effort and a lot longer to learn the basic skills. And probably they have got to concentrate much more of their school curriculum on those basic skills rather than getting them into conceptual subjects which they are never going to understand. (RP, II4:4)

One company described what happened when they recently offered some engineering apprenticeships:

> When we came to test these lads they were clueless, completely and absolutely clueless. The test we gave them was by no means difficult – we could do them mentally and we left school a long, long time ago – things such as the area of a circle; the application of Pythagoras; metric to imperial conversion; decimal to fractions. (RP, II,4:3)

I put this to teachers who had been planning and developing new courses in science and mathematics and asked them what sort of considerations had gone into determining the character of these courses.

Paul Francis as a head of science might perhaps have been expected to be reasonably sympathetic to an industrial perspective on the curriculum and indeed, on his own account, this is something to which he gave serious consideration in planning a new school's science programme:

I really wanted to know what sort of things employers wanted, to help us plan our courses and look at which kid should be going into which groups, and tell us into what sort of employment they are going. So, that was my initial interest.

Paul Francis went on to describe in some detail the series of consultations that he engaged in – with other science teachers, the head, science advisers and employers – before drawing up the programme. It is worth listing some of the considerations that he took into account:

timetable constraints

the desirability of an integrated science course

the imaginativeness and interest of different syllabi

the suitability of courses to different levels of ability: I wanted a course that would cater for a fair band of ability at the top rather than just the highflyers. I didn't want people just struggling through.

the fit of the course with the interests of the teachers

the acceptability of courses in a context of university entrance

the requirements of employers

Although he did take some account of employers' concerns he made it clear that this was in no way an overriding consideration. In fact it seems that his first loyalty was to his own conception of what would constitute a legitimate representation of science:

I think we would have to be honest and say that we are interested in educating pupils in science so that they have a basic understanding of a fair number of the basic areas, the fundamental areas of science that hopefully will carry them through for quite a number of years in their general lives. We certainly wouldn't be specifically training them just for a job in a factory, but we have to some extent borne that in mind – the fact that for example employers would like people who want to go into engineering apprenticeships and technician apprenticeships to have an education in physics – by allowing that option to be available. (RP, II4:4)

Some of the mathematics teachers I spoke to gave a similar impression on the lines that they were aiming to develop in all children an understanding of mathematics as a discipline, of mathematical operations, of what some people referred to as 'conceptual mathematics'. They sought to join to this what they recognised as the legitimate demands of employers and others for certain kinds of arithmetical skills. They also sought to persuade employers not to assess children's mathematical ability simply in terms of their facility with these exercises.

Employers, by contrast, wanted all children to be taught basic arithmetic – and saw 'conceptual mathematics' as something appropriate only to a small minority who might for example be going on to do mathematics or science at university. This, for example, was the view expressed in a comment by one local employer:

> Going back to mathematics. One feels that if children come out of school without a mastery of the basic arithmetic they are going to be at a disadvantage throughout life. There are very few jobs in industry in fact which call for much more than basic arithmetic. And conceptual mathematics are really for this tiny minority. One should be regarded as a necessity [basic arithmetic] and the other should be regarded as an advantage [conceptual mathematics] (Production Manager: RP, II 4:3)

4. The gap between teachers' and employers' attitudes towards the values and importance of the world of industry and commerce

> They complain about teachers being almost anti-industry. . . .
> I think I could be accused of that. I really wouldn't defend myself against it.' (Teacher: RP, II4:4)

Employers we interviewed were often looking for more willingness on the part of teachers to present a positive picture of the world of industry and commerce in schools, to show its positive importance and the personal satisfaction it can provide. There was a strong feeling among them that teachers, perhaps through ignorance, perhaps through the bias of their own essentially academic background, undervalue the world of industry and commerce and present a somewhat disparaging picture of this world in the classroom.

Employers picked out a number of different dimensions of this problem. One of these was *the disparaging picture which schools present of conditions in factories*.

> I think that unfortunately schools tend to look very much down on factories and shops. Not all schools, but some do. I think they put an umbrella over all factories as being what I call the old-type Lancashire cotton mill – girls with curlers in their hair, cigarettes falling out of the corner of their mouth – clog feet – you know. That type of set up. Very old-fashioned ideas. OK there are those industries around. I think by the very nature of the jobs they do there will always be noisy factories, there will always be dirt where there is machinery and so on. But equally, if you take the other side of the coin, there is a fair amount of industry which by its very nature has to be clean. This happens to be one of them. It's not noisy. Some of the work is boring, but equally a lot of the work can be very interesting. (RP, II4:3)

A second aspect of concern was the way in which *schools seemed to encourage criticism of aspects of the capitalist industrial economy without establishing any basic understanding of its rationale*.

> They have terrific debates about – the unacceptable face of advertising and things like that. I think they should think about these things. But they start to come in on what is a good, critical angle without knowing the basic foundations. Because there are some extremely unfortunate things done in advertising, it doesn't mean that people who advertise, the objectives of the organisation that is advertising, are wrong in themselves or are wrong in general for all competitive based, capital funded production units. (RP, II4:3)

A third aspect was the way in which *schools and educational institutions generally seemed to admire occupations associated with spending surplus capital rather more than those concerned with its creation through the successful manufacture of things that people wanted to buy*. In this way they devalued the social value and importance of the manufacturing industry.

> I think the schools encourage a feeling that work in a factory is somehow less desirable than white-collar working for the

government. Whereas I would put just the reverse. It is easy to go and divide up the wealth. Being creative takes much more guts, a lot more involvement, a bit more risk, it takes more skill, I think. (RP, II4:3)

A fourth and closely related aspect was *schools' seeming reluctance to encourage in particular their more able pupils to think in terms of a career in industry and commerce or study in higher education with a more directly industrial or commercial application.*

One employer complained that he had never had a single student from a particular school applying for an HND apprenticeship. 'Why do you think that is?' he was asked. 'Because the school wants them to go to university.' He went on to tell the story of one of his HND apprentices who had gone to a local meeting of sixth formers to talk about his experience but was told by two sixth form teachers that 'he had talked a lot of rubbish' and was 'more or less told to shut up'. (Jean Graham-Cameron interview, L, p. 7)

Not all teachers would accept this characterisation of their attitudes. Nor of course would those in industry and commerce want to argue that all teachers were like that. In interview employers tended (rather bewilderingly, I sometimes found) to present these characterisations as pictures of what teachers in general were like but immediately to make an exception of the teachers in CAP schools of whom they had direct experience.

But some teachers freely accepted the characterisation provided. One who did so was in fact a head of English – on his own account one of a generation of English teachers trained in the 1960s who came to see a close relationship between the teaching of literature and social criticism. This is how he began to express his attitude in interview:

> I realise now – I'd never thought of it before – but I'm really very much the sort of teacher of the sixties who had this sort of view that it's our job to get them to think about the sort of society they are in and to say 'why?' . . .
>
> I feel myself you have a duty to make them think about the society they live in. I think English is a subject which is particularly well equipped to provide that. . . .
>
> All this guff about the British not working – when you think of the jobs many Britons are asked to do, I'm not surprised if they don't work. It amazes me that anybody really expects

them to put their backs into this. Which I suppose is implicit in my view of what I teach, really, and how I teach it. But it really amazes me if you can hear them going on 'you really have to work harder' and what they mean is drill ten holes instead of nine. And in a way again I feel what we do in school is often negated, what I do is negated by the set-up they enter. . . .

In school we say 'Do your best'. The idea of planned obsolescence as such is a denial of doing your best. In that sense it strikes me as though often you are working against society. That sort of sums it up. . . .

And this is probably why they complain. And I suppose in a way I could be accused of fostering the view that they dislike, I don't do it overtly, but implicitly it's there – I wouldn't deny that. (RP, II4:4)

This kind of stance, mistakenly viewed by some people outside schools as evidence of Trotskyite infiltration, is conservative rather more than revolutionary in character. The love of the products of man's artistic imagination and sensibility; the scepticism of authority; the questioning of taken-for-granted assumptions; the humanitarianism and the anti-materialism – this is the stuff of what Raymond Williams calls 'the old humanists'* and nineteenth-century liberalism rather than revolutionary socialism. But, let us not mince matters, what is just as relevant in this context is that without a doubt it is the stuff of a kind of schooling which stands firmly against anything which will produce a grateful and amenable work force for the assembly line. And it is precisely this sort of conflict of values and purpose which has led some people to pose the question I want to turn to in my final section: whether it should be left to teachers to determine the kind of values and aims that are promoted in schools.

Accountability and control of the curriculum

I have illustrated in this chapter a considerable number of areas of educational concern in which there is evidence of discrepant and

* Williams distinguished three groups which he called respectively 'the old humanists', 'the industrial trainers' and 'the public educators'. His discussion of their respective attitudes in historical settings is very illuminating of the kind of issues which in this paper are located in contemporary case study.

even contradictory opinion on the part of teachers and employers in industry and commerce. We have observed significant differences of opinion over the aims and purposes of education; the personal development of children; people's evaluation of the world of industry and commerce and its social importance; knowledge and its utility; and the content and structure of the curriculum. There is not a clear and unified opinion either among employers or among teachers. The situation is much less tidy than that. We very often found in our interviews that both teachers and employers found themselves articulating unthought-out positions for the first time. Nevertheless both those in schools and those in industry and commerce believe that there are differences of opinion between them and we found sufficient statement of them to suggest that they are neither mythical nor insignificant.

Now one response to this observation is to suppose that people would think differently if only they understood better the other side's point of view. Our studies suggest, however, that it may be naive to assume that the gaps in attitudes and values would in practice be narrowed by closer familiarity with each other's world. It is true that employers spoke with special approval of the careers work of one school where a number of the teachers involved did have previous industrial/commercial experience. But we also came across teachers with previous experience outside school who had come into teaching precisely because they could no longer stand what they saw as, for example, the harsh commercialism of the business world and were looking for a more caring and humane community. The effect of visits by teachers to local factories was as often to deepen their disquiet at the conditions of work inside them as to allay ungrounded suspicion.* The sort of (quite proper and indeed important) public relations exercises which both schools

---

* It is interesting in this connection to note a caution entered in the interim report of the Schools Council Industry Project:

> There is a danger that in the assumption, which now appears very general, that liaison between schools and industry is inherently a good thing, we may overlook the possibility that close liaison could hinder or frustrate this process by encouraging young people to adopt stereotypes prematurely, and before the schools have had a chance to develop abilities and expectations. (op. cit. p. 26)

Might not the same apply to teachers?

and business concerns set up for each other's benefit, the polite niceties of mutual hospitality, the exploration of ways in which each could be practically helpful to the other – all of these can overcome some quite unnecessary misunderstandings, generate a great fund of goodwill and an important sense of mutual understanding and cooperation. But all of this can be achieved (and is often designed to be achieved) without really touching on the underlying issues of what each party stands for. The careful way in which these issues are avoided on such occasions suggests to me that a real understanding of each other's values and purposes would be as likely to widen as to close the much publicised gulf between 'education' and (to use the arrogantly assumed title) 'the world of work'. Fortunately or unfortunately communications rarely if ever in our observation got that far.

An alternative and fairly natural response by employers to the observation that schools seem to be failing in various respects to turn out the 'products' they required might be for them to seek a larger and more positive role in shaping school policy. One of the questions we tried to answer was what evidence there was of employers themselves drawing this conclusion and seeking more influence over what went on in schools.

We found little evidence to support the view that employers wished to be involved directly in the management of schools or in schools' decision making. Jean Graham-Cameron interviewed a group of local employers associated with Holbein school and Rex Gibson summarised their views as follows:

> As far as I can judge, *all* employers welcomed receiving information about the curriculum and felt that 'schools in general' should produce literate, numerate students. *None* wanted the right to control the curriculum ('up to the schools') but wanted some way in which they could express views of satisfaction, dissatisfaction, particular needs. All five would welcome being consulted on aspects of the school curriculum. (HO, 5)

Jennifer Nias reported from Highstones that:

> The questionnaire that they filled in made clear that very few employers want to have more influence over what goes on in school. Rather, what they seem to want is to feel that the

school understands what they are trying to do, and their point of view, and that teachers represent both fairly to their pupils. (HI, 2B7D)

In my own interviews with employers connected with Robert Peel School I collected a mixture of hesitant responses which levelled some criticism at what went on in schools (in general) but stopped short of seeking control.

A number of my conversations with employers followed the same, and I think rather revealing, pattern:

Employer: (complains bitterly about the inadequacies of present-day schooling and offers clear and concrete suggestions for what should be done.)

David Bridges: Is this what you are calling for schools to do?

Employer: Certainly.

David Bridges: What if the schools say 'no – we don't accept what you propose. We think what we are doing is better'?

Employer: Well, I would want to know why.

David Bridges: What if they give you their reasons, but you are not convinced by them, you do not think they meet your case?

Employer: I would say so.

David Bridges: What if they are still quite unconvinced?

Employer: (looks puzzled.)

David Bridges: Would that lead you to take the view that people like yourself ought to have more power to require schools to do what you are arguing for?

Employer: (looks distinctly uncomfortable at this suggestion. No, this is not what he wants – at least he didn't think he did.)

My own impression of the employers' standpoint on accountability and control can be summarised in these terms:

a. Employers did feel that some general changes in the curriculum (of the sort already indicated) were required.

b. They wanted more opportunity to present the case for changes of this kind to the schools.

c. They anticipated that given this opportunity and the (to them) eminent reasonableness of their case, the schools would respond favourably to their arguments. In other words they relied on dialogue rather than power to compel to bring about the changes they thought desirable.

d. They did nevertheless emphasise the importance at the more political level of the school's responsibility to or accountability to the wider community, including as a significant part of that community the world of work.

In the end, however, and perhaps ironically, it may be market forces rather than reasoned principle that will determine whose view of education and the curriculum will prevail. When work is plentiful and labour scarce young would-be employees can get away with a more independent attitude towards their employers; parents are less anxious about what the schools are doing to ensure their children will get a job; and schools can confidently pursue goals which they value even if they are only very remotely related to the demands of employment. When work is scarce and labour plentiful, as a number of employers we spoke to have already begun to observe, attitudes change: the boot is on the other foot. In the end, perhaps, schools may come to feel that they are as squarely located in the market place as British Leyland or Marks and Spencer.

10

Two worlds – some employers' views of teachers

Dave Ebbutt

The views upon which I wish to concentrate were expressed by employers from a range of industry and commerce. While not held universally, they were encountered commonly enough to deserve consideration. The view-points are uncomplicated and can be summarised thus: teachers know very little of *the realities of life* in the world *outside*. Employers putting forward this view characteristically supported it with the following observation. The normal training and career progression for a teacher commences when he or she enters infant school, moves through compulsory schooling before entering college or university and subsequently back to school – it is seen as a total immersion in the world of education to the exclusion of everything else.

As a site manager of a large national building contractor said:

> My feeling is that it is a cocoon. I know from my experience at school. I found it difficult, and I didn't want to leave. There was plenty of sport to play. You couldn't do exactly what you wanted, but you had no sense of responsibility. I think it is a cocoon at school . . . the teachers leave school; they go to college; and they are back in school. They *don't* really know what *outside life* is really like. (S 4; my emphasis)

A managing director was more polemical:

> School teachers, I know a fair number of them. I don't think they should be allowed anywhere near children. . . . But school teachers should have to work in industry. That's part of

the social background that they are preparing kids for. If they haven't experienced it themselves – they've got all their lives to be school teachers. . . . And I don't think you can *really* prepare children *for life without having had some prior personal* experience. . . . And therefore all school teachers to get their Dip. Ed., or whatever, should *go out* and do a minimum of say two years in industry. And see if they can find an interest in, and understand what is going on. (RP, I4:4; my emphasis)

Jennifer Nias noted:

Several times I heard the view, 'Teachers don't know what business is, or industry. . . . You've got to have a readiness to fight. . . . It's a hard world. Teachers seem to think they can sit around and do the nice things all their lives.' (HI, 2D)

Reporting on an employers' afternoon at Highstones, she commented that she frequently overheard the following observation by employer guests:

Nothing but good can come of this exercise. We live in *two separate* worlds. Clearly this is all wrong . . . we ought not to. Obviously we need to know more about each other. (HI, 2D; my emphasis)

As a first step towards bringing the two worlds into dialogue, I shall put forward possible arguments as to how these views come to be held and suggest appropriate strategies for resolving misunderstandings.

The first argument is that these employers are correct. The views express a more or less accurate picture of the outlook of many teachers, and accurately capture the nature of the relationship between many schools and much of industry and commerce. Circumstantial evidence to support this explanation comes from the comments of two employers, both representatives of a nationalised aerospace consortium. They saw the careers department of one of the CAP schools as atypical because it was staffed by teachers who had both had prior experience in industry. In conversation they remarked:

Employer 1: . . . which of course is quite unusual.

Employer 2: . . . these people who have worked in industry, or in the world of work, are already inclined in this way, to look beyond the school. (unpublished data, Uplands)

Further, it is perhaps significant that another CAP school which annually sends up to 250 pupils on a highly successful week of work experience with local employers, does so under the combined aegis of its Business Studies and Careers departments. Both departments are staffed by teachers with previous commercial or industrial experience.

If the employers are wholly or partly correct in their view of teachers, then a resolution of misunderstanding could result from a strategy mentioned by the employers themselves, short periods of work experience for teachers. All five employers with whom Rex Gibson or Jean Graham-Cameron spoke in gathering data for his case study thought that work experience for teachers was a useful idea. The employers with whom I spoke echoed this opinion.

This strategy places all its emphasis on teachers coming to know the world of industry and commerce better, and might therefore be a necessary but not a sufficient means towards dialogue. The explanation given above may in fact be an oversimplification. The employers may be correct in their observation, and yet draw from it doubtful inferences. I have in mind that their observations could be used to reinforce a chain of argument which Stake *et al.* (1978) maintain to be current among sections of the American public:

> The youngsters are in trouble because they are idle; they are idle because they do not work; they do not work because they are ignorant and lazy; they are ignorant and lazy because the schools have failed to do their job [and – my addition – they failed to do their job because teachers have no experience of the real world outside].

As Stake points out, there may be some truth in that line of reasoning, but not much. It fails to take account of current political and socioeconomic trends and their effects upon the attitudes and life chances of young people. However, if such reasoning is implicit in the employers' views, work experience for teachers is unlikely to have any impact and greater reciprocity may be necessary. Perhaps representatives of industry and commerce could also be released to teach for short periods in schools: school experience for employers. Only one employer with whom we talked raised this as a possibility, when he suggested that he would actively support middle management from his firm going into school to work for a limited period. Such a reciprocal arrangement deserves serious consideration because it has the potential to fulfil one of the basic criteria for a meaningful dialogue: equal access to information.

A second, more convoluted argument is that the employers are incorrect. This depends on two anecdotal experiences (neither deriving directly from CAP work) which would seem to be pertinent. The first concerns the use of the word 'outside' and in a similar context to that in the extracts above. Apart from in television drama documentaries ('faction') featuring prisons, I have encountered the word used in that sense only in one other context. That happened in discussion with naval personnel who were considering career moves subsequent to the termination of their period of engagement. Their conversation contained many references to 'going outside' and 'life on the outside'.

The second anecdote concerns the manner in which some pupils, especially those below second year of secondary school, from time to time make such comments to teachers as, 'I seen you on Saturday, Sir.' These express surprise at the realisation that teachers do not cease to exist after 'going home time', i.e. surprise that teachers have a life separate from their institutional existence. It seems to me that it may be significant that the navy and prisons are total institutions and it might well be that, from the perspective of pupils, so is the school.

What is clear is a feeling we all shared on the project, namely that people tend to evaluate schools and teachers, at least informally, in the light of their own past experiences at school. Indeed this in itself is not surprising in that the classroom places pupils, for the first time in their lives, in a unique position to evaluate adults at work. So powerful is this extended evaluation role that the literature documents its significance even in terms of how young teachers make judgements about teaching:

They talk about assessments they made as youngsters as currently viable, as stable judgements of quality. What constituted good teaching then, constitutes good teaching now. (Lortie 1975, p. 65)

The explanation I am moving towards is that the employers are like Lortie's young teachers, articulating a pupil's-eye view of teachers and the job of teaching built up during their own schooling, albeit viewed retrospectively through an adult employer's lens. But this pupil's-eye view has been generated over time within an environment perceived by the pupils as something akin to a total institution. This helps towards explaining why the words used by employers are more or less congruent with the terms used about total institutions such as the navy or prison. Lortie further remarks that the young teachers who he was studying: 'underestimated the difficulties [teaching] involved' (ibid.). I suggest that the difficulties Lortie's teachers encountered arise from exposure to similar, though by no means the same, socialisation pressures as those young employees in industry and commerce experience. Both have to make the transition from a pupil's-eye view to an employee-worker's perspective on the institution for which they work. In this respect it is interesting to note how one head of a CAP school, at a meeting for parents of prospective pupils, publicly characterised his school:

We are also the largest employer of labour – highly skilled labour – in Antheath, apart from —— Engineering. (S, 2)

It is interesting to note that where both David Bridges and John Elliott document the effects of the teachers' industrial action of May 1979 on parental opinion, they show how fathers are in general more understanding of the teacher's position. Elliott comments:

None of the fathers I talked to appeared particularly disturbed by the manifestation of militancy in the staffroom. 'Industrial action' was something they were used to in their own work situations and perhaps they did not expect teachers to 'be different'. (U, 14)

Thus in the eyes of the fathers mentioned the teachers were understood as fellow workers or as fellow employees or were understood in the same terms as are their own employee-workers.

The preceding argument is grounded in the notion that the employers' views reported at the beginning of this chapter are based on a distorted view of the world of teachers and schooling. If this is so, then the need is for a strategy which would allow employers to refocus their perceptions, to experience first hand the employee-teachers' world. School experience for employers potentially fulfils this.

The third argument regarding the employers' views is as follows. The two worlds do exist, but they reveal and reflect distinctions erected by society about how people are employed. I have in mind such distinctions commonly made by politicians, economists and the media, between the private sector and the public sector; between profit-making and non-profit making institutions; between manufacturing and service industry. On such a classification our teachers operate within a public sector non-profit making service industry. Perhaps these are the key indicators of a great divide between the two worlds. These indicators in fact reveal deeper distinctions about the nature of the accountability operative in the two worlds. In the world of the employers, based on such evaluation procedures as profit and loss, cost benefit analysis and input-output measures, accountability at its simplest and most tangible is ultimately *accounting to* the shareholders, in cash terms. Employers have to *account to* the bank and the shareholders, as well as the possibility of *giving an account* or *being called to account* by the workforce or by consumer bodies representing the public.

By way of contrast the world of education is markedly less tangible, less concrete. One of the project team (Gibson, internal project issue paper, May 1980) saw it like this:

> . . . education and the expertise teachers possess is high on intangibility: increasing professionalisation increases mystery. Thus teachers can lay claim to knowing these abstract, intangible things that non-experts, non-professionals don't know. It's inherent in what it is to be a teacher.

A managing director put the contrast more simply:

> . . . I do meet occasionally, two or three times a year, teachers and they are very knowledgeable people – heaven forbid. But I think that as to what it is like to be in Industry and to what it is like to say that you have to turn X number of pounds over X

times a year to produce something that is going to be profit-
able. . . . I don't think that they have very much idea at all. (S,
4)

There are endless arguments regarding evaluation going on within
education. It is not surprising that accountability within this
world is also problematic. There are, it seems to me, at least two
dangers concerning teacher accountability to employers which
flow out of this problematic nature of accountability. The first is if
teachers hide behind their professional status in order to frustrate
public debate about their accountability to employers. Kennedy
(1980), writing about the accountability of the medical profession,
accuses doctors of indulging in this. Such strategies, he maintains,
give rise to paternalism, to a bland giving of account, which he
believes carries the risk of 'infantalising' the recipients of the
account. The second danger stems from any attempt which might
be made to impose, unmodified, the *accounting* model of accountability from the tangible world of industry onto education. Neither
of the two strategies put forward earlier – work experience for
teachers; school experience for employers – for increasing the
quality of dialogue between the two worlds is invalidated by this last
argument. But by the same token, no additional strategy suggests
itself.

11

The role and tasks of school governors

Dave Ebbutt

> **Governor** – A self-acting contrivance for regulating the passage of gas, steam, water etc especially in order to ensure an even and regular motion in a machine. (*Shorter Oxford English Dictionary*)

The original stimulus to write this chapter was provided by a teacher governor in one of the CAP schools, who raised this deceptively naive question during an interview:

> Well I would want to know what the specific status of the governing body was. What is it there to do? *I mean what is their role in life?* (OT, 7; my emphasis)

This chapter is a descriptive analysis in which I hope to throw a little light on that question as it concerns six secondary schools in the early 1980s. I will also attempt briefly to relate this analysis to the constitutional position of school governors as it appears in the wake of the Taylor Report (1977). I have drawn on two categories of evidence: first, what governors say they, or other governors, actually do as governors; second, the reactions governors visualise they might make in hypothetical situations. (Throughout, the use of the word 'role' is based on my commonsense understanding of the term, as are the labels I have used to pick out the tasks I will describe.)*

---

* There are several useful background sources for the historical, constitutional and legal position of school governing bodies. The Taylor Report gives an informative post-war historical resumé (pp. 5–11). Wragg & Partington (1980) entertainingly present similar information with more

The pattern which will emerge in this description arises out of a series of ambiguities and contradictions which currently surround the work of governors. Such ambiguities reside, to a great extent, in the lack of power which governors feel able or willing to wield, as opposed to the power with which they are actually invested. At its simplest the contradiction is between the dictionary definition of the verb 'to govern', and what governors say they do. The Shorter Oxford English Dictionary interprets the verb thus:

> **Govern** – To rule with authority, especially with that of a sovereign; to direct and control the actions and affairs of (a people etc) whether despotically or constitutionally; to regulate the affairs of (a body of men).
> To sway, influence, to direct, guide or regulate.

Although varying from LEA to LEA, the powers the governors do have constitutionally are quite extensive. They have a degree of power over:

staff appointments and dismissals
finance
the physical condition, maintenance and use of school premises
the suspension of pupils
the conduct and the curriculum of the school

These powers are enshrined in the LEA-produced Articles of Government, which must have approval from the Secretary of State. Nevertheless they are heavily hedged about with provisos. Such provisos or conditions serve to limit the power of governors *vis à vis* the power of the LEA, as this extract from the County Articles of Government (1955) for one of the CAP schools indicates:

> The Governors shall, subject to any direction of the Local Education Authority, determine the use to which the School premises, or any part thereof, may be put out of School hours.

emphasis on the legal and constitutional aspects, together with an interesting appendix of the 1977 Nottinghamshire Instruments and Articles of Government. Sallis (1977) gives a very tight and pithy historical account (pp. 117–119) together with revealing glimpses concerning the 'hidden curriculum' of the Taylor Committee.

Similarly the power of governors *vis à vis* the head is also delimited:

> . . . it is not the Governors' function to give instruction to the Head and his colleagues regarding the exercise of their professional skill and judgement. ('Role of Governors' in the same County's *Notes for Guidance*)

Governors we spoke to were not unaware of their lack of power.

> Dave Ebbutt: You say that in practice it has very little power.
>
> Teacher Governor: It seems to me that it does.
>
> Dave Ebbutt: Is that true?
>
> Teacher Governor: Yes, because basically it has no financial control over the school. I mean the greatest decision we take every year is to allocate the contract for cleaning the windows, and we can witter on until we are blue in the face about things, but those in County Hall make the decisions. (S, 5)

Articles, advice and guidance such as this serve to point up what I see as another ambiguity affecting governors of schools: the relationship between lay governors and professional educators:

> Governor: There is an awful danger in involving lay people in matters which, quite frankly, they're not capable of even looking at from an educationalist's point of view. (HI, 3A10)

This issue is of particular significance because of the way in which the job of the teacher (as opposed to teaching) has become increasingly professionalised over the last twenty years. Such professional specialisation has resulted in bewildering divisions of labour and esoteric role titles which serve, I would speculate, to distance the professionals from the lay audience. A similar process has occurred within the LEA administrative arm. The Taylor Report has this to say about the situation immediately prior to the setting up of the committee of enquiry.

> Governing and managing bodies consequently found that they had no indispensable role to perform within the executive structures set up by local education authorities (op. cit. p. 8)

It is also clear, as Rex Gibson's case study points out, and as the Articles of Government underline, that the relationship between chairman and head is especially close. This is so in terms of the frequency of contact and the quantity and quality of the information which passes between them. Before examining the role and tasks of the governors in general, I give the following example to illustrate this particular aspect of the head–chairman relationship:

> Head: The Chairman or Vice Chairman I can talk to and with, which is often a help, for example with a delicate staffing decision, in order to have the view of someone outside the situation. (OT, 5)

The governing bodies of all the CAP schools show some post-Taylor features of membership. All have either one or two teacher governors or teacher representatives (representative signifies non-voting membership). All have one or two parent governors or representatives. One of the schools has pupil governors, invested with the same powers as other governors except over staff appointments. Most of the others invite pupil observers to governors' meetings. Important though these post-Taylor changes have been, the situation remains that political appointees continue to form a majority on CAP governing bodies. I have collectively referred to all governors who have some political affiliation, even down to parish council members, as 'political'.

1. The Representational Role

What all the members of a governing body have in common is that they are representatives of some other group or organisation. For example, the parent association, the teaching staff, the parish council, the county council, higher education or industry. The one role of governors which subsumes all other tasks is the representational role. This is seen by Rex Gibson to be divisible thus:

The Representational Role

(A) Representative (at)
   (the governors)

(B) Representative (of)
   (the governors on
   behalf of the school)

The governors we interviewed explained the two facets of the Representational Role in their own words. For example:

(A) Representative (at)

I am a councillor and therefore I feel that most of what I do is either full representation of my political party or full representation of the people who I represent – primarily. Therefore, I am interested in making sure that my electorate – be they parents – do have what they want from the education system. (HO, 3)

To try and represent their [parents'] views . . . to see that they [children] receive the sort of education that their parents want. (HO, 3)

(B) Representative (of)

Teacher Governor: I mean that is the way the school can ask the county, via the governors, about various things. (OT, unpublished)

Parent Governor: I don't really know [the other governors] very well yet. . . . But at the meetings I've been to they do seem to get involved and they say 'we'll do this and I'll do that'. They don't hold back, they do take a very active interest. (RP, II2)

The representational role would appear from these extracts to be unproblematic. However, examination of the range of tasks which are performed by governors within that role reveals a more complex picture. The tasks which are illustrated below should not be thought of as necessarily discrete. Indeed both of the first two self-explanatory tasks can be performed simultaneously.

(i) The Continuity Task

Parent Governor: So you can in fact have a complete turnover once every four years, but with parent governors, you are getting a change, perhaps in two years, perhaps less. I think there is something there that should be looked at, because I don't think it is good for the governing body. I think we should work as a group, as a team, and it is difficult when you keep having changes. (HI, 3A8)

(ii) *The Balance Task*

> Governor: [I see my role as] acting as a balance to the political
> element on the governing body. (HO, 3)

(iii) The Transmitter of Information Task

Another relatively unambiguous task to describe is one which was
most easily observed by the project when applied in particular to
teacher and parent governors. In practice their position can be
highly ambivalent if the necessary forums for collecting and
reporting back information do not exist. This ambivalence is
further intensified by their relatively short period in office, and by
what one governor saw as an imbalance of power between these
groups and the head. Both were seen as to some extent 'hostage' to
the head.

> Parent Governor: . . . asked if somebody would come along to
> the PTA and tell them what went on at Governors' Meetings.
> (RP, II2)

> Parent Governor: . . . watching brief on affairs, express the
> views of PTA, report back. (OT, 7)

A more difficult task to categorise neatly involves governors in the
imparting of advice. In this context I don't mean 'second opinion'
advice such as that which the head I quoted indicates as characteristic of the relationship with the chairman, but rather advice about
special skills, or technical advances or innovations from the world
beyond school. In the context where governors performing this
task were observed – a sequential series of governors' meetings –
the advice imparted was of a technical nature involving the choice
of the most suitable computer for the school. There were strong
implications underlying the imparting of this advice of a desire, on
the part of several of the governors, to initiate curriculum change.

(iv) The Advisory Task: curriculum initiator

> Political Governor: . . . and she [another governor] has been
> wanting to get computing taught at that school for a long time
> and I too want computing in that school . . . and we have been
> sniping on this for a very long time because I think it is very

important for young people in this country to have education in computing. (OT, 7)

One of the CAP governors suggests that only 5 per cent of the time at governors' meetings is given to discussion of such important educational issues, and he would see the following task afforded much more time at Governors' meetings:

(v) The Advisory Task: systems maintenance

Political Governor: Some of these formal meetings are an absolute pain in the neck. One sits the whole bloody evening, talking about painting bits of wood and so on, which has to be done, but I am sure that is not what we are there for. (U, 20)

That school has evolved a strategy of holding two types of governors' meetings, formal and informal. It is in the former that the bulk of the advisory systems maintenance task is effected. Of course, in that informal governors' meetings have no decision making function, such a strategy could be viewed as further limiting the power of governors with respect to the head on curriculum matters.

(vi) The Safety Net Task

John Elliott coined this term in his case study. He sees this task as resting on the assumption that governors, acting in the representative (of) role, will catch the school if it suffers from what one governor euphemistically called a 'wobble of confidence', or before the school falls from grace, or to protect the school against public representations which are damaging. Such representations can, of course, emerge from any quarter, but the press is a good example. Here a Chairman of Governors explains what he sees as a relatively ineffective safety net strategy:

Chairman: One tries to keep the press informed. Ultimately you are in their hands entirely because they [do what they] want, and if you in fact then write a letter the following week to try and correct things – invariably people don't read that. Or if they do – one article with a banner headline on the front page and your letter is on page 10. So I think it is far better to try and keep the press informed, to create a good relationship with the press and then hopefully you will get good coverage. (S, 5)

(vii) The Finding Out/Curriculum Oversight Task
Several of our case studies document the type of questions asked of the head (and heads of departments) at those governors' meetings at which part of the proceedings were given over to consideration of a particular curriculum or policy area. At one meeting I observed the Religious Education curriculum was being discussed. These are the types of questions that the governors were asking:

Do you tackle the Science/Religion issue?

Is Religious Education in Year 4 on every option?

Do you cover Church History particularly with reference to movements in Europe?

Similar questions (but in this second example requiring a degree of justification) were recorded at a governors' meeting at another CAP school, this time about the Schools Council History Syllabus:

How do you explain your approach (to teaching the subject) to parents who have been taught history in a more traditional style?

Why did you decide on this (Schools Council) approach?

It is interesting to note how one governor's comments about the quality of the information exchanged at this sort of meeting compares with curriculum information given to parents:

Governor: [You could ask] as a parent, but you wouldn't get the same answer. (HO, 3)

I suggest that all the tasks which have been listed so far have several features in common, other than simply fitting under the representational role. They all are tasks which governors say they actually do at one time or another. Moreover the *mode* or manner in which the tasks are performed is essentially supportive to the school (although this begs the important question of who is the school: the collective, or the head?). Here are two governors talking about the *supportive* mode:

Governor: I think the role for the governor in this school is slightly different from an established school. . . . I think my prime objective was to be supportive to the school in every possible way I could be . . . to be as supportive as possible. (HO, 3)

Parent Governor: I think I see it [the governors] largely as a supportive role to [the Head]. It has not taken initiatives, it has always been responsive. (OT, 7)

Further, the psychological climate in which these tasks are performed is, I suggest, characterised by trust; trust, that is, in the professional judgement of the head. This in turn carries with it implications about the type of accountability in operation. All the tasks so far show the school (the head) operating what one governor referred to as 'accountability in the soft sense', where the school gives an account and the governors are responsive or reactive to that account. Nevertheless, there are indications of tension within this facet of the representational role which becomes increasingly evident within the Finding Out Task as this extract shows:

Industrial Governor: As an employer I have felt that educational standards maybe – I know 'everything in the past is always better than in the present' – but I have felt that education standards have gone down and I wanted to find out some first hand information. Whether anything was being done. (HO, 3)

Here there are implications of a degree of mistrust of the school's accounts, and the germ of a feeling which expresses itself as heightened concern for the interests of the group which that governor represents.

(viii) The Investigative Task

It is in the transition zone between the Finding Out Task and what I have termed the Investigative Task that the tensions of the representational role would become apparent. I use 'would' here because this situation was not observed in any of our study schools. However, governors were willing to speculate about this hypothetical eventuality. It should be emphasised that many governors

would feel unsure about exercising the aspects of the representational role which are described below. Such uncertainty raises
again the point made earlier about the problematic nature of the
extent and limits on governors' power.

> Governor:. . . I would not be inclined on my own initiative to
> start probing and prying. I would only do so if I felt that there
> was a genuine concern amongst a large section of parents over
> a lack in a particular area. (U, 20)

Flowing out of the Investigative Task, governors envisaged two
other subsequent tasks:

(ix) The Questioning Decision Task

> Parent Governor: I suppose if [the Head] decides to do
> something that is absolutely scatterbrained, I suppose actually
> that the governors might decide to come down with a hard
> hand. (OT, 7)

(x) The Curriculum Judgement Task

> Political Governor: Then I would see it as our responsibility to
> make ourselves sufficiently knowledgeable on the subject to
> make a judgement. And so on. . . . I would be calling in
> people to advise us and I would expect the governors to make
> that decision. But that way round rather than us going off and
> saying 'well, which method of maths are you teaching?' (S, 5;
> in response to a hypothetical question)

Here radically different tasks are being considered, in the light of
something hypothetically going wrong. The psychological climate
is now one of *mistrust* in the professional judgement of the
head/school. Similarly the mode in which these governors visualise having to operate has also changed from the *supportive* to a
corrective mode. In turn the form of accountability has also
changed, for here we see the 'hard' sense of accountability, of the
school being called or held to account for its actions or its perceived
shortcomings.

In conclusion, figure 1 summarises the above classification.

	Climate	Manner of Operation	Form of Accountability
(a) Tasks Governors Do			
(i) The continuity task			
(ii) The balance task			
(iii) The transmitter task			
(iv) The advisory task: curriculum initiator	Trust in school/head	Supportive of school/head	'Soft' sense; school gives account
(v) The advisory task: systems maintenance			
(vi) The safety net task			
(vii) The finding out/curriculum oversight task			
(b) Tasks Governors Might Have to Perform			
(viii) The investigative task	Mistrust in school/head	Corrective of school/head	'Hard' sense; school called (held) to account
(ix) The questioning task			
(x) The curriculum judgement task			

Figure 1.

The representational role of school governors and its constituent tasks

12

School Accountability to Governors

John Elliott

The representational role of governors and accountability

In the previous chapter, Dave Ebbutt listed the variety of tasks governors across CAP schools see themselves performing. He argued that in mode or manner of execution they tend to be supportive of the school, and that the tasks many governors cited are viewed by them as compatible with both aspects of their representational role. He claimed that such a view is grounded in an attitude of trust in the work of the staff.

According to Ebbutt, some governors in certain CAP schools refer to their investigative task, which involves probing, questioning and judging the policies and practices of the school. He suggests that when governors take this task of calling the school to account seriously, a tension or conflict is introduced into their representational role. This is because *calling to account* expresses an attitude of mistrust, and although such an attitude may satisfy the functions of the *representation at* aspect of the governors' role, it is not consistent with the functions of the *representation of* aspect. The latter essentially assumes a supportive and trusting attitude.

Certainly there is evidence in the CAP case studies which suggests that at least some school staff view being called to account as 'interference', or 'prying', and indicative of mistrust in their professional competence. However, our case studies also provide evidence of staff perceiving being called to account by governors as satisfying a supportive function. This is clearly illustrated by Rex Gibson's observations on a governors' meeting at Holbein School.

All questions were regarded as legitimate by staff and governors. Clearly, the governors felt they had a right to ask them, and equally clearly the staff felt – not simply that they *should* answer the questions, but that they *wished to* – that they welcomed the opportunity to explain and justify.

> . . . the 'tone' in which the questions were asked appeared to be positive and supportive, genuinely concerned to 'find out' rather than to 'needle' or 'score points'. . . . All I can do is to assert my impression (borne out by later asking the participants for their own impressions), that the general atmosphere was one of trust, where the governors were not trying (and did not expect) to 'catch out' the staff. Accounts were asked for – and were willingly given. (HO, 3)

Similarly at an Uplands School governors' meeting some staff expressed a desire to have governors observing their classrooms and questioning them about what was going on there:

> Mr Carpenter (teacher): I've often wondered what a governing body thinks about a school, its staff, its functioning. We never see you in classrooms.

> Chairman: A personal view. I personally feel it's rather an intrusion to go around the classrooms on a 'I'm a governor, what are you doing?' exercise . . .

> Governor: If I said 'Can I visit your class?', what would you want me to do?

> Mr Carpenter: If he/she came into the classroom and sat, listened, saw exactly what happened, and commented 'Do you think the children understood that, because I didn't,' it might jolt us into further thought . . . (U, 20)

Some staff, therefore, perceive being called to account by governors as a potentially supportive exercise, and not in the least suggestive of an attitude of mistrust, while others do not. Those who view the investigative task thus would disagree with Dave Ebbutt's contention that probing, questioning and judging are indicative of mistrust on the part of governors. It seems to me that this perception of the supportive function of being called to account is valid.

In calling the school to account, the governors may well be

responding to mistrust felt by their 'constituents'. In other words the shift towards a more investigative stance by a governing body is likely to reflect a certain lack of public confidence in either schools generally, or in its school in particular. The shift indeed stems from the 'representative at' aspect of the governors' role.

The following excerpts from our interviews with CAP governors demonstrate the fact that, for some governors at least, the motive for moving towards a more hardnosed investigative mode of accountability does stem from perceived public mistrust.

> A lot of parents are reluctant to see their children taught in a different way from how they were taught . . . this worries them and I think it's only fair to reflect their views, although one may not necessarily agree with them . . . one is trying to reflect the views of the people. (HO, 3)

> . . . whereas it is my business to find out what that is, and how the structure goes, I would not be inclined on my own initiative to start probing and prying. I would only do so if I felt that there was a genuine concern amongst a large section of parents over a lack in a particular area. (Vice-Chairman; U, 20)

When public confidence is low the public representatives at the school, the governors, may feel they need to investigate the extent to which this is merited. But the probing and questioning orientation governors adopt as a result does not necessarily indicate mistrust on their part. Calling the school to account certainly involves a temporary suspension of any trust governors feel towards the school. But the suspension of trust is quite different from expressing mistrust (for as at Holbein School it remains in the background as a mutually understood context). Indeed the investigative task requires governors to display qualities of *open-mindedness* and *impartiality* that can only be expressed by setting aside both feelings of trust and mistrust. When governors allow their investigation to be distorted by the loyalty to the school they fail to carry out their 'representative at' functions, and when they allow it to be distorted by prejudices they share with their constituents they fail to carry out their 'representative of' functions. But by adopting the impartial standpoint required by a genuine calling to account exercise, governors indicate to their 'constituents' that they are not going to be 'fobbed off' by the professionals while at the same time indicating to the professionals their refusal to be blinkered by public prejudice.

From the standpoint of a school which is confident in its ability to do a reasonable job, being called to account by public representatives displaying qualities of impartiality and open-mindedness can be viewed as a means of increasing public recognition of its merits. In other words the investigative task of governors can be seen by teachers to serve a supportive function.

Some teachers are well aware that when public confidence in their work is low 'soft accountability', in which they exercise total control over what to tell and when to tell it, will have little credibility for the public. Accounts are likely to be more credible if they are known to be elicited by public representatives under conditions where they are subjected to critical scrutiny and appraisal.

> I would expect them to bring along the remarks which are common in the media and ask me what my opinion is on those things. What does fly about in the papers and on the BBC is so wrong. I would expect them to bring those things along, the things that parents might bring to them and ask if this is the case in Holbein School and insist that I've an answer for it or put the record straight or say where the 'Panorama' programme was wrong with regard to this school, for example. That's the sort of thing initially . . . they ought to have the right to be able to investigate anything that we do. They ought to sit in on our meetings, they ought to come in and turn over students' exercise books. Now that doesn't mean that I expect them to go off and tell all and sundry what they learnt. I then expect them to come back to me as Head of Department and say 'we're uncomfortable about the work that has been done in this aspect of the [subject] Department and we want to go into it further'. (Teacher, HO, 3)

The example of teachers at Holbein and Uplands welcoming being called to account can, I believe, be explained in terms of teachers desiring greater public recognition for their work at a period when public confidence is on the decline. In the Uplands meeting I have referred to, when both governors and teachers seemed divided on whether the former should observe classrooms, one governor commented, 'people need to have contact from above'. Certainly, as one of those present, I felt that teachers who asked for observation and comment on their classroom practices were seeking recognition for their work at a time when public confidence was low. In fact, after the governor's comment about 'contact from above', I expressed this view at the meeting. The intervention met with a chorus of approval from some of the teachers present, and was referred to later at a subsequent point in the meeting.

Of course, every school and group of teachers can recognise that a shift towards a more investigative stance on the part of governors places them as professionals in something of a dilemma. If the outcomes of investigations by governors are positive then a school may expect support from its governors in promoting a favourable image of its activities amongst their constituents; with corresponding increases of public confidence in the professional competence of the staff. However, if the outcomes of investigations are negative, then they can be used by 'constituents' to urge some form of external intervention in, and control over, the activities of the staff. A vote of no confidence from governors could result in some degree of external interference in matters normally considered to be the preserve of the professionals.

Shifting from 'Giving Accounts' to 'Being Called to Account'

I suggest that the case studies indicate that school staff are likely to welcome being called to account by governors, as an acceptable level of risk they ought to take, if the following conditions obtain:

1. They perceive a lack of confidence in schools to exist amongst certain influential sections of the community, and are concerned lest it distort a true appreciation of their work.

2. They are confident that they are doing a reasonable job, and that public mistrust is unwarranted in their case.

3. They perceive governors to be capable of influencing public opinion where it counts.

4. They trust governors to exercise qualities of impartiality and open-mindedness when calling them to account.

I would argue that all four conditions must obtain before a school is willing to risk being called to account by governors in contrast to

merely giving accounts to them. The CAP research clearly indicates that the second condition obtained in all six schools. But the
first condition did not exist to any great extent in two schools.

A basically trusting attitude towards the professionals appears to
persist within the local communities of these two schools. At Old
Town this governor's comments appear to sum up the general
attitude towards the school:

> . . . by and large the governing body and the Parents Associa-
> tion are really very happy to leave most of the decisions
> relating to the school, to the curriculum, to staffing, to . . . the
> school – things like mixed ability. All these are regarded as
> very strictly professional decisions . . . but in fact there is no
> real discussion at that level. No real discussion at the level of
> any changes or any policy decisions of that kind'. (OT, 7)

At Highstones Jennifer Nias reported:

> Overwhelmingly parents felt that 'teachers should teach and
> we should leave them to get on with it'. . . . I certainly did not
> find parents clamouring for greater control over the school.
> Even those who wanted to be consulted did not 'think parents
> would have the expertise to make decisions'. (HI, 2A3)

In the circumstances cited, of considerable public confidence, the
provision of information is under the control of the professionals.
Accountability manifests itself as giving an account rather than
being called to account. Both Old Town and Highstones emerge as
very accountable in the former sense of informing parents and
governors about their activities. Presumably there are schools
operating in a similar trusting context who are not so good; perhaps
because they are less confident in their professional competence.
This trusting context, however, provided little incentive for the
governors at Old Town and Highstones to shift towards a more
investigative stance or for the staff to see much point in welcoming
such a shift.

At Robert Peel, a new school anxious to establish confidence
with employers, David Bridges documented a move by the school
towards welcoming a more probing, questioning stance from
employers, and by the latter towards encouraging opportunities
for this:

My general impression can perhaps be summarised in these terms:

a. employers did feel that some general changes in the curriculum (of the sort already described) were required;

b. they wanted more opportunity to present the case for changes of this kind in schools;

c. they anticipated that given this opportunity and the (to them) eminent reasonableness of their case the schools would respond favourably to their arguments (in other words they relied on dialogue rather than coercion to bring about the changes they thought desirable);

d. they did nevertheless emphasise the importance at the more political level of the school's responsibility to or accountability to, the wider community, including as a significant part of that community the world of work.

> . . . all my evidence indicates that this will meet a ready response from Robert Peel . . . the school has indicated . . . its readiness to make public its policies and the thinking underlying them, to listen to comment, criticism and suggestion and to discuss what it is doing with relevant interest groups. (RP, 4)

Indeed the section of this case study relating to employers was used by the school as the basis for a first meeting with them; one designed to foster the kind of dialogue cited above.

But David Bridges provides little evidence that such a move towards being called to account by an important section of the local community was reflected in the proceedings at governors' meetings. Would this be the case if a substantial block of employers were represented on the governing body? At least one employer cited by Bridges felt that governing bodies did not do a very good job at representing industry:

> I don't think boards of governors today, without really knowing a lot about it, do succeed in producing people, young people, who are adjusted for society today. . . . They [governors] are there to call the employees and the school staff to account. I feel, in the end, the governors must respond to their responsibility. (RP, 4)

In the case of Robert Peel one might argue that, since the section of
the community it wishes to establish confidence with are employers, a shift towards being called to account through its governing body would depend on influential employers being well
represented on that body. This points to the significance of my third
condition. If a school does not perceive any of its governors to be
influential where it counts it is unlikely to welcome, or even see the
point of, a more investigative stance by them. And in turn this raises
a critical issue about the representativeness of governing bodies.
For if a school's 'significant audiences' within the community are
not well represented by their influential members on its governing
body, it will tend to account to them independently; as Robert Peel
appears to with respect to local employers.

The 'danger' of separate accountability systems emerging for
different groups is that there is no mechanism for coordinating
conflicts of interest between them.

By far the heaviest representation on most governing bodies is
'political', in the sense that about half of the members tend to be
nominated by county and district councils. Not all, but some, of
this group will be councillors. Currently many teachers feel they
are unjustifiably mistrusted by local government politicians, and
consequently feel threatened by the prospect of greater political
control over their professional activities. Given the amount of
political representation on governing bodies, the latter are increasingly viewed by heads and their staff as a potential mechanism
for rectifying this impression. In these circumstances one can, I
think, expect discussions at governors' meetings to be skewed in
favour of the interests and concerns of the political representatives.
For in this context they are the people who matter to the school. For
example, in the Uplands case study, I wrote:

> My colleague Dave Ebbutt, while observing a governors'
> meeting, noted that 'the Head tends to talk to the half of the
> room from which speakers have volunteered. So far two
> members on the other side haven't spoken and don't seem to
> be being talked to'. Later he again noted that the Head 'still
> speaks to his left side, ignoring the other side'. Having sat
> through a number of formal governors' meetings I had also
> noticed that the dialogue was frequently between Philip King
> and a particular group of governors of whom I was certainly
> not one. I felt they were essentially the local politicians on the

body, who might be useful in furthering the school's interests with respect to its problems with the LEA. (U, 20)

The 'problems with the LEA' tended to determine what was talked about at formal governors' meetings in Uplands. These meetings were largely concerned with perceived deficiencies in the provision of necessary material, financial, and manpower resources. This kind of 'systems maintenance' orientation was not always to the liking of those governors who were more interested in the 'educational' aspects.

Richard Ball (Further Education Representative): In fact it's remarkable how little information governors get with respect to teaching methods. . . .

Governor: Some of those formal meetings are an absolute pain in the neck. One sits the whole bloody evening talking about painting bits of wood and so on, which has to be done, but I am sure that is not what we are here for.

Views like these tended to be shared by the parent educationalist and community 'representatives'. There was a tendency for such people to view the headmaster as deliberately concentrating attention on the 'systems maintenance' problems in order to deflect attention away from what one governor called 'the essential educational issues'. But, in the light of the conditions I cited earlier, a rather different interpretation is possible. The 'systems maintenance' problems are, given the present economic climate, increasingly real and urgent ones. The 'governors' is the only meeting where the staff of the school encounter face to face the *nominated* representatives of the body which ultimately controls the money supply. These representatives are in a position to influence the distribution of scarce resources by LEA administrators. In the eyes of the headteacher they may provide the school with some protection against the worst effects of the cuts. It is therefore 'natural' for a headteacher to view governors' meetings as a way of getting governors to exercise this supportive function, and to provide them with the necessary information ('ammunition') to do so.

At Uplands at least, the non-political representatives tended to be relatively powerless to change the agenda, because they lacked

the necessary legitimation required to exercise strong representational functions. They tended to be selected, as representative of
their constituents, by the school. As far as I am aware the governors
from further and higher education, and those who might be
considered to represent parents, employers and the local community, had not been formally nominated by their constituents. This
must inevitably limit the capacity of these governors to exercise
'representative at' the school functions. Even if they are personally
inclined to shift towards a more investigative stance and probe the
'essential' issues, they cannot with confidence claim any formal
right to represent the views of their constituents in doing so. This in
turn places limits on their capacity to represent the school to the
constituents. If they are not elected to represent any formally
constituted body they are unlikely to have access to procedures for
reporting back to it.

Moreover, the official parent on the governing body at Uplands
had no voting rights. Other governors at Uplands were also
parents, but their voting rights derived from their status as
representatives of another group, e.g. the county council or further
education. Several governors wore two or more hats, and this did
not always help them to sort out whose interests they ought to be
representing at any one time. Thus Richard Ball, an Uplands
parent and FE representative, commented:

> I find I suffer the most enormous role conflict in the gov-
> ernors – I mean from the points of view of parent, governor
> and professional educationalist. I find it extremely difficult to
> know which hat to wear. One of the things I was very acutely
> conscious of is that if there were any debate about the
> curriculum in the governors there would have to be a lot of very
> hard spade work done first to bring all the participants of that
> debate to a level where some dialogue could take place. You
> know, myself included, we would all have to do our home-
> work. (U, 20)

The official parent-observer felt that although several other governors doubled as parents they did not wear that hat at meetings.
She would have welcomed a second 'official' parent on the
governing body:

> I think then you can discuss things. If I look at the governing body; they have known each other for years and years as members. Then I came along as a parent. OK. I knew quite a lot of people, but if you want to talk to parents on the governing body, different governors are parents but they are like Mr Ball or Mr Dodd, he is a councillor and his interests are more different than my interests sometimes. (U, 20)

The 'doubling' as parent and something else tends to further weaken the extent to which parents can be represented at governors' meetings.

The way the governing body was constituted at Uplands, which I have no reason to believe is untypical within the particular LEA concerned, supports the representational functions of political governors but not those of governors representing other groups. This explains why systems maintenance problems have tended to dominate proceedings. However, these proceedings have largely taken the form of the school giving accounts of such problems to their governors. This highlights the supportive role of the political nominees as 'representatives of' the school at local government level; the agenda being largely controlled by the headteacher.

> John Elliott: . . . who sets the agenda for the governors' meetings. I mean, I have never seen anyone asked for items for the agenda. So the impression I get is that the Head – perhaps in consultation with the Chairman and you – prepares the agenda.

> Vice-Chairman: I think in that sense you are right. I have never been consulted about an agenda either. So I think that must be right. I don't even know to what extent the Chairman is consulted – I guess he must be. . . . I would certainly agree with your indication that all the governors should have the opportunity for adding items on the agenda. But there again – I don't think one should excuse oneself . . . the facility is there I believe if one chose to use it. (U, 20)

However, at least one influential governor in local politics wanted to move the agenda in other directions:

> I also feel the information presented at governors' meetings is extremely guarded, and prepared at a specific level for the

governors. Probably a lot of what we should be informed about or should be informed on, is not presented to us. That is just a feeling. I have no evidence. (U, 20)

As the cuts in local government spending bite deeper into the educational system the systems maintenance problems increasingly impinge on central education questions surrounding the curriculum. Politicians want to know how resources are being deployed in this area, whether schools are deploying them efficiently and what their curriculum priorities and policies are. At Uplands there were signs that some political governors, not all, wanted to do more probing and questioning in this area. Their focus of interest to this extent began to merge with the concerns of some non-political governors. However, unlike the latter, the political nominees had a greater capacity to act as 'representatives at' the school.

The school's response to this situation was to institute informal governors' meetings, in addition to formal ones, each term. The 'informal governors' is open to all the staff of the school as well as members of the governing body. It takes place over 'wine and nibbles' and focuses on a particular area of school life. Governors are asked to suggest topics for such meetings. The intention is to allow them opportunities to discuss a particular topic fully, frankly, and in depth with staff. No formal minutes are taken. During the two year period of the CAP research at Uplands the following topics were discussed:

The Cambridge Accountability Project
Religious and moral education at Uplands
Provision for sick and injured children at Uplands
The HMI survey of secondary schools
Should the governors observe classrooms at Uplands?
Case histories of pupils in the school (fictionalised)

These meetings were generally well-attended by both governors and staff, and amongst the former the following comment was a fairly typical one:

. . . these informal meetings are so self-evidently better, for want of a better word, than any formal meeting could possibly be. I am sure everybody gets more out of them. Certainly people put more into them. The input is of higher quality, better quantity. (U, 20)

It was not simply the topics talked about, but the quality of the talk that was different. In the formal meetings the school's relationship to its governors continued, to a large extent, to consist of giving accounts. But the governors had more control over the topics discussed at informal meetings, and felt freer to question and probe.

The emergence of the informal meetings did indicate an attempt on the part of the headteacher and staff at Uplands to open up 'professional matters' as topics for full and frank discussion with governors. Behind this attempt was, I believe, a desire to demonstrate the professional competence of the staff to those in a position to exert political influence. But this innovation also indicated a certain crisis of trust between the school and its governors. The crisis was precipitated by the introduction of a number of Conservative party members on the governing body, and a subsequent 'Tory coup' whose outcome was a new chairman and vice-chairman. The former chairman – a Labour councillor – was replaced by a Conservative councillor, and the new vice-chairman was also chairman of the local Conservative party. The coup was supported by another new governor who happened to be the leader of the constituency Conservative party. As I observed in my case study (U, 2) the headmaster had been somewhat concerned about what all this meant for the future of governor–school relations.

These circumstances perhaps explain the rather controlling, giving-accounts style of communication at formal meetings which was indeed interpreted, by the governor who led the constituency Conservative party, as 'extremely guarded'. They may also explain the institution of the informal meetings. The 'new governors' were politically influential, and the head and his staff faced the dilemma of wanting to demonstrate to them their professional competence, while at the same time feeling rather wary about their intentions towards the school. The informal meetings, where proceedings were 'off the record', enabled the head and his staff to assess the extent to which members of this newly constituted governing body could be trusted to adopt an impartial and open attitude towards central educational issues, while at the same time ensuring that the risks of opening up such issues for discussion were minimal.

Many of our case studies show how teachers' feelings of accountability towards others depend on personal knowledge, and indicate that one of the major obstacles to staff feeling more accountable to governors lies in the absence of such knowledge. The 'informal meetings' at Uplands provide a context in which governors and teachers can feel free to shed their roles and loyalties and emerge as persons in a way which is not easy at the formal meetings. This was well illustrated by the informal meetings on 'Governors observing classrooms', where people felt free to agree or disagree with each other on an entirely personal basis.

The 'informal meetings' have enabled individual staff and governors to get to know each other, and to demonstrate such personal qualities as impartiality and open mindedness. The result has been the development of high quality discussion in which individuals feel free to question, challenge and probe on fundamental educational issues. The meetings also provide a context in which the non-political governors feel freer to express their personal views.

However, the most politically influential governor did not attend the informal meetings for some time. The fact that some staff exerted considerable pressure on him to go perhaps indicates the extent to which he was perceived as an integral part of the 'experiment'. He tended, at least initially, to question the split between formal and informal meetings:

> . . . where do you draw the line on priorities? And why do you put either in where you do? (U, 20)

It is certainly true that the confinement of certain topics to informal meetings suggests a reluctance to place them on the official agenda of things governors ought to discuss with staff. However, there were increasing signs that the informal meetings were beginning to influence both the content and quality of the formal meetings. Said a parent governor:

> I think it is getting better in the formal as well. I am sure the informal meetings have something to do with it. . . .

One might view the split meetings at Uplands as an imaginative and constructive response to governors who are shifting in the direction of calling the school to account, in a situation where the fourth condition I cited earlier was at stake, i.e. staff trust in governors' impartiality and open mindedness. Its ultimate potential as a response is its capacity to integrate the content and style of informal meetings into the formal proceedings; a state of affairs which appears to obtain at Holbein School. However, at Holbein there is what I would consider to be a functional equivalent to the 'informal governors' at Uplands. This is the close 'off stage' relationship which exists between the headmaster and his chairman of governors. Just as the formal proceedings at Uplands are increasingly influenced by the mutual respect and trust developed through the informal meetings, so at Holbein the formal meetings reflect similar qualities which are created and sustained by encounters between the headteacher and his chairman of governors. Rex Gibson noted:

> Although I personally have seen few Headmaster–Chairman meetings, it is clear that the relationship is close and friendly, based on frequent meetings and conversations. A high degree of mutual respect characterises the relationship. It seems obvious that this trust and confidence in each other arises from the concern of the Head to 'keep the Chairman fully in the picture about all aspects of the school' and from the fact that over several years they have discussed and acted upon many issues relating to Holbein. (HO, 3)

The extent to which a school allows its governors to call it formally to account will depend on interpersonal knowledge generated in less formal contexts.

13

Teachers and Advisers

Rex Gibson

This chapter concerns itself with Local Education Authority Advisers. It is in three sections: first, a brief review of the nature and function of the Adviser's role; second, a report of evidence from the CAP schools, showing how teachers in those schools view LEA Advisers; and finally a description of an accountability exercise jointly undertaken by one CAP school and a team of LEA Advisers – an exercise that represents a significant development in professional accountability.

1. LEA Advisers

LEA Advisers are almost invariably former teachers with substantial practical experience. There is no doubt that Advisers identify strongly with schools: their past, present and future activities are firmly centred in them. All view their principal task as helping to ensure the continued improvement of the education of children in their Authority's schools. To achieve this task, Advisers are concerned to build a relationship of mutual trust and confidence with heads and teachers, by offering advice, guidance and support. However, Advisers are clearly aware that they are, by virtue of their central task, the major channel of external professional accountability between school and LEA. Thus, they are not simply 'the link between the Administration and the schools' (East Sussex 1979: 18), but are inevitably required to monitor and report on standards in schools.

There are, therefore, two given inescapable elements in the Adviser's role: to advise and to inspect. These two functions present an uncomfortable dilemma for many Advisers (Bolam 1978: 18): as former teachers they wish to support and help their ex-colleagues, but the role requires them to make judgements on those former colleagues and, in some way, to act upon those judgements. They are the 'quality control' agents of the LEA (Pearce, 1979) and, increasingly in the 1980s, are under pressure to develop their inspecting role as the eyes and ears of their Authority. This unavoidable tension makes the role a delicate and demanding one, and the fact that Advisers' experience and sympathies are in and with the schools makes successful performance fraught with difficulties at a time of demands for greater teacher accountability.

Central to the thinking and behaviour of Advisers is the notion of 'good relationships': a concern to maintain friendly, warm, supportive contacts with teachers. Without such relationships they feel their work would be vitiated. Evaluate they must; but if judgements are to issue in effective action they must be made in the context of good relationships with teachers and schools. Weak teachers are to be helped to become good teachers, poor schools aided to raise their standards. The emphasis is invariably on positive, facilitating action; dismissal or similar drastic action must be preceded by sustained attempts to help teachers or schools to help themselves. Thus, all the respect for the notion of colleague autonomy that attaches to the word 'professionalism' serves to inform Advisers' beliefs and actions.

2. Teachers' views on LEA Advisers

What do teachers say about Advisers? From interviews with teachers in the six CAP schools it is possible to identify typical views:

(a) Advisers as busy people
There is no doubt that teachers recognise how very active Advisers must be:

> They've simply got too much to do. Every school would like to see more of them but they can't get round. . . . They are over-stretched.

The sheer number of schools and their geographical distance meant that, in practice, Advisers were sometimes difficult to contact:

Like all the advisers she is never there when you ring up. She has a very wide area – she does all of the county.

Little resentment was expressed at this. Teachers accepted that Advisers were out in schools somewhere, but that it was well-nigh impossible to visit all schools frequently. When they did call, their visits were often seen as concerned with particular groups. Thus, apart from the head and probationers, Advisers were seen to spend more time with senior staff:

Occasionally he comes round. He doesn't have a lot to do with me – invariably the Head of Department.

(b) Advisers can have too many responsibilities

There was recognition that Advisers are sometimes called upon to undertake tasks that are not strictly within their professional expertise:

Mr [Adviser] has tried his best but of course he is not a [subject] adviser, so he had extra to do.

The fact that Advisers could be called upon, because of the exigencies of staffing, to take up additional responsibilities was acknowledged:

He is also [subject] Adviser. He knows nothing about it. . . . I don't think it's one of his interests really. I think he has just got lumbered with it because the guy who was doing it retired, and they didn't feel that they could – having had teachers nagging at them for years to have a [subject] adviser – they felt that they couldn't just let it drop they had to give the responsibility to someone else.

(c) Good personal relationships are vital

Advisers' emphasis on the importance of good relationships is strongly echoed in teachers' comments. Teachers judged an Adviser very much on his or her personal qualities:

It entirely depends who they are. It entirely depends on the person.

> . . . the whole question hinges around personal relationships
> and I suppose that what I realised is that the Adviser's first job
> is to build up relationships with colleagues. . . .

Tact is of great importance and some Advisers clearly exercise
thoughtful discretion:

> My particular adviser is very careful not to be pushy.

Such typical comments however must not be taken to imply that
teachers judge Advisers solely on the basis of their personalities.
Professional knowledge and skill is greatly valued for, whilst
teachers invariably stated what they thought of an adviser as a
person, they usually went on to comment on the Adviser's particular subject expertise.

(d) Advisers' wider knowledge of schools affords greater objectivity

Teachers recognise that, by virtue of many school visits, Advisers
have extensive knowledge of practice. Thus, the Adviser is deemed
to have a wider view, one that is potentially more objective than a
teachers' relatively school-bound one:

> . . . I felt that because [the Adviser] goes round to a lot of the
> schools, and sees a lot of what goes on, I was quite happy to
> listen to [the Adviser] and respond to things that [the Adviser]
> suggested and advised. . . .

> the Adviser. . . as an outsider can look at the work that we are
> producing, in a far more objective way than I can by working
> inside the department everyday.

(e) Teachers reserve their right to accept or reject advice

Teachers are very conscious of what they see as their own professional autonomy. Certainly, they look to Advisers for advice,
but the (often-stated) implication is that they are free to take it or
leave it according to their own professional judgement. Teachers
wished to be responsible for their actions and were not happy to
think an outsider – even a fellow professional – was taking decisions for them:

If I didn't like the advice obviously I wouldn't take it.

I listen to them and then decide. . . . It has to be really. . . how can you teach it if you don't believe in it?

If I make a decision that someone else really has made for me then I wouldn't feel responsible for that. . . . I would see [the Adviser's] role basically as an adviser.

However, on a number of occasions Advisers were reported to have played an important role in aiding subject departments to take decisions. The head of a major department pinpointed an instance where he and his colleagues had sought advice:

I think they are here *as* advisers. For instance when [the Adviser] came in and we got to a point in a faculty meeting – about curriculum where we were divided and we weren't sure – we asked for advice . . . when you ask the adviser it means you are already open and likely to receive it and accept it.

(f) Advisers are professional colleagues; but their being external to the school has consequences for accountability relationships

The status of Adviser as fellow-professional was much stressed by teachers, often in contrast to other external groups:

I suppose I'm very wary of parental or even governors' involvement in what I consider to be a very specialised area of the curriculum. . . . I would respect the viewpoint of a fellow teacher or of an adviser far more than an interested amateur.

Teachers' comments often showed clearly the delicate tightrope the Adviser treads in relation to issues of authority relations and professional autonomy. Although acknowledged as an experienced professional, the Adviser is *external* to the school, and this fact weighs heavily. Teachers are in no doubt as to where their major professional accountability responsibilities lie: they are *within* the school:

I feel [that] in a school . . . the Head tends to be autonomous . . . if he gives the OK, then it's OK. I think the Adviser is what [his title] says: an 'adviser'. He can advise, but the decision finally is [Head's or teacher's].

Nonetheless, Advisers are seen as important in the accountability process, even though teachers were rarely clear or specific as to quite how they did or should operate (William Tyndale was often cited, but as 'an extreme case'). Mention was made of their role in the appointment of staff, help for probationers and in-service courses. In all these, as in school visits, teachers felt there was an accountability element, even though it was indirect and rarely or never seen as the major purpose of such activities. Rather, the reciprocal nature of the accountability relationship was stressed:

> The Authority in [subject] owes us quite a lot in the way of support for [activities we do]. . . . But I feel equally that we are accountable to them: very much so. And perhaps they don't make enough demands on us . . . I'm thinking not just of the *local* Authority but at national level. . . . I'm very concerned that perhaps we have not had enough – direction is not the right word – but *guidance*.

The careful avoidance of 'direction' by this highly qualified and successful head of department, simultaneously linked with a desire for more demanding accountability procedures, shows some of the ambiguities and ambivalences inherent in teachers' attitudes towards Advisers. In secondary schools the chain of command and responsibility is usually very clear. The relationship with 'outside' professionals is far less certain. Such uncertainties arise from many sources that can only be hinted at here: they include the diverse elements in the Advisers' inspector–adviser role; the ambiguity that attaches to 'authority' in present-day society; and the notion of 'professionalism' itself.

(g) Advisers should advise: teachers should ask for advice

Although the difficulties of the Adviser's role has been stressed, there is no doubt that teachers do want advice ('that's their job') and when they get it they can be generous in their praise:

> With regard to equipment in the department I took a lot of his advice. . . . He gave me some ideas what to get for and what material to buy and to stock up and start off. I was grateful for that.

One teacher was critical of teachers who did not take positive action to get advice:

It's no good us sitting back in school and saying, 'We never see the Adviser'. I think, if you need them, then they are very good.

The evidence of the CAP interviews suggests that the 'good relations' Advisers seek with teachers genuinely do exist, and there is often a high level of mutual respect. Teachers who have regular or significant contact appear to understand the difficulties Advisers face in successfully performing their diffuse and delicate task and see them as valuable colleagues not simply because they can make available materials and equipment, but also because they can and do offer helpful advice and support in less tangible ways.

3. One School's Accountability Exercise

What follows is a description of an experiment in school-Adviser relationships, a venture that, potentially, marks a significant step towards the practice of self-accounting schools. The comprehensive upper school involved opened in 1976. In September 1978 it had 900 third, fourth and fifth year pupils. Committed to a policy of keeping parents fully informed, it had already developed an extensive and effective system of teacher-parent communication (Gibson 1980). The headmaster felt the time was opportune for the school to take stock of its development by means of a joint assessment programme. This involved inviting in the entire LEA Advisory team to help staff assess the work they were doing. The exercise, spaced over two terms, was conceived as being of value to both the school and the Advisory team. It was a novel experience for both, and represented a cooperative venture which would reinforce links between teachers and Advisers. In the head's words:

> The coming months seem to be a very appropriate time to strengthen our relationship with the Advisory Service and to begin to make greater use of the service which they offer. (HO, 4)

In each subject department the head of department and Adviser engaged in a programme of joint observation and consultation. The Careers Department, Resource Centre and pastoral system were also studied. Although the pattern obviously varied from department to department, typically it involved the Adviser in lesson observation, participation in departmental meetings, study of syllabuses and other documents, and discussions with individual teachers. With the major aim of examining the work and organisation of the department, particular attention was paid to how work was developed for pupils of all abilities; to identifying instances of good practice; to resources; to identifying causes and suggesting remedies in areas of agreed weakness; and to indicating directions of development. The outcome in each case was a written agreed statement, prepared jointly by the head of department and the Adviser. These statements were discussed with the head, appropriate deputy, and occasionally, the Acting Chief Adviser. A report on the whole exercise expressed the views of the headmaster and heads of department. The Acting Chief Adviser also reported his general observations to the school.

Significant features mark out the enterprise as an important step in school accountability:

1. The exercise took place at the initiative of the school. Thus it signifies a *professional* rather than a *lay* concern for assessment.

2. It was largely a process of self-assessment. Thus, it involved teachers looking directly and consciously at their own practice, and attempting, in cooperation with an external professional (the Adviser), to give an account of that practice.

3. It was conducted for *school* purposes. Thus, the individual subject department reports were compiled for school, not LEA, information and use.

4. It was conceived an an exercise of mutual benefit to both school and Advisers. Thus, not only was it seen as a joint undertaking by professional colleagues, but also it was viewed as potentially significant as a *team* exercise for the Advisers.

5. It represented a coordinated attempt to provide a picture of the school as a whole at a particular stage of its development. As such it was concerned both to assess past and present performance, and to guide rational decision-making for future development.

6. It had, as a particular aim, the strengthening of relationships between teachers and Advisers.

7. It was conceived as a process, rather than as an event. Thus, the exercise stretched over two terms, involved a variety of practices and was viewed as part of a continuing relationship between teachers and advisers.

What were the views of the teachers? Characteristically, staff comments were favourable. It was typically thought to be 'an eminently worthwhile exercise' and individual teachers made many positive comments:

> Gave particular support over timetabling problems.

> Made us reflect on and reappraise aims, objectives, syllabuses.

> Useful to have a sounding board.

> . . . I think the best thing that's come out of it is probably better relations with [Adviser]. . .

Many comments suggested that the most important features were the building up of personal relationships and the opportunities for discussion with a fellow professional who had wide experience of other schools. Over and over again teachers interviewed in the CAP have made the point that in everything to do with school 'personal relationships' are paramount. This comment was made with equal force about the accountability exercise: that 'getting on', 'feeling in sympathy with', 'liking', 'respecting', were the vital ingredients for success. Personal relationships seem to be a crucial key in explaining not just the quality of teacher–pupil interaction, but all others: teacher–teacher, teacher–head, teacher–Adviser. The accountability exercise appears to have gone a long way to cement such good relationships.

There were, however, criticisms of the exercise. In particular, teachers felt that it was rare for advisers to pinpoint weaknesses of which the teacher was not already aware:

> [Adviser] confirmed our own criticisms.

> Told us little that was new.

> [I was] already aware [of weaknesses or opportunities].

> I don't think [the Adviser] picked up much that we weren't already worried about . . . we had a pretty good idea before [of the practices] we should tighten up on or improve.

Further specific critical points were made: that observed lessons were 'somewhat artificial', that there was insufficient time for discussion, that more advice could have been given on classroom use of materials, and that there was some lack of appreciation of the pastoral responsibilities of subject teachers. There was a worry that Advisers might feel they had 'done' the school and that they might not be in again for a long time (in the event, an unsubstantiated fear). However, far the most telling criticism was:

> I should have liked it to have a bit more bite.

This comment was fairly common. Staff claimed they would welcome 'harder', 'more searching', 'deeper', 'more critical' discussions with Advisers. Thus, because the teachers had confidence in what they were doing, they felt they would not feel threatened by closer critical probing, particularly by their professional peers, the Advisers. The head of department who wanted 'more bite' was quite specific about his expectations:

> I shouldn't like an Adviser to be able to come to me and say 'You will teach . . .', but I think if I was doing a very different course, he ought to be able to bring a lot of pressure on me to move away from what I was doing . . . If I'd made the wrong judgement . . . he could say '. . . I can tell you what other schools do and what they think is successful' . . . [the Adviser] has got to be able to suggest a compromise with a bit of clout!

Such an expectation illustrates the delicate balance of teacher–Adviser relationships emphasised throughout this chapter. It demands much respect, goodwill and give-and-take.

The demand for more searching criticism invariably carried the qualification 'as long as it is justified'. Advisers thus have their own 'Morton's fork': when they offer advice they are in danger that teachers will find those bits they agree with 'obvious', and those they disagree with 'wrong' or 'not appreciating all the particular circumstances'. Although some such criticisms were made of the accountability exercise, nonetheless it was clearly a successful enterprise. Such a conclusion not only witnesses to the professional and social skills of the Advisers and teachers concerned but also indicates ways in which professional accountability may be more practically effected.

14

Structures of accountability

Rex Gibson

What sort of 'theory' relates to accountability? The evidence of the six case studies is practical; each one shows teachers facing certain practical problems in their relations with parents, governors, employers, and dealing with those problems in commonsense, pragmatic ways. Rarely, if ever, do the teachers speak of 'theory'; the closest they get to it is when they state the principles that guide their actions, the most typical being:

The parents have a right to know.

The same is true of parents, governors, employers, students, LEA Advisers and others interviewed in the project. Again, there are statements of principle:

Exam results aren't everything in a child's life.

The school has to come to the community.

[Schools] are accountable to the governing body really in a very global way.

But nowhere is there what might be described as a theory of accountability. Neither teachers nor others see it as their task to produce theory: elaborated, abstract, systematic, complete, internally coherent, predictive, universalisable, expressed in technical, self-conscious, precise language. Rather, what they talk about are principles of the type noted above and the actual practice of the schools they are familiar with. Certainly, the tone is usually reflective; certainly, generalisations are made, but the content of what is said relates to this school, these teachers, these children: i.e. particular people in particular schools facing and resolving particular problems.

Thus, experience is drawn upon, actual instances are recalled, and these are sometimes used to illustrate or derive principles. But, in the formal sense of my earlier paragraph, 'theory' is missing. And yet what is present in each case study is a regular pattern. Each researcher has 'told a story' about his or her school: a fairly clear narrative line emerges from each. Whilst much variability of views and attitudes is evident in each study, there is even more evidence of order and coherence. Thus, teachers and parents and others generalise and prescribe on the basis of their experience and themselves clearly see pattern, system, typicality. Further, in selecting quotations, in ordering our case studies and frequently in using such words as 'typically' and 'characteristically', as case study researchers we have presented a picture that is not random but coherent and systematic. To put it simply: like parents, teachers and others, the members of the CAP see things 'hanging together' as meaningful, as somehow ordered. But does this constitute a theory of accountability?

It is certainly not my intention to put forward a theory of accountability; indeed I would confidently assert that there is no such thing as *a* theory; and I am sceptical as to whether there are even theories of accountability in any strict scientific sense. But I am confident that what can be perceived in the work of the project are certain structures which are significant in explaining school accountability. These structures can be seen underlying, inform-ing, influencing practice in each of the CAP schools; and they similarly underlie, inform and influence practice in all English schools. I am putting forward theory in the sense of identifying abstract, not directly visible structures which produce order and pattern – and which can be used to explain such consistency. But while these structures make for pattern and system, it is central to my thesis that, because of their nature, they also result in great complexity and variability of practice. Such complexity and varia-bility is the major feature of school accountability – indeed, of any social practice – and I do not intend to underestimate it or to seek to diminish it. Such diminution is all too often the effect of theory and theorising: a striving for intellectual neatness that, in its passion for tidying-up, trivialises and reduces human activity to a uniformity it does not possess. My claim, rather, is that significant structures do exist, and do shape the action of teachers, parents and others, but the very nature of the structures guarantees both patterns and variation.

A note on 'Structures'

The problem with using a word like structure is that it implies rigidity and something clearly discernible. To assert, as I do, that there are structures which underpin and influence human behaviour is to put myself in danger of being accused of reducing such behaviour to something puppet-like: man controlled by impersonal, non-human forces, merely responding to such forces; dancing to society's tune. The word structure conjures up such images. But this does not represent what I intend, or what I think is evidenced in the case studies of the CAP schools. There is not space to explain fully why I have chosen to adopt such a potentially misleading word as structures. I have set out my reasons in some detail elsewhere (Gibson 1981). Here I would refer to the fact that my thinking has been influenced somewhat by the recent writings of Raymond Williams (1977, 1979, 1980) and Anthony Giddens (1976, 1977, 1979); that I see structures as essentially man-made and man-changeable; that they are rooted in history and represent forms of organisation, thought and feeling which take material and cultural expression; that they are drawn upon, expressed and recreated in every human interaction; that they are always in dialectical relation, existing independently neither of each other nor of man. Their relationships are complex and interactive, allowing of no simple interpretation or prediction, for they correspond to, and embody, that complexity which is social life itself.

What must now be done is to set out some of the substance of, and evidence for, this claim. Thus, for the remainder of this chapter I shall argue that accountability in English schools in the late 1970s and early 1980s is conditioned by certain structures and that these are evidenced in the CAP research. Four structures will be examined: of competence, of social organisation, of thought, of feeling. Any understanding of school accountability must take account of these structures and their complex interrelationships.

Structures of competence

The notion of competence is all too often the missing assumption in social theory. Sociologists, psychologists and others have been prone to write as if the persons they discuss, collectively or individually, are 'cultural dopes' or beings without minds or purposes of their own. Such devaluation is done in both gross and subtle ways: to label an individual the 'subject' of a psychological experiment is as potentially dehumanising as any slipshod reference to 'classes' or 'masses'. The concept of the *competent social actor*: of the individual as a highly skilled, resourceful and *resourcefull*, meaning-seeking and meaning-endowing, valuing and evaluating *person*, is, I would claim, central to any understanding of social affairs. It is the lynch-pin of social understanding: a recognition that every human being in every utterance, and almost every action, draws upon huge cultural resources. This competence is all too easy to overlook and, indeed, both in social theory and in everyday life, is all too readily taken for granted and consequently neglected. And yet it is the central connecting term in the relationship between language and utterance, past and future, institution and individual action; between the abstraction that is 'society' and the concrete visible transactions that make up daily life.

The CAP case studies are rich in evidence of this competence. Thus, when teachers, parents or others are interviewed, or when the case study writer records a particular event (parents' evening; governors' meeting), what we are most obviously presented with is evidence of social competence: competence that is structured most evidently as linguistic skills, social skills, intellectual skills, emotional skills, evaluative skills. Each individual performance, seemingly unremarkable, is in fact a simply dazzling display of competence, and would be recognised as such if it were not for the everydayness, the sheer ordinariness of the feat. But it is a crucially significant feat that must be kept at the centre of attention in any attempt to explain social behaviour.

Qualities of competence are displayed by all those interviewed or observed in the Accountability Project. Even when effective communication is not achieved, or when social relations break down, the 'structure of competence' is still there in the recognition of such failure, in the evident possession of criteria by which such failures are recognised, or in the recognition that failure is the result of incompatible, uncongenial (or just different) 'views'. An interview with a 'non-attending parent' shows that this diffident, reluctant-to-attend mother evidences competence.

> I would get a bit nervy. I don't like 'phones anyway. But if I had to I would because of John. I want to know all about him. How he is getting on. Because when my husband was home that was all right because he had a car and we used to go to the school. . . . (RP, II2)

She has her point of view, motivations and judgements and she knows how to express them. Although the reader may feel she lacks, say, certain social competences ('nervy'), it is still my claim that, in her own awareness of those inadequacies, competence is once again evidenced. The important point is that life has its meanings for her – and they are meanings she has constructed out of her experience.

What is the importance of structures of competence in the explanation of school accountability? First, because it roots any explanation in human activity: in the beliefs and actions of particular persons. Second, because it is its engagement with other structures that are evident in schooling, that produces, in a very wide variety of expressions, the demand for accountability. More directly: it is because Mrs Smith's son John is taught by Mrs Jones in an English comprehensive school in 1980 that all three will – inevitably – have particular views of what happens in the school and on what should happen. All three will, in some way, *do* something about these views, and no explanation must lose sight of Mrs Smith *et al*. For what the case studies provide is massive evidence of the Mrs Smiths, the Mrs Joneses, the Johns, all making sense of their surroundings, all with their viewpoints, all with their competences, actively seeking and establishing significance and meaning in themselves and their world.

Thus it is human competence that actively mediates and works within and upon other structures I shall now examine: structures that have particular application to school accountability.

Structures of social organisation

These structures are the most immediately obvious, providing at once the framework and the mechanisms for school accountability.

They are clearly evidenced in the roles and the social positions, in the bureaucratic and organisational features of schooling. To speak of 'teachers', 'parents', 'governors', 'employers', 'pupils', is at once to identify the structure. All are social positions held at particular times by unique individuals and they are at once three things: the *means* by which relationships are effected, the devices that both *constrain and enable* individual behaviour, and an important *source of the demand* for accountability. I will confine my analysis to the working out of these three processes at school level, but before doing so it is necessary to indicate two other levels at which structural analysis of accountability can be undertaken.

The first level relates to *institutions* and would locate schooling within the structure, i.e. the education system, and would further locate that system in the structure of institutions of society (religious, political, economic, etc.). The second level would take a more radical stance than either approach so far identified, rooting itself in the material, economic structure, i.e. in *social class*, and interpreting accountability in terms of that structure (Gibson 1981).

To be a 'parent at Uplands School' is to belong to a social category. To be a 'teacher at Uplands School' is to belong to another. The effect of such categorisations is to call up a complex set of expectations and beliefs, and to establish normal, conventional ways in which individuals can relate to each other. Such expectations and conventions will be mediated by each individual parent or teacher: the 'competent social actor' identified above. But – and it is an important but – the basis of the relationships of these unique, purposive individuals is their roles. Fundamentally, the individuals meet *as* parent and *as* teacher: they have expectations for each other as parent and as teacher; they judge each other as parent and as teacher. Indeed, the basic reason they come into contact at all is because of their respective positions as 'teacher/parent at Uplands School'. Although there will be great variation between individuals in *how* they play their roles, nonetheless the bedrock of that relationship, the underlying structure, is the role-system. Different parents will have very different views of the school (good – OK – bad); will talk with teachers in very different manners (deferential – equal – superior); will place very different emphasis on goals (academic success – happiness – fitting in); such differences are an inevitable part of what it is to be human. But what those differences have in common is the social organisation – the role structure – within which they are expressed. In short, teachers are held accountable *because* they are teachers: a remark that is not as tautologous or banal as it might at first sight appear.

What the CAP research reveals is that teachers and parents actively seek ways of reducing the formality of the role relationships. Thus teachers typically seek to 'get to know' the parents and to show that 'we too are human'. Similarly, parents are concerned with the personal qualities of teachers and enjoy it when a 'good relationship' on 'easy friendly terms' is established. The case studies provide solid evidence of attempts to bridge the gap, to reduce role-distance, to create friendship: PTAs, social evenings, concerts, outings; the list is very long (Gibson 1980). But in spite of such efforts the gap remains for some parents:

> The teachers are strangers to us – they're not like ordinary people . . . they even marry other teachers. (HI, 2A3)

Such a comment begins to hint at something that is even more marked in the CAP case studies: this friendship, this informality, is very much secondary to the judgements that parents make of teachers as teachers, and the judgements teachers make of parents as parents of pupils. Here, the influence of the underlying social structure is exceptionally strong: parents never lose sight of the fact that schools have particular jobs to do, however different individual prescriptions might be (in fact there is much agreement). And teachers' tasks are held to be similarly self-evident. Almost every parental remark recorded in the case studies bears witness, directly or by inference, to this structure; to role performance:

> She is a very good head of lower school . . . also quite a strict disciplinarian.

> He's approachable isn't he – as a Headmaster? (U, 12)

Similarly, teachers are rarely under any illusions as to the bedrock of the relationship. They make their expectations (about appropriate behaviour) clear to parents through brochures, newsletters, reports, parents' meetings, and whilst they too judge parents on personal qualities their prime orientation is a structural one: is the role being played appropriately? Is this parent behaving as a parent with a child at this school should behave? Awareness of the structural relationship is ever present:

> I think that most of the parents of children who do SCISP [integrated science] are happy with it as a course but some may not necessarily be happy with it as exam results. (U, 10)

and at a parents' evening for fourth year parents:

> Unless we are in total agreement with each other and prepared to air our problems the child will suffer. . . . I want the most enthusiastic, committed and happy fourth year we've ever had. (Head of Middle School; U, 17)

What is evident is that every remark is made in context, and that context is an educational one: teachers, parents, pupils going about the business of schooling. The exercise, however, is never merely mechanical; the particular context is this school, these teachers, these pupils; indeed most usually it is this teacher, this child, these parents, this subject; and although each individual plays his role with his own unique emphasis, those personal competencies are exercised within the framework of the role structure. Mrs Smith, Mrs Jones and John are vividly alive to each other in their personal encounter, but that encounter is mediated in their roles. This framework necessitates stereotyping: thinking and speaking of 'the teachers', 'the parents'; aggregating individuals on the basis of their temporary social category. Such aggregations take the form of images of schools recorded in every case study.

But what is clearly evident in those images is the factor of human competence. Mrs Smith and Mrs Jones engage with each other. The role structure and other social structures play their part, but what comes through unmistakably are the personal qualities of individuals: personalities, actions and judgements of particular teachers and parents:

> The discipline comes over pretty strongly. . . . I get the feeling when Mr King puts across that he wants smart clothes worn, that is the order of the day. (U, 12)

> First of all we were told that we mustn't bend the child to our will. Secondly we were told that the child must have a broad

education which would include English/Maths, the Arts, Languages and something practical, something artistic, using the hands. So my son had to go into one of these craft subjects and he said, 'I don't like any of them and if I have got to do one, it can only be Technical Drawing . . .' that was his attitude and so I didn't want to bend him to do something he didn't want to do, and I couldn't resist pulling the school's leg on that point. (U, 17)

It is in the last remark that we see clearest evidence of the need in any theorising about accountability to ensure the centrality of the competent human actor. However, the most aware human lives within social structures, and the role structure constrains each individual by virtue of the expectations, rights and obligations that attach to each role. In a sense, Mrs Smith and Mrs Jones are forced to talk about mathematics – or at least, John's success or failure at it. But the structure also enables each individual to achieve his own purposes, through his unique conception and realisation of those expectations and duties. Thus power is a function neither simply of personality *nor* of role: but of their interaction with each other and a host of other structures.

Structure is not simply external to the individual, for it is historically, humanly constructed. But it provides the necessary continuity in human activities: Mrs Jones is the temporary holder of that post, year tutor, that outlasts her. But because of the structure – a structure created by, drawn upon, reproduced by the competent social actors who are embedded in it – because of the very different tasks of teachers, parents, governors, the demand for accountability will always be there: the forms of its realisation will depend on the complex interrelations of individual action, social structures and other structures to which I now turn.

Structures of thought

The least visible structure that influences school accountability is what I shall call structures of thought. By this is meant the ways of thinking, the modes of intellectual expression current in a society at any particular point of time. Such structures lie far beneath the surface of everyday behaviour and are invariably taken for granted. Of particular importance are language itself and the nature of school knowledge. Space does not permit any adequate discussion of language. I have attempted a preliminary analysis elsewhere (Gibson 1981). However the second, school knowledge – the curriculum – is distinctively relevant to accountability.

What is evident in the CAP case studies is that when knowledge is structured in particular ways it reduces the degree of accountability that is demanded or seen as possible or desirable. Thus the more abstract or specialised the knowledge, the further removed it is from commonsense everyday knowledge, the more theoretically complex, intangible and systematised it is, the more it removes itself from lay accountability. Conversely, where particular structures of knowledge overlap with similar structures in everyday experience: where commonsense, practicality, 'obviousness', applicability, can be declared as evident in the structure, the more open that particular area of school knowledge is to accountability demands.

How are these assertions supported by case study evidence? In the very frequent comment of both parents and school governors that curriculum matters are for teachers, not others, to decide:

That's a professional matter. It's for the teachers.'

'We pay the Headmaster.'
(Governors at Holbein, Ch. 3)

'That's their job – what they're paid for to teach.'

'We know what we want [child] to do for the exams – but I couldn't do it!'
(Parents at Holbein, Ch. 2)

And teachers are firm in their resolve to protect curriculum from lay interference or judgement. They are willing to discuss and justify, but they reserve the right of decision over curriculum matters:

'We provide the menu and the parents choose the dishes'

'The decision as to what was taught and how it was taught . . . should be within the professional staff of the school'. (HO, 2)

Justification for protecting curriculum from accountability lies in the teacher's claim to greater knowledge, superior technical skill, more complex understanding of particular structures of thought than the layman can possess. Such understanding, it is held, is called for by the very structure of the knowledge itself: for it is non-everyday, not concrete and visible, not 'easy' or 'simple'; rather, it is far removed from daily life, requiring long study, special vocabularies and concepts, self-consciously theoretically under-pinning. Such characteristics are evident in two particular areas: curriculum construction itself (after all, the study of 'curriculum' is now a very prestigious enterprise); and in subjects which have clear and well-established theoretical structures: for example, mathematics and science.

It is in those areas where the teachers' structures of thought are shared by parents, governors, employers; where claim can be laid to equality of understanding; where it is much harder to defend special expertise, specialised knowledge; where tradition denies special privilege to teachers; in these areas accountability claims can be and are – pressed. Thus, in financial matters school governors claim equal – often superior – knowledge to teachers. Their experience as councillors or businessmen, or the legitimation that their position *as* governor affords, serves as their own claim to expertise. Similarly, in the non-curricular practical activities of school, participation demands can be pressed more easily: dress, meal and bus times are practical matters that can be (but very rarely are) discussed with claim to equal expertise. But it is the matter of behaviour that is most open: morality is not seen as a 'reserved' area. Everyone can – and does – have their views about pupil behaviour and these are central in the image of any school:

> Seeing them going in and coming out of some schools – when you are driving around as I do – you see the kids coming out of the school like lunatics and running across the roads not looking where they are going, but I don't get that impression at Uplands. (U, 12)

Pupil behaviour is a particularly interesting item in the school accountability debate, for with the growth of pastoral care systems in schools and with the vast array of 'technical knowledge' that *can* be called upon (e.g. psychological theory), teachers can and do make special claims to expertise. Such claims are however much more open to dispute by outsiders. What needs remarking upon is that it is the *structure of knowledge* that is held to legitimate protection from lay judgement and to modify the strength of accountability demands. These conclusions about *structures of thought* can be inferred from the case studies.

It would be inappropriate to conclude this section without reference once again to structures of competence: to the active, purposive individual. Thus, what is most evident in the CAP case studies is that whilst teachers and parents do typically take the structures of knowledge for granted, nonetheless they actively and consciously – against the background of that taken for granted knowledge – negotiate solutions to particular problems. Hence, every parent, vitally concerned about his or her child's wellbeing, seeks to ensure that 'the best' is being done within the structure of options that exist. For the great majority of parents this comprises limited choice, guided by teachers and children, of particular curriculum patterns. For a very small minority, who see much of schooling as irrelevant, it entails opting out or putting up with as little fuss or involvement as possible. But in every case each parent is thinking of their particular boy or girl, attempting to figure out, in the face of the evident complexity that is curriculum choice, a 'right' path for their child. Such choices are made in terms of structures of thought that do not correspond to the structures of school knowledge: in everyday knowledge, in knowledge of one's own child. In these there is at once a comprehensiveness, an indefinability, an *irrationality* that is common property. Such knowledge makes it possible to demand accountability which cannot be wholly resisted by differently structured 'expert' knowledge. To return to the analogy invoked by a teacher on p. 198 above: the parents exercise their right to choose the dishes; the teachers decide the menu.

Structures of feeling

These would be called by some 'ideologies', by others 'beliefs', and by others 'attitudes'. Without offering elaborate definition or justification I prefer the term 'structure of feeling' because it emphasises affective rather than cognitive states (cf. 'structures of thought' above); because it draws attention to those springs of impulse and restraint that move individuals to act or withhold from action; because such individual motivations, though not necessarily consistent, appear to be or arise from organised sentiments; and because such motivations can be seen as manifestations of more generally held beliefs about human conduct. 'Feeling' serves to remind us that general sentiments, ideologies, find individual expression. Indeed, as I have implied throughout, any individual is embedded in, and embodies, certain traditions, certain structures, but it is through his or her activity that those traditions and structures are simultaneously drawn upon and eventually transformed. What is true of social structures and structures of thought is even more true of structures of feeling. Thus, it is my claim that, evidenced in the case studies, we can clearly perceive four (at least) main structures of feeling that greatly influence school accountability: professionalism, individualism, community, democracy.

a. Professionalism

Mention has already been made of the expert knowledge to which teachers lay claim. It is this esoteric knowledge that is held to justify protection from lay interference and judgement: in other words, professional knowledge limits accountability. But professionalism is much more than possession of a corpus of theoretical knowledge. It constitutes a set of beliefs about *relationships* with others. The literature on professionalism is well known and there is no point in recapitulating it here. All that needs pointing out is that a profession claims, apart from specialised knowledge, *autonomy* (i.e. regulating entry, exit and role behaviour), a *service ethic* in relation to its clients and *high status and reward*. Hence it asserts monopoly of practice and protection from lay evaluation.

What the case studies show is that this general structure of beliefs is held by almost all teachers, even though it is accommodated to, or held in tension with, other beliefs. Thus, every teacher interviewed claimed professional status. However, as all were committed to some form of accountability, their professionalism was contested or modified by a concern for informing and involving 'the laity': parents, governors, etc. It is fair to claim that the great majority of teachers had made a satisfactory accommodation of their belief in their own professionalism with other, potentially conflicting, beliefs. One typical view was that reasonable discussion would overcome difficulties:

> It's a long job, but we've got to educate parents, talk to them, listen to them, give them confidence in themselves and us. (HI, 3A11)

Another view was that democratic control was not really what parents (or others) wanted:

> Surely most parents wouldn't want to have that kind of control over school? They would want to have their particular point of view listened to, but I think most people would then be prepared if the school said 'Right, thank you very much for making that point of view, but we don't do that', to say 'OK'. (HI, 3A11)

What is impressively demonstrated in the case studies is that the teachers' view of themselves as professionals is held also by parents, even when that view is threatened by apparently 'non-professional' behaviour. Thus, a parent on teachers' industrial action:

> I sympathise with them but I think you think of a teacher as rather a special profession, rather like a Doctor and so forth, and I think it is rather diminishing to them really. (RP, III3)

Further, it is usual for parents to acknowledge teachers' professional knowledge ('they know their stuff'), but Jennifer Nias draws attention to how some parents sharply perceive the monopolist aspects of professional control:

> My son put down what he wanted but when they actually came to it they told him that he had to change it and do what they said.

> Regardless of what we think, they'd do as they want anyway.

> The teachers might listen [to parents] but not do anything. . . . They all stick together. (HI, 3A11)

There are therefore three tasks that still need to be undertaken in any adequate theorising about school accountability. First we need to know much more about those structures of feeling parents draw upon when thinking of teachers. This section has directed attention to a crucial ambivalence that seems to exist: between 'trust' and a feeling of powerlessness. Second, we require a mapping of the educational assumptions of secondary teachers. What I have in mind is the identification of a set of beliefs corresponding to those set out and justified so meticulously by Ronald King (1978) as 'the ideology of infant teachers'. And third, we need to understand more clearly how such structures of feeling interact with other material and social structures to produce, in particular comprehensive schools, in the 1980s, the modes of accountability that exist and are possible.

b. Individualism

If feelings about professionalism are a major influence on teachers' views and practices on accountability, so too are those structures of feeling that relate to individualism. For parents its effects are probably even more significant. The notion is a very complex one that has taken a variety of expressions historically and cross-culturally (Lukes 1973). However, certain key features can be discerned, much evidenced in the case studies.

First, the idea of *personal autonomy*, of the right to determine one's own life, take one's own decisions. In certain respects it appears to fit neatly with teachers' conceptions of professionalism. Thus, in the professional-layman relationship the issue is seen as clear cut: teachers decide (albeit after much consultation and involvement). But when a fellow professional is involved, individualism is called into play. Thus, speaking of LEA advisers:

> If . . . someone else really has made [a decision] for me then I wouldn't feel responsible for that. (HO, 4)

However, when the role-structure of the school itself is invoked, the effect is lessened: individualism loses ground to bureaucracy and professionalism ('That's the Head's job').

For parents, the concern for self-determination is evident: schooling should be about parents getting what they want for their own children. They may not express it in such formal language as 'independence', 'self-direction', but it clearly lies behind the wish for children 'to get on well'. There is, incidentally, an interesting paradox here: for this rugged independence of parents often sits oddly with their critical, demanding attitude towards (their own) children ('such liars', 'need pushing', etc.). Further, it could be claimed that 'getting on well' often means 'fitting in'. But to take this view would be to deny that, whatever conception of 'getting on' parents hold, their concern is for the realisation of what they see as best: a clear expression of individualism.

The second component of individualism is the idea of *human dignity*; of the intrinsic worth of each individual. In the case studies neither teachers nor parents put it in such high sounding terms, but the evidence is there. The unique importance of each individual pupil is enshrined in school aims, in teacher-parent communications and in the pastoral care system of any school. In the second half of the twentieth century it is part of the belief system (and rhetoric) of all teachers. For parents, the matter is clear cut: 'Our John' is the touchstone of the school's success, the criterion by which accountability is ultimately measured:

The main thing is to know how the boy is getting on

You do want to know how your children are doing

As far as our child is concerned . . .

We've a very bright boy . . .

Third, individualism implies the right to *privacy*: liberty of conscience, of thought and feeling; freedom of opinion and freedom to live one's life in one's own way. The pluralism expressed by teachers, the tolerance of other points of view, the right of the individual child to make up his own mind to choose his own way of life, is, once again, part of the structure of secondary teachers' beliefs (and rhetoric). And, again, such views are clearly expressed in teacher–parent communication. Similarly, what is evident in all parents' remarks is that they regard their own views as privileged. That is, although some may argue for more discipline and control in school (and they do), although their views may be anti-libertarian, nevertheless each parent regards his or her right to hold and express them as natural and proper. Even if they show little tolerance of other viewpoints, the claim of their right to their own is marked.

Finally, but not exhaustively, individualism enshrines the notion of *self-development*; of the unfolding of personal talents. It is not necessary to spell out how this too is enshrined in the structure of teacher beliefs; and the case studies contain much corroborative evidence. Similarly, parents expect that schools will enable their children to 'make the best of themselves'.

What is clear is that the structure of feeling that is individualism – autonomy, dignity, privacy, self-development – actively promotes demands for school accountability. Teachers quite explicitly include it in their conception and stated aims of education, and hence imply criteria by which a school can be judged. Parents find in it (albeit unselfconsciously) both the motivation for, and criteria of, holding the school accountable. Individualism has a very long history in England (Macfarlane 1978); it is a crucial part of the fabric of our culture. As such, it is not surprising that, as a structure of feeling, it is massively evident in schooling and is a vitally important factor in accountability.

c. Community

But if individualism gives rise to accountability claims, so too does its seeming opposite: that structure of feeling that is associated with the word 'community'. The history of the term is long and complex, its meanings and expression having an almost infinite variety and resonance. But its central notions are clear: 'belonging', 'caring', 'concern', 'commitment'; and there is no doubt as to its importance both in the culture at large and in schooling. It conventionally begins any statement of school aims as, for example, at Highstones:

> To develop in the school an ordered, caring community, based on good personal relationships, and with the highest possible academic, cultural and sporting standards. (HI, 2B2)

And it is a structure of values that underlie many headteachers' statements about their schools:

> it is our job as teachers to care for every child. Every child . . . making the school a welcoming place when parents come in. (HI, 2B2)

The commitment to the notion of 'school *as* a community' is very strongly held by almost all teachers, and even if it takes somewhat different expression, the elements of belonging, caring, concern, are always present. It is also evidenced in the concern for the school to serve the local community:

to develop the school as the servant of the local community and
to encourage community use of the school. (HI, 2B2)

What is less remarked upon is that as a structure of feeling it is in
tension, if not in direct conflict, with that of individualism. For
whilst community stresses getting on together, fitting in, an active
concern for group aims, individualism stresses getting on, getting
out, non-conformity, competition. Both are deeply rooted in our
culture, and both therefore find significant expression in our
schools. It is yet another mark of human competence that the two
coexist, are accommodated together in beliefs and in action.

   Parents too are much concerned with community although they,
unlike teachers, rarely use the word. Typically, this concern is
manifested in three ways: 'fitting in', 'control' and 'the future'. The
first, 'fitting in', is associated with the universal wish of parents: the
happiness of their children. The case studies are full of evidence
that parents want their children to get on with their teachers and
their peers, to enjoy good relationships, to be happy. This would
appear to entail a tempering of individualism. The second, 'control', was frequently expressed as a concern about discipline,
order:

   There's too much freedom in the classroom . . . the teachers
   should have more control over the children. (U, 12)

Here, 'belonging' takes on a sharper, conforming edge: and the
notion of community is some way removed from warm, organic,
friendly relationships. The third, 'the future', stresses the school's
role in preparing children for work (I write this with a sinking
feeling in early 1981). Thus, the taken for granted assumption of
the great majority of secondary school parents is that schools
should be happy, ordered, friendly places, but that the central task
is one of preparation for a future: the world of work or of higher or
further education, and that is a serious and demanding business.
There is, for example, in some case studies, talk of 'pushing the
kids'. This, and other parental expressions, is clear evidence of a
future orientation: the idea of community is there; but the structure
of feeling in which it is embodied embraces a world far wider than
that of the school.

   The structure of feeling expressed by 'community' is another source of accountability claims. For a school to profess commitment to 'community' is to impose upon itself an obligation to be accountable to that community. And such obligation and its reciprocal expectations will issue in accountability practices different in form, function and nature from those which arise from individualism – or from that structure of feeling closely allied to it: 'democracy'.

d. Democracy

The structure of feeling that embodies democratic sentiments is inextricably and centrally part of English culture. It is usually acknowledged as the source of accountability demands. Calling our rulers to account, and each individual possessing the right to participate in deciding matters affecting him, is deeply embodied in popular belief and practice, even if the sceptic occasionally thinks the exercise more a necessary fiction than a substantive reality. But it would be a mere cynic who held such a view consistently for, however imperfect the realisation, democratic assumptions and practice characterise British social life.

However, the relationship between school accountability and democracy is both uneasy and complex. The case studies provide much evidence as to how, in practice and in principle, that relationship is at once tenuous, uncertain and intricate. For example, seldom, if ever, are the words 'democracy' or 'democratic right' used in the case studies, and it is clear that limits apply as to how far the analogy of democratic procedures can be applied to schooling.

School governors are, of course, the prime example of the workings of representative democracy. They are usually held to be the formal expression of how 'the people' control education. Thus, their legal obligation is:

the general direction of the conduct and curriculum of the school (DES circular 14/77)

But in practice their powers and importance appear very limited. Certainly, for teachers, governors rank low on their list of accountability priorities. Characteristically, when teachers were asked to whom they were accountable they would reply:

> Mostly you're accountable to your pupils, to each other to the
> Head and to parents. (U, 22)

Teachers are overwhelmingly in agreement with this view. Others: governors, LEA advisers, came far below these four categories. To put it bluntly, the notion of democracy – if it means effective lay control of school – is anathema to teachers. A polite expression of such feelings is:

> I would prefer however the governing element of the schools
> (if it is not to be the Headmaster) to be a group of educated
> professionals. (U, 22)

Thus, for teachers, democratic structures or feeling are subordinate to that of professionalism, to the structure of bureaucratic organisation, and to the personal loyalties felt to *our* pupils and *our* parents. And it must be noted that such personal loyalties do not take democratic form. At its starkest: no teacher would be willing for curriculum (or many other matters) to be decided by majority vote of non-professionals. Governors themselves are well aware of the uncertainties that attach to their role, of the limits of their powers:

> But what *could* you do?

was a much repeated example of governors' self-questioning. And the answers they gave were, with very few exceptions, qualified and tentative. They too, in matters of curriculum, saw strict limits to any democratic decision-taking: it was something to be left to the professionals. However, governors clearly are much influenced by the democratic ideal, for they see themselves clearly as representatives at the school:

> To try and represent parents' views to see that their children
> receive the sort of education that their parents want. (HO, 3)

I have set out elsewhere (HO, pp. 31–50) details of how school governors see their functions and how they work out in practice. There is no point in recapitulating that analysis here, examining as it does the detail of how application of the notion of democracy takes different forms in relation to particular issues: curriculum, standards, staffing, discipline, financial matters. It is sufficient merely to point to three further problems that serve to qualify 'democracy' as a structure of feeling influencing school account- ability. First, there are in practice very strict limits as to how far a governing body really is representative of the people's (parents?) wishes. Thus, not only are political governors' appointments notoriously subject to change after small swings in local govern- ment elections, but this very indirect system of appointment (rather than election) means that very few parents know who most members of the governing body actually are. Only parent gov- ernors are directly elected by parents. Second, although schools are institutions in our democratic society, it is very misleading to think of them *as* democratic. They are not. Other structures of feeling predominate. Third, the curious blend of trust and mistrust that is embodied in 'democracy' ('you can vote the beggars out of office') applies very uneasily to schools that are staffed by full-time qualified experts claiming distinctive skills and knowledge, and who are committed to building a relation of trust and consensus with parents and pupils.

To return to the question posed at the start of this chapter: what sort of 'theory' relates to accountability? There is no simple answer other than that any simple 'cause-effect' theory will not do. Rather, any explanation of accountability must be a complex, delicate matter that takes account of material, social and cultural struc- tures – but which, above all, places a consideration of individual purposive, meaning-seeking action at the centre of explanation. The notion of parents, teachers and others as competent social actors is, quite simply, indispensable. With this concept of struc- tures of human competence, explanations can then be offered of its engagement with other structures which have particular relevance and application. Such structures bear with different weight on different people at different times, but they constitute the inescap- able social, shared pressures which both confront and exist within each unique individual.

Any future theorising about school accountability would seek to explain how local expression of the structures examined above (and others e.g. material, demographic) both constrain and enable unique individuals to exercise their competences and so to acquire power, influence and authority that will help to secure their purposes. There is thus clearly much scope for further investigation that synthesises the particular and the abstract: the relationships of these parents and these teachers within structures that find expression in their actual behaviour.

15

The nature of trust

Jennifer Nias

> The desires of the heart are as crooked as corkscrews,
> Not to be born is the best for man:
> The second-best is a formal order,
> The dance's pattern; . . .

W. H. Auden

Understandings are reached; decisions are made. School account-ability rests upon understandings rather than decisions. Therefore, provided the means exist for understandings to be reached, schools have no need, for purposes of accountability, of decision-making machinery. This oversimplification of a familiar argument reflects a characteristically English suspicion of 'formal order' and a prefer-ence for 'trust'. Yet this is to beg the nature of trust. In this chapter I suggest that trust means predictability; that, in institu-tional terms, it implies being able to make accurate predictions about: individuals' attitudes, reactions and technical competence; the consistency of norms and of patterns of role-behaviour within the institution; procedures and forms of organisation. However, people and routines become predictable only as one gains know-ledge of them. Thus formal accounting devices can be seen as a means of ensuring regular, stable contact between individuals. In this sense the 'dance's pattern' serves the dual purpose of express-ing the need for predictability and ensuring it.

Trust has a second necessary condition – perceived agreement over ends. Since schools provide an essential public service, both teachers and their clients are likely to prefer conflict about ends and means to take place outside the school and in such a way that the education of pupils is disrupted as little as possible. The existence of an auditing system removed from the classroom allows this to happen. Thus another way of viewing formal procedures is to see them as a culturally-sanctioned device for regulating conflict over values and removing it from the schools. If this is true, then the less the agreement among participants about the essential purposes of schooling, the greater the need for an effective auditing system will be.

In the past, schools have been protected to a large degree by an unspoken agreement over ends, an understanding which exists between teachers and society at large that both will work towards the best interests of pupils. External demands for accountability call the tacit nature of this contract in question. Thus it is at the core of teachers' sense of moral responsibility as 'professionals' that they stand at the present moment most in need of the protection afforded by a new 'formal order'.

Formal procedures and the interpersonal knowledge which grows from and supplements them are the interacting means by which predictability is established and maintained, and agreed goals are negotiated and reaffirmed. By formal procedures I mean forms of organisation which are built into the functioning of the school (e.g. parent associations; employers' meetings; heads of faculty meetings) or which routinise or give bureaucratic recognition to existing informal arrangements (e.g. numbering and ensuring regular publication of newsletters; publishing an annual programme of parents' meetings or the arrangements for pastoral care; giving an informal staff group the name and status of a working party). The characteristics of formal procedures are as follows: they take place at time and places advertised in advance and usually at pre-specified intervals; membership (of meetings) or attribution (of publications) is publicly recognised; attendance (at meetings) tends to be regarded by participants as morally or as constitutionally obligatory; writers (of documents) and participants act in role. Thus when individual parents offer each other lifts to meetings, this is an informal arrangement, but when the PTA Committee establishes a rota and a neighbourhood organisation it becomes a formal procedure. Similarly, when governors attend school plays or meet the staff socially they are acting informally; the formal procedure is the termly meeting of the Governing Body. An ad hoc interview between an anxious parent and the head is informal, whereas when the same parent meets the head as part of

	High predictability of personal and institutional behaviour	*Low predictability of personal and institutional behaviour*
High agreement over ends	No felt-need for formal procedures	Felt-need for personal contact
Low agreement over ends	Felt-need for formal procedures	Felt-need for formal procedures *and* for personal contact

organised referral arrangements, a formal procedure is operating.

The relationship between predictability and agreement over ends may be expressed as follows:

A high level of agreement over fundamental aims and a strong degree of interpersonal predictability reduces participants' felt-need for formal procedures. Much is left to tacit understandings; the occasional ambiguity or disagreement can usually be resolved through a personal exchange. By contrast, conflict over ends coupled with uncertainty over likely behaviour increases protagonists' felt-need both to increase interpersonal knowledge (often possible in the first instance only through formal procedures) and to govern one another's actions by establishing rules and conventions. Yet to some extent the two factors are independent. It is possible to have a situation where disagreement can be highly predictable, in which case formal procedures help to regulate and ritualise the resulting conflicts; or one where tacit agreement over goals is accompanied by an erratic use of means, in which case interpersonal knowledge becomes critically important.

Predictability of personal behaviour and technical competence

The commonsense way of establishing certainty in relation to the behaviour of significant others is to 'get to know them', either directly or through the reports of others. Predictability relies heavily therefore on personal contact over time. As an employer said of the staff of a new school:

It takes time to build up liaison; you have to know who you're dealing with and what to expect from them. (HI, 2D)

Given the opportunity to establish such personal knowledge participants looked for certain reassurances. Consistency between word and action was felt to be particularly important. Examples illustrating the need to feel 'that when they say something will be done, it damn well will be' (U, 8) occurred in relationships between schools (S, 3), within schools (HI, 1A), between the press and teachers (RP, 113) and in parents' dealings with teachers (U, 8).

Knowledge of how individuals were likely to behave was often however the first step towards building up stable expectations of a role. As a teacher at Highstones School said in an unpublished interview:

> [Last year] it wasn't that decisions weren't being made. It was that we didn't know who was making which decision. We had to get that straightened out before we could get on with working together.

Head and governors at Old Town held highly congruent views 'of the role the other is expected to play', whereas at Highstones a parent was worried by her uncertainty about:

> 'the relationships [between teachers and pupils] . . . I often wonder what sort of relationship there is. (HI, 2A2)

Parents often wanted teachers to act in role on all occasions, and the latter realised this:

> Their expectations from the *Sun* or *The Times*, if they buy them on the market, is quite different from what they expect from the school. And if you had me topless in the middle of the school brochure it would shock them, even though they would love it in the *Sun*. (U, 5)

Parents and others sought also to discover teachers' level of technical competence. Individually, they read reports, studied homework, went to parent association 'teach-ins', questioned teachers at employers' or governors' meetings, talked to teachers at consultation evenings, sized up the school on open days and evenings. Desire for 'technical' predictability may also be why many parents supported the publication of public examination results. Anxiety about levels of competence was particularly noticeable in the CAP's two new schools (Highstones and Robert Peel) and may well account in part for the very high turnout at both schools for all types of parent meeting.

The need to establish predictability in relation to behaviour and technical competence also explains the significance which parents attached to stability of personnel. For example:

> The question I asked [the Head] was 'Are you going to stay in this area, or can I expect you to be pursuing promotion and moving off to another school as soon as the opportunity offers itself?' And he said he intended to put his roots down, and stay here, and he is the sort of man I would like to have to guide my child's education. (U, 11)

Predictability of institutional behaviour

Participants also need to feel that systems work predictably. Parents in all the CAP schools obviously understood how the schools were organised. They were able to describe with assurance 'how things worked'. Many of the means of communication (e.g. newsletters) used by the teachers to 'give account' of their work were routinised:

> The Head's policy is to get it out every week, and you can see the reason why. Once you start missing an issue here and there, the children and parents might cease to expect it. . . . Break the continuity and parents won't know where they are. (U, 14)

According to John Elliott, the extent to which the school was well-organised was 'an important reason for [parental] choice' (U, 9), and the head of Old Town Girls' School claimed:

> It is through the teaching staff that the school's accountability to the girls is effected. The school *works*. I see it as my role to make it possible for them to work effectively. . . . (OT, 5)

In general participants liked 'to know what to expect'. On several occasions parents expressed dissatisfaction with meetings because the purpose of them had not been clearly spelled out in advance. Employers argued that schools were letting pupils (and employers) down by failing to tell the former what life in paid employment would be like. One claimed:

> It's a hell of a shock for them when they suddenly come to work and find that they have for instance a foreman telling them what to do. (RP, II4)

Many parents took every opportunity they could to find out more about their children's work. As David Bridges reported at a parents' evening:

> One or two parents specifically made the point that they would have liked to have been able to see a copy of the overall syllabus for the year, so that they could see where the children were going as well as understand where they were and where they had come from. (RP, III2)

Predictability and 'time-lag'

Expectations, built up over time and through personal contact, persist. Indeed they can adversely affect the attempts of a school to change its image (e.g. U, 7) or to establish new forms of accountability. As the head of one new school said:

> I think one of the things we have in mind here is to try . . . to help them understand the kind of things that we believe in . . . it is difficult because all the time when people think about school they are going back to their own experience which is likely to have been very different. (RP, I)

In the other new school, several teachers brought to their relationship with their head expectations of authoritarianism built up through previous experience in other schools (HI, 1A). This situation was mirrored in the same head's attempt to let parents hold him to account. Discussing a meeting with parents from a feeder middle school, the foundation year tutor argued:

> It didn't become a unified discussion group – people talking together for a common purpose. . . . Because I don't think the parents were used to that. . . . They are still used to being talked down to by a teacher behind a desk, and having to talk up to him.

For some of them the only language they do understand in schools is us and them. And they find it very difficult for that to be broken down – particularly when it gets to the upper school. If they have had 'training' in the previous school, by the time they get to us it's not too bad. But if the other schools don't work that way either . . . then really it is quite difficult to change their opinion. (HI, 2B4)

Agreement over ends

To speak of agreement over goals is, in one sense, to extend the scope of participants' mutual predictability. When members of a system have the same ends in view there is much that they can take for granted about one another's actions. Nevertheless, although agreement may result in predictability, the converse is not true: conflict often results from situations in which individuals can predict that their fellow participants will have different goals from their own. Thus agreement over ends is a second vital ingredient of 'trust'. Like predictability it grows from and depends upon 'formal procedures' and interpersonal knowledge.

Members of all the CAP schools and their audiences showed themselves keenly aware of the importance of agreement over goals. From among many instances I have taken three, from different members of the school's accountability networks:

Head, in address to new parents: We ask for your support in this, we hope we will get it. If you lay down your standards which are in conflict with ours – then it may be too late when you need help. It is a partnership. (S, 2)

Teacher: I would have thought parents expect certain things of teachers. . . . No, I don't object to that. The things I think they would generally want are things everyone would want. (HI, 3A)

Governor: The governors can only try and ensure that the education offered in school fits in with what the community seems to want. (OT, 7)

By contrast, in his study of employers' perspectives, David Bridges argued that a major cause of industrialists' distrust of teachers was their feeling that schools misrepresented their values

and systematically alienated pupils from industry. Similar views
were voiced by employers of pupils from other schools. Yet,
despite their suspicion of 'teacher propaganda', they wanted not
more control over the school, but assurances that their point of
view was being 'fairly represented'. Formalised and personal
contact between the two types of institution were perceived as the
means of ensuring this. Similar views on the dual importance of
personal knowledge and formal procedures came from a teacher
who, in explaining his distrust of his school's 'closed' decision-
making procedures, claimed:

> Well one likes to feel that one's own point of view is repre-
> sented at the highest level – I have no guarantee that it is.
> (HI, 1A)

Given shared goals, members of a school's 'accounting system'
also need to feel confident of the capacity of the head to lead the
school towards them. In all the CAP schools, this confidence
existed, as one typical comment suggests:

> Vice-Chairman of Governors: I suppose it amounts to the fact
> that I have confidence in the Headmaster and his staff to put
> together a curriculum that is going to meet the aims of the
> school. (U, 20)

However, a reputation for self-confidence appears to be equally
important, perhaps because it helps to generate confidence
in others. Contrasting views from two schools make this point:

> Teacher: [the Head] has a sense of confidence that he does
> really know what he is trying to do . . . (U, 4)
>
> Jean Graham-Cameron: Why do you think they are having
> frequent meetings and not making decisions?
>
> Teacher: Inexperience.
>
> Jean Graham-Cameron: Because it's a new school?
>
> Teacher: Yes and they are new to their jobs – new Head-
> master, new Deputy – they are still feeling their way. (HI, 1A)

Open communication plays an important part in establishing
and maintaining a reputation for self-confidence. In the project

schools, giving information was seen as an indication of acceptance, while to withhold it was to suggest lack of trust:

> I was asked to write this report, and then I was given some
> vague outlines as to why they wanted it and then eventually I
> went to the Head and he did eventually tell me. I felt that what
> he was basically saying was that I couldn't be trusted with this
> information. (U, 10)

In two descriptions (too long to quote in detail) of the relationships
between the governors, the chairman of the governors and the
headteacher, Rex Gibson elaborates this point:

> In short the Head looks to [the governors] for advice, support,
> interest and involvement and sees it as his responsibility to
> keep them fully informed about all the activities of the school.
> It is clear that he has set out to establish a climate of confidence
> based on knowledge of the school's activities. . . . I have
> never seen the amount or quality of information afforded to a
> governing body of a school that Holbein provides. Further, I
> have only rarely seen such a positive desire to answer (and
> encourage) questions from governors. (HO, 3)

In other words, in some situations open communication becomes
not just a means to an end, but an end in itself: to be open indicates a
readiness to be held to account by others because one has nothing to
hide. Formal procedures thus help to build a sense of shared
purpose and, simultaneously, signal that it exists.

Tacit contracts

Until recently, there has been little public demand to place
responsibility for the goals of education anywhere but in the hands
of teachers. In part this is due to the implicitly contractual nature of
the relationship between schools and society. Thompson (1967)
suggested that organisations seek to impose certainty upon their
environments by a number of means (contracting, cooptation,
coalition) which vary with the degree of uncertainty which they
perceive to exist. Schools have tended to operate in highly predictable environments. They have therefore relied upon contracting –

the simplest form of uncertainty-reduction – to provide them with a satisfactory level of environmental control.

Two such contracts usually ensure for schools a high degree of implicit agreement over ends. First there is the contract made between teachers and parents (and governors on behalf of the parents) when a child enters a school (especially if the parents have chosen the school) (U, 22). Teachers assume the obligation to do the best that they can for the child and in return parents (and governors) offer patience and support. The head and chairman of the governors at Holbein School described their relationship as one of 'reciprocal obligation' (HO, 3) while the head of Old Town Girls' School saw her governors as 'friends of the school' (OT, 7).

Underpinning this tacit contract is another, even more fundamental. All participants are pledged to give priority to the interests of the children. Thus the head at Uplands was able successfully to reassure mothers, during an industrial dispute, by telling them that 'he was doing all he could for the welfare of the children (U, 14), and teachers often expressed views such as:

Well, ultimately you're working for the children, so you'd both try and see what was best for them. (HI, 2B4)

On this shared responsibility for children is built a network of other obligations, summed up by one head:

All those concerned (in the education of the pupils) do feel and act in a spirit of accountability and responsibility to each other. (OT, 5)

These contracts – that everyone will 'do their best for the children', and that teachers can count upon public and parental support as long as they are perceived to be doing this – provide important safeguards for schools, ensuring that they operate within fairly wide boundaries of tolerance, and that consensus and compromise are usually preferred to conflict. Indeed, as accounts of Old Town, Holbein and Highstones indicate, differences of opinion, and even of value, can result in constructive outcomes as long as the protagonists remain faithful to the mutually, though implicitly, agreed constraints within which they are working.

However, the fact that the work of school is tacitly rather than openly contractual is, in one sense, a major handicap for teachers. One of the defining characteristics of a professional is normally taken to be client-orientation. Although teachers do not take any educational equivalent to the Hippocratic Oath, they frequently regard themselves as morally bound by and to their pupils. Dave Ebbutt suggests that teachers' sense of professionalism contains:

> a deep sense of personal moral responsibility to pupils. When parents 'interfere' they are making inroads into the core of the teachers' professional self-image. (OT, 2)

Their sense of professionalism is also built upon access to a store of 'expert knowledge' (of children, the learning process, subject matter, teaching methods, educational issues and the workings of schools). In all the CAP schools researchers found teachers defending their right to autonomy on the basis of this knowledge, and parents, governors and employers ready to accede to their claims. Yet, as schools wrestle with the problems of dialogue and as in doing so they tacitly encourage parents and others to hold them to account, they make it increasingly likely that lay persons will call into question both their expert knowledge and their right of sole access to it. Now the possession of knowledge is not a matter of ethics. One can question whether or not a doctor has made the right diagnosis without casting aspersions upon his moral worth. Unfortunately, since the term 'professional' tends to mean both client-orientation and specialist knowledge, and since many teachers see themselves as professionals, a parent (or other) who calls in question the expertise of a teacher may be understood to be attacking the basis of concern and responsibility for pupils upon which the teacher believes his work to be built.

By itself scepticism about the 'expert knowledge' of teachers might not matter. Indeed, it could be argued that the decisions of specialists are often the better for an injection of lay opinion. However, if Leakey (1981) is right in assuming that altruism is as basic an instinct in man as aggression is now taken to be, to call in question a teacher's sense of moral responsibility for his pupils is to threaten his claim to humanity. Thus, as long as the meaning of 'professionalism' continues to be confused and inexplicit the ethical commitment of teachers will be open to attack because of its reliance upon their status as 'experts'.

The situation is compounded by the absence of ways in which teachers can either 'give account' or 'be held to account' as professionals. Between their practice and every aspect of account-ability teachers erect the barrier of professionalism. They set limits to their legal accountability to governors and to the LEA by referring to their status as professionals. Their moral account-ability to clients and consumers is similarly circumscribed. Moreover for the most part, the school's 'audiences' accept teachers' claims to professional status at face value. But teachers do not have any widely-accepted set of formal procedures through which they can make explicit or vindicate these claims. Thus when the crowd begins to cry that the Emperor has no clothes, teachers have nothing but their own protestations of professionalism with which to disguise their nakedness.

Trust, I have argued, depends upon the predictability of personal and institutional behaviour and of technical competence, and upon an awareness of shared goals. Yet in the educational system of a pluralist society there is bound to be conflict over the aims of education, and thus over the conduct of the schools (especially secondary comprehensive ones). To claim that this conflict can be resolved by mutual trust rather than by 'formal procedures' is to be guilty of circularity. It is also to ignore the part played in the establishment of trust by forms of organisation. In a world which is 'crooked as corkscrews', accountability must be expressed in part through formal order. The latter allows antagonists to negotiate agreed goals without interfering with the direct educational pro-cess and helps to establish the predictability of the systems and personalities through which a school interacts with its 'audiences'. In other words, formal procedures and the interpersonal know-ledge which they promote are not the antithesis of 'trust' but the necessary conditions for it. Moreover, they act upon each other. Formal procedures facilitate the growth of trust and help to ensure its survival. Without trust, forms of organisation become empty rituals. Similarly trust by itself fails to meet society's need for the audit of public institutions and, in the absence of appropriate mechanisms, may easily degenerate into mistrust. Although teachers still take for granted their sense of moral responsibility for pupils, members of the public rely less obviously than they have done in the past upon the tacit contract which ensured for schools widespread agreement about their fundamental purposes, and secured for them a high degree of public trust. Yet teachers, as 'professionals', are reluctant to commit themselves to further formal order, thus fuelling demands for their accountability.

Tension will always exist between 'the desires of men' and the pattern of the dance to which they are committed. Viewed this way, accountability becomes not a question of power but of identities.

The extract from the poem 'Death's Echo' on p. 211 is taken from *The Collected Poems of W. H. Auden* (ed. E. Mendelson, 1979) and reproduced by kind permission of Faber & Faber.

16

Accountability, Communication and Control

David Bridges

At least part of what it means to be or to become accountable is that one will give some kind of account, report or explanation of what one is doing to some other body, group of people or, in our slightly jargonistic terms, 'constituency' or 'audience'. In our experience with the CAP schools, those giving the accounts have been head-teachers and other (mainly senior) teachers; the audiences have consisted mainly of parents, governors, local employers and LEA officers and advisers; and the accounts have taken a wide variety of forms ranging from formal reports, through newsletters, brochures and special meetings to demonstration lessons. For these schools, their accountability has manifested itself most obviously in terms of this great array of *communication*, of attempts by the school staff to get across, to report, or explain to one or more of its audiences some aspect of its life or activity. The concentration of attention in our case studies of individual schools appears to confirm the impression that the project team and the schools came to treat the problems of accountability as almost synonymous with the problems of communication.

But although accountability has a lot to do with communication, this is surely not all there is to it. In particular, an explanation of educational accountability couched simply in terms of a school's concern to communicate what it is doing to an outside audience fails to tell us enough about educational accountability as a political concept located among discussions about the *control* of education and, more particularly, among complaints about the failure of schools to deliver the goods in terms of the attitudes or skills demanded variously by national government, employers, parents or some ill-defined but frequently referred to 'society' at large. The call for schools to be more fully accountable is surely not to be disassociated from other contemporary calls for wider powers for, and more democratic representation on, governing bodies, closer parental involvement in school decision-making, an extension of central government influence on the curriculum, closer LEA supervision of the curriculum or more responsiveness of schools to the needs of industry. In other words, for a school to become either more or less fully accountable to an outside body must surely mean among other things some shift in the distribution of responsibility for and control over its affairs.

But is this necessarily the case? And what more precisely is the relationship between accountability, communication and control in the educational context? These are the questions I want to explore in this final chapter.

1. Who initiates the accounting procedures: offering account and being called to account?

All the CAP schools have chosen of their own will to develop (meaning: expand and improve) the procedures they had for giving accounts of their work to their defined audiences. They wanted their audiences to understand more fully, more clearly or more reliably what they were doing. They chose to provide this information in a context in which they might have been free to choose otherwise. They wished to make themselves more fully accounting (if not accountable).

Now it seems to me that this situation stands in quite significant contrast to one in which an institution is called to account for itself by some outside group which is in the position of requiring it to explain events or activity which it had not itself chosen to explain.

In the first case the voluntary offering of an account might be thought to represent an act of professional confidence which indicates a relationship of mutual cooperation and trust between the accounting body and its audience:

One might justifiably argue that it is precisely because one is trusted that one feels obliged to give account. (John Elliott; U, 22)

On the face of it at least the offering of an account is an act which reasserts rather than undermines the autonomy of the institution. However, by being called to account the institution is being reminded of its political subservience to an external authority; the call threatens rather than reaffirms the autonomy of the institution. It will be difficult for the institution to avoid interpreting the call as an indication of a lack of confidence or trust in its own proficiency, even if the authority concerned only sees itself as exercising its responsible surveillance of institutions in which it has every confidence.

> . . . I don't mind in any sense talking to parents about details and matters relating to the syllabus of whatever subject it is and so on. But . . . there are some parents who . . . are always checking on this and checking on that and so on, and I would tend to get a little irritated with that small minority which expects that amount of accountability. (U, 22)

In his study of Old Town Girls' School, Dave Ebbutt related the distinction between offering and being called to account very firmly to the distribution of control:

> In 'held to account' type accountability initiative and control lies outside teachers, whereas 'giving an account' locates initiative and control with teachers themselves. (OT, 2)

But he also suggested, on the basis of teachers' explanations of how they saw their accountability, that the relationship implied in a context in which one was held to account was 'structurally hier-archical' and 'ultimately legalistic', whereas offering account was associated with the recognition of some kind of moral responsi-bility.

I am arguing, then, that the political significance of a school's extension of its accounting or communication depends on, among other things, whether it is voluntarily and willingly proffered or whether it is a response to outside demand. But the picture I have presented is over-simplified. In practice we found that at least one of the schools' motives for developing their accounting procedures was to anticipate or perhaps forestall possible external demands. In this way they sought to preserve at least the appearance of independence which might have been more seriously and explicitly threatened if they had waited for some outside agency to call the terms of their accountability. If this observation is right, it prompts the questions: is it only the appearance of professional autonomy which is protected in this way? Has the development of self-accounting procedures entailed in practice some diminution of the school's autonomy? These are questions to which I shall return in section 4 below.

2. Who provides the accounts? Self accounting

All of the schools we have been working with have been involved in the business of self-accounting. By this I mean that it has been the schools themselves that have been producing, in one form or another, the accounts of their work. They have been deciding what will be reported on and by and large producing the reports. In this respect the form of account differs from one that might be provided by some outside 'accountant', as in the traditional form of HMI inspection or through an LEA inspection or even by the publication of exam results or children's scores on some kind of standardised test. The schools have not had to submit their accounts to outside and independent auditors. The schools have retained a good deal of control over the process and content of communication. Self-accounting in this sense is a further expression of professional autonomy, which could be much more severely threatened by alternative forms of e.g. external auditing.

This general observation concerning the schools' control over communication requires qualification of an important kind. Those involved in the project have come to attach considerable significance to the distinction between the formal channels of communication between a school and its audiences (e.g. newsletters, meetings, open days, etc.) and informal channels (the picture of the school taken home by children, children's behaviour in town, gossip transmitted in all sorts of social encounters in a local community).

It is not easy to control the informal channels through which a picture of a school is conveyed, though schools made some attempts at this.

We try to prevent malicious rumour or incorrect rumour from being spread. I think definitely we are making more effort on that side of things than we did last year, trying to counteract wrong impressions. (HI, 2B)

In one instance a school restricted its pupils' access to town at lunch-time at least in part for fear of the misbehaviour and damage to its reputation which might ensue. It was one of the pupils who explained:

What they're worried about is if we do things like thieving and that it gets back to the school. It's bad publicity for the school. (RP, II1)

If the school cannot control all informal channels of communication, perhaps the best it can do is to counter as far as possible any undesirable or misleading messages conveyed through the informal channels by ensuring comprehensive and efficient communication through its formal channels. A concern by staff to communicate what they saw as a 'proper' picture of the work of the school (as contrasted with the 'misleading' picture which might be conveyed through informal channels) was indeed a recurring motive among our schools for the development of their own self-accounting procedures – the letters, brochures, exhibitions, open days, meetings, press releases which presented evidence of the work of the school and to one degree or another an 'official' interpretation of the evidence in terms of the policy, philosophy or intentions of the school.

I think the more you inform them about what's going on, the less likely gossip, rumours and misunderstandings will be to arise. (HI, 2B3)

The development of fuller accounting procedures by schools can then be reasonably interpreted as associated with a desire to control more effectively the kind of picture of the school which is communicated to outside audiences.

3.   Communication and decision-making

I have written so far about the control of communication. I want now to turn to certain aspects of the question as to what extent the

communication embodied in the kind of self-accounting procedures indicated impinges on the decision-making and practice of
a school.

Three sets of considerations will help in the analysis of this
relationship. First there is the question, at what stage in the process of:

deliberation – decision taking – implementation and practice – review

should the school's policies be communicated. In particular I would
attach very different significance to the timing of an open meeting
or even a letter to coincide with the following different stages in the
process:

1. at an early stage before the staff themselves had come to
   any opinion on an issue (this would be presented as a
   genuine consultation at a stage which allowed the possibility of influencing teachers' opinions)

2. after staff had developed a proposal but in plenty of time to
   allow revision of that proposal if strong opinion or evidence were brought against it

3. just before implementation when it was too late to do
   anything about it

4. after implementation, i.e. the outside audience was hear-
   ing retrospectively of something the school had done

Secondly, and closely related to these considerations, there is the
question of the extent to which and the way in which the style of
communication encourages or allows audience response. How far
is the audience expected or allowed:

1. to be a passive recipient of information?

2. to ask questions with a view to a better understanding of the
   information or practice?

3. to question (see, U, 15 on the distinction between 'asking
   questions' and 'questioning') the information or practice of
   the school, i.e. to criticise or challenge it?

4. to develop positive proposals for new practice?

Thirdly, we need to set alongside these considerations those to do with the extent to which the school is disposed to respond to the opinions and arguments of its audiences, by changing its practices. How far is the school:

1. indifferent to or uninterested in the opinions of outside audiences (seeing perhaps their expressions as no more than a useful letting off of steam); deeply sceptical of the possibility that any lay group could contribute to the improvement of its own professional practices; feeling neither obligation nor necessity to take any notice of them?

2. disposed to review and change its practice in the light of outside opinion to the extent that the professionals themselves can be persuaded of its wisdom and reasonableness?

3. disposed to review and change its practice out of respect for the interests and concerns of the outside group (independently of whether the school agreed with them and even where the school did not feel compelled to do so)?

4. sensitive to the personal or political 'muscle' which might be wielded by some individuals or groups among its audiences and disposed to review or change policy when this was what was threatened?

Now one can obviously generate from these three sets a variety of patterns of ways in which outside audiences are involved in communication and decision-making. For the moment I want to restrict myself to three patterns which I shall call: the professional/isolationist; the professional/rational; and the professional/participatory. More especially I want to illuminate and then go on to discuss the professional/rational pattern which is I think characteristic of the style of accountability that the CAP schools were trying to develop.

Briefly, the *professional/isolationist* pattern has the following characteristics. If outside groups are informed at all of school practice (which they may very well not be) this will be once the practice is firmly established *de facto* and when it can be changed only at great cost. Those informed are not encouraged to seek further information though there may be some restricted opportunity to do so. They are particularly discouraged from questioning the practice. The professionals are largely unconcerned with the opinions of outside groups and certainly feel no need to seek them out as a basis for determining present or future practice. If a school in this mould is at all 'accountable' it is only in the minimal sense of occasionally releasing information about its practice.

The *professional/participatory* pattern, at the other extreme, has the following characteristics. The school consults with relevant outside audiences at an early stage in the formulation of policy. Those consulted are encouraged to examine current practice critically and develop suggestions for change. The professionals feel an obligation to be guided by the opinions of their audiences not just in relation to their apparent reasonableness but out of respect for the right of these audiences to share in the formulation of the school's policy. On this view, as John Elliott expresses it:

> The involvement of parents in policy decisions would be a necessary condition of exercising accountability to them. (U, 19)

The *professional/rational* pattern, as I shall call it, is characterised in different terms. The school, being fairly confident of its own right and responsibility to develop and implement practice, typically sounds out the opinion of any outside audiences after the practice has had chance to run or at least when it is thoroughly thought out. The school provides a battery of information on its work and opportunities, for its audiences to seek further information, clarification or explanation. Being confident too of its capacity to justify its policies and their intrinsic reasonableness it is not wholly averse to engaging in critical dialogue. John Elliott's 'dialogue' model of accountability has indeed much in common with what I am elaborating here in somewhat broader terms (see U, 22). The pattern nevertheless expects those so engaged to recognise the limits of their own as against the teachers' professional expertise and not to press their questioning too far or too tediously.

Teachers subscribing to this set of opinions and practices acknowledge the importance of public support for the work of the school and recognise that this entails understanding but are not in general able to accept the kind of equation which Joan Sallis (1979e) offers in favour of direct lay-participation in educational decision-making:

The case is essentially that the job schools now have to do cannot be done adequately without more support from parents and the community in general. Support means consent, consent means understanding, true understanding can only come from responsibility.

Such teachers may however accept a measure of direct lay participation in decision-making in aspects of school life which are not central to its strictly educational concerns and where consequently it does not challenge the *educational* expertise of the professionals.

At the risk of gross oversimplification I see the set of attitudes and practice which I have called professional/isolationist as that which has characterised and perhaps still characterises a majority of schools but one from which many have moved in recent years and many more are under pressure to move. I see the practices of the professional/participatory model as ones for which there has been some enthusiasm among some lay audiences and ones to which the Taylor Committee gave a cautious measure of support. They are, however, practices widely opposed by many of those in teaching who see it as threatening their professional autonomy.

The professional/rational pattern is one many of those who were associated with the project preferred as a representation of the character of both their professional authority and their professional accountability.

John Elliott, for example, summarises the attitudes of Uplands staff thus:

On the basis of the evidence I have cited in this study, I would conclude that Uplands as a school shows signs of moving away from simply giving accounts to parents, towards a dialogue model; particularly with respect to its curricular and organisational policies.

What he means by dialogue model he explains in terms which, as I have already suggested, include many of the features which I have expressed as characteristic of the professional/rational pattern of decision-making and accountability:

On this interpretation it is the accountable subject who decides what he ought to do but in doing so acknowledges an obligation to explain and justify his decisions and actions when challenged. This kind of willingness to engage in dialogue or argumentation about his policies and practices assumes the desirability of proceeding with them on the basis of their acceptability to others. It also assumes being open to the possibility of modifying his policies and practices in the light of dialogue. Dialogue is the process by which a self-determining agent validates his policies to others. Through dialogue others are given 'a say' in what the agent decides and does but it is one which flows from 'the force of the better argument' rather than the exercise of power. (U, 22)

Rex Gibson summarised the attitudes of staff at Holbein School (in this particular case in relation to their governors) in not dissimilar terms:

that the staff are strongly committed to 'the right to know' philosophy

that they feel a strong responsibility and desire to *explain* all aspects of the school to the governors

that they are ready to be *influenced* by the governors' views and comments

that they feel ambivalent over Taylor's recommendation that the school's aim should be set by the governors

that they feel their prime accountability responsibility is to the head

that they strongly feel that the pattern and implementation of the curriculum is the teachers' responsibility

that they would generally welcome increased contact with governors

that they would generally welcome governors into their classrooms during school hours, but would wish to discuss what was seen with the governors to ensure that the governors were fully appraised of all the factors influencing what had gone on

and that they feel that teacher accountability necessitates teacher responsibility for decision taking (HO, 3)

On the view that I have called professional/rational, accountability to outside bodies is one thing; sharing in responsibility for school decision making is another. But of course, like everything else in the murky waters of educational politics, it is not as simple as that. What I want to explore in the next section are some of the ways in which the professional/rational pattern of school management and accountability involves some devolution of professional independence at the same time as its defence.

4. The rational professional and professional autonomy

A pattern of school decision-making and accountability on the lines of that which I have called professional/rational has the apparent characteristic, which may appeal to many teachers, of leaving intact their professional autonomy. They accept the need to engage in some kind of dialogue with their lay audiences but retain the power of decision, at least in relation to those decisions which are made at school level.

But is this how it will work in practice? Our experience with the CAP schools gives us some basis for appreciating some of the ways in which what is overtly a professional/rational pattern of decision-making and accountability nevertheless involves in practice some concessions away from professional autonomy.

First, let us note that in so far as teachers' right to decide is based upon their professional expertise in the area of education, then that right is not readily extended to decisions which are not regarded as centrally or essentially educational ones. Parents may claim for example (and teachers may agree) that what children wear to come to school is not an issue on which teachers' opinions should outweigh parents'. At least two of the CAP schools allowed this particular decision to be made by a vote of parents, feeling that this concession in no way seriously undermined their autonomy on matters of more central educational concern. One headmaster said:

> . . . the uniform . . . let's be quite honest, that is not something that interests me very much in the sense that I don't want it to be a major issue. . . . The approach to school uniform was very much pragmatic. It was obviously an important concern in the minds of governors and parents. . . . We conducted a referendum. . . . I was glad to make this frankly a non-issue so that we would try to get back to what I see as much more central to our main function as a school. (RP, I)

Second, and more significant, it became quickly obvious as we came to see more of schools' decision-making that even where outside audiences were not directly or knowingly party to decision-making, they were often there as a ghostly presence. What I mean by this is that their known or supposed opinions or reactions were commonly referred to, anticipated and where necessary taken into account.

In general I think the schools we worked with sought consensus rather than conflict with their outside audiences. If part of this process involved careful communication designed to persuade them of the wisdom of the school's practice, another part involved anticipating and if possible forestalling powerful objections. At the same time as exposing themselves to criticism the schools hoped to avoid it. And so they researched and prepared their policies and rehearsed their defence with sufficient care so as to avoid being caught out at, for example, an open meeting for parents or a governors' meeting by any damaging and especially any concerted and widely based criticism. It is one thing to act without the approval of e.g. a governing body or PTA; it is an altogether different thing to act in the face of their public disapproval. In other words, once a school begins seriously to allow comment on its policies and practice it becomes increasingly difficult to disregard these comments – and once it habitually opens up issues to discussion it loses the option of acting without risking that disapproval. If it invites comment and criticism it is surely irrational to ignore it when it comes, and the school risks presenting itself as autocratic and unreasonable rather than professional and rational. Better by far to anticipate the criticism and either adjust one's practice accordingly or prepare a really rather compelling answer to it.

> Teacher: As long as you can turn round and say 'Yes, we're doing this because . . .' and give a good reason which the majority of the population, if they don't absolutely agree with, wouldn't object strongly to, then you've got some justification and some backing. (HI, 3B)

If the school is successful in anticipating sources of discontent in this way, then parents or governors are merely agreeably aware that the school is either doing what they would like it to do anyway or seems to have some very clear reason why it is not. This gives them the reassurance, which most lay people seem to want much more than they want control, that the schools can be trusted to get on with the job. In this way perhaps the institution of professional autonomy is preserved at the cost of some largely invisible concessions to lay opinion.

These considerations lead me to a third observation on the limitations of professional autonomy or, more strictly, professional independence within the rational professional pattern of decision-making and accountability. This starts from the consideration that on this view the professional authority of teachers is based upon their special knowledge and understanding and hence the claim that their judgements will better withstand the tests of reasons, evidence and argument than will (in general at least) those of the lay community. Along with this claim is set, for self-accounting professionals, a readiness to make public their judgements and the reasons underlying them.

It seems to me that as soon as teachers claim that the authority supporting their policies is not simply their personal, social or professional authority as teachers ('this will be done because I say so/I know best/I am in charge') but the authority of reason ('they are rationally defensible/they are supported by the evidence/they are more justifiable'), then they introduce a court of appeal to which parents, governors and others can also refer. Moreover it is a court which with all its imperfections can offer at least some procedural rules which can be used to contradict and overrule any other authority which holds itself answerable to its rules.

For example, a school which publicly defends its policy on the science curriculum by reference to the requirements of local employers or university admissions opens itself to challenge in the face of evidence that its interpretation of those requirements is erroneous. A school that defends its arrangements for combinations of subjects which can be taken at 'A' level on the basis of claims that these are the combinations most commonly preferred by its pupils has its position undermined by unambiguous evidence that these are not in fact the combinations which are sought by its pupils. A school that defends its policy on school uniform on the grounds that this is what parents prefer might reasonably be expected to produce evidence to support this premise. A school which proclaims itself firmly against a practice which it nevertheless permits, or one which expresses in its objectives concerns which it shows no sign of pursuing, offends at least against the elementary but ubiquitously demanding principle of consistency. In this way is not the professional independence of teachers subject to, or limited by, objectively or at least publicly grounded criteria of reason?

Well, in practice, again, it did not seem to work out quite as simply as my examples might suggest.

To begin with, even where a school was sensitive to outside opinion this did not necessarily mean that it was the weight of argument which prevailed so much as the persistency or stridency of the complaint. One headteacher, explaining how she had resolved a question as to what combination of subjects could be taken at 'A' level, acknowledged that one of the considerations which influenced her decision was

> which parent was going to make the most fuss if his daughter couldn't do it easily! (OT, 2)

More interestingly perhaps is the observation that though many teachers indicated a readiness to submit their practice and policies to rational scrutiny, this was characteristically combined with an *almost* unchallengeable assumption that (i) the evidence would indeed vindicate the teachers' judgement and (ii) that anyone questioning them must submit to the teachers' ruling on the matter.

> We're quite prepared to listen to their ideas but we are still the best judge of whether those ideas are worthwhile or not. We're the professionals (HI, 2B6)

> I think it is difficult to listen when you feel that what you are doing is right. You can listen and then say 'That's a load of codswallop', which to a parent would probably mean you are not listening. (HI, 2B6)

> I'd answer any questions. I can justify everything I do. (HI, 2B3)

> I would say that I am willing, very willing, to discuss with parents [and] if parents pointed out a significant flaw . . . I would respond. But, clearly, I am hoping and expecting that within the school we'll be evaluating what we're doing and that we ought to be in a better position to judge than the parents whether we are doing a good job or not . . . (HO, 2)

Perhaps I have to acknowledge that when it comes to educational judgements, teachers' claim to professional expertise involves not only a special qualification to make those judgements but also the right to be the final judge of their reasonableness in the event of their being questioned. The 'court of reason' is the staffroom and the judge the headteacher.

Nevertheless I offer for consideration the perhaps optimistic thesis that once a body of people advertise themselves as ready to listen to argument, concerned to base their judgements on evidence and amenable to reason, they cannot entirely define the terms of this reason in their own favour without total loss of credibility.

Besides, my own experience on the project has left intact my early opinions that, within the ordinary limits of human fallibility and frailty, many of those with positions of responsibility in education *are* trying to test their judgements against publicly identifiable criteria of evidence and reason and are not entirely obstinate in the belief that their own opinion and practice wholly defies improvement. It may be a naive hope, but it is one worth hanging on to nevertheless, that the opening up of dialogue about education within schools as well as between schools and the wider community might have the effect of shifting consideration from the question of *who* should determine educational practice to the more fundamental question: *how* can educational practice be rationally determined?

Select bibliography

ADVISORY CENTRE FOR EDUCATION (1979) *School Governors: Partnership in Practice*. London: ACE.

ADVISORY CENTRE FOR EDUCATION (1980) *Guide to the Education Act 1980*. London: ACE.

ASSOCIATION OF ASSISTANT MISTRESSES (1976) *An AAM Discussion Document*. London: AAM.

ATKIN, M. (1972) *Accountability Defined*. Los Angeles, CA.: University of California, Centre for the Study of Education.

ATKIN, M. (1979) Education accountability in the United States. *Educational Analysis* 1 (1).

AULD, R. (1976) *William Tyndale Junior and Infants Schools Public Inquiry*. London: ILEA.

BAILEY, C. H. (1980) The autonomous teacher. In H. Sockett *et al.* (1980).

BAINBRIDGE, J. (1977) The adviser: no school is an island. *Education* 150.

BARRELL, G. B. (1978) *Teachers and the Law*, fifth edition. London: Methuen.

BEATTIE, N. (1978) Formalized parent participation in education: a comparative perspective. *Comparative Education* 14 (1).

BECHER, A. and MACLURE, S. (eds) (1978) *Accountability in Education*. Slough, Bucks.: NFER.

BECK, J. (1981) Education, industry and the needs of the economy. *Cambridge Journal of Education* 11 (2).

BLACKSTONE, T. (1979) Parental involvement in education. *Education Policy Bulletin* 7 (1).

BOLAM, R., SMITH, G., CANTER, H. (1976) *LEA Advisers and the Mechanism of Innovation*. Slough, Bucks.: NFER.

BRIDGES, D. (1979) Some reasons why curriculum planning should not be left to experts. *Journal of the Philosophy of Education* 13.

CASEY, J. (1971) *Morality and Moral Reasoning*. London: Methuen.

CYSTER, R. *et al*. (1980) *Parental Involvement in Primary Schools*. Slough, Bucks.: NFER.

(DES) DEPARTMENT OF EDUCATION AND SCIENCE (1977) *Education in Schools: A Consultative Document* (Cmnd 6869). London: HMSO.

DEPARTMENT OF EDUCATION AND SCIENCE (1979) School/Industry links. *Trends* 2.

DEPARTMENT OF EDUCATION AND SCIENCE (1981) *The School Curriculum*. London: HMSO.

DES and the WELSH OFFICE (1979) *Local Authority Arrangements for the School Curriculum*. London: HMSO.

EAST SUSSEX LEA/UNIVERSITY OF SUSSEX (1979) *Accountability in the Middle Years of Schooling*. Brighton, Sussex: The University.

EDGLEY, R. (1977) Education for industry. *Educational Research* 20 (1).

ELLIOTT, J. (1976a) The problems and dilemmas of mixed ability teaching and the issues of teacher accountability. *Cambridge Journal of Education* 6(1).

ELLIOTT, J. (1976b) Preparing teachers for classroom accountability. *Education for Teaching* 100.

ELLIOTT, J. (1977) The conditions of public accountability. *Cambridge Journal of Education* 7 (2).

ELLIOTT, J. (1979a) Self-accounting schools: are they possible? *Educational Analysis 1* (1)

ELLIOTT, J. (1979b) Accountability, progressive education and school-based evaluation. *Education 3–13* (7).

ELLIOTT, J. *et al*. (1981) *Case Studies in School Accountability* vols I, II, III. Cambridge: Institute of Education.

ELLIS, T. *et al*. (1976) *William Tyndale: the Teachers' Story*. London: Writers & Readers.

GALBRAITH, R. E. (1978) An accountability checklist for parents and teachers. *Social Education* 42 (7).

GARVEY, A. (1977) Do children want parents in school? *Where?* 125.

GIBSON, R. (1980) *Teacher-Parent Communication*. Cambridge: Institute of Education.

GIBSON, R. (forthcoming) *Social Theory and Social Understanding*.

GIDDENS, A. (1976) *New Rules of Sociological Method*. London: Hutchinson.

GIDDENS, A. (1977) *Studies in Social and Political Theory*. London: Hutchinson.

GIDDENS, A. (1979) *Central Problems in Social Theory*. London: Macmillan.

GLASER, B. & STRAUSS, A. L: (1967) *The Discovery of Grounded Theory*. Chicago: Aldine.

GOACHER, B. & WEINDLING, R. (1978–81) *School Reports Newsletter* 1, 2, 3. Slough, Bucks.: NFER.

GRAY, J. (1979) The statistics of accountability. *Education Policy Bulletin* 7 (1).

GREEN, L. (1975) *School Reports and Other Information for Parents*. Home and School Council.

GREEN, L. & MARLAND, M. (1970) *School Reports: A Home and School Council Working Paper*. Home and School Council.

GRETTON, J. & JACKSON, H. (1976) *William Tyndale: Collapse of a School or a System?* London: George Allen & Unwin.

GRIFFIN, P. (1978) The future of Taylor. *Secondary Education* 8 (3).

HABERMAS, J. (1968) Technology and science as 'ideology'. In *Towards a Rational Society*. London: Heinemann.

HABERMAS, J. (1973) *Introduction to Theory and Practice*. London: Heinemann.

HAMMERSLEY, M. (1979) Research methods in education and social sciences: analysing ethnographic data. DE304, Block 6, Part 1. Milton Keynes: Open University Press.

HARLEN, W. (1979) Accountability that is of benefit to schools. *Journal of Curriculum Studies* 11 (4).

(HI) Highstones: Mirror-images and reflections; case study by J. Nias. In J. Elliott *et al.* (1981).

(HO) Holbein case study by R. Gibson. In J. Elliott *et al.* (1981).

HOGGART R. (1955) *The Uses of Literacy*. Harmondsworth: Penguin.

HONEYFORD, R. (1974) Progress reports in English teaching. *Use of English Quarterly* (25).

HOUSE, E. R. (1972) The dominion of economic accountability. *Educational Forum* (37)

HOUSE, E. R. (1973) *The Price of Productivity: Who Pays?* (Mimeo). Urbana-Champaign, Ill.: CIRCE, University of Illinois.

HOUSE, E. R. (1974) *The Politics of Educational Innovations*. Berkeley, Calif.: McCutcheon.

KAY, B. (1976) The Assessment of Performance Unit: its task and rationale. *Education 3–13* 4 (2).

KENNEDY, I. (1980) Consumerism in the doctor-patient relationship (from the Reith Lectures). *The Listener*, 11 November.

KING, R. (1978) *All Things Bright and Beautiful?* London: John Wiley.

KOGAN, M. (1975) *Educational Policy Making: A Study of Interest Groups and Parliament*. London: George Allen & Unwin.

LAWSON, K. (1979) The politics of primary curricula. *Education 3–13* 7 (1).

LEAKEY, R. E. (1981) *The Making of Mankind*. London: Michael Joseph.

LEE, D. (1979) What is school for? The views of some parents. *Bulletin of Educational Research* 17.

LELLO, J. (ed.) (1979) *Accountability in Education*. London: Ward Lock.

LEVIN, H. M. (1974) A conceptual framework for accountability in education. *School Review*, May.

LORTIE, D. C. (1975) *Schoolteacher – A Sociological Study*. University of Chicago Press.

LUKES, S. (1973) *Individualism*. Oxford: Basil Blackwell.

MACFARLANE, A. (1978) *The Origins of English Individualism*. Oxford: University Press.

MACDONALD, B. (1978) Accountability, standards and the process of schooling. In A. Becher & S. Maclure (eds) (1978).

MARLAND, M. (1974) *Pastoral Care*. London: Heinemann.

MCGRATH, K. (1974) Who's assessing who? *Observer Review*, 14 July.

MORRIS, M. (1977) The teacher: watch us by all means but don't interfere. *Education* 150.

NATIONAL ASSOCIATION OF INSPECTORS AND EDUCATIONAL ADVISERS (1977) *The Role of the Chief Adviser*. NAIEA.

NEWELL, P. (1979) What to do to get things changed – who to see, where and when. *Where?* 145.

Open University (1981) *Governing Schools: A Home Study Course*. Walton Hall, Milton Keynes: Open University Press.

(OT) Old Town Girls' case study by D. Ebbutt. In J. Elliott *et al.* (1981).

PARTINGTON, G. I. (1976) Community school and curriculum. *Forum* 18 (3)

PEARCE, J. (1979) Advisers and inspectors. In J. Lello (ed.) (1979).

PETERS, R. S. (ed.) (1976) *The Role of the Head*. London: Routledge & Kegan Paul.

(RP) Robert Peel case study by D. Bridges. In J. Elliott *et al.* (1981).

(S) Springdale case study by D. Ebbutt. In J. Elliott *et al.* (1981).

SALLIS, J. (1977) *School Managers and Governors: Taylor and After*. London: Ward Lock.

SALLIS, J. (1979a) The parent: schools must earn parents' trust. *Education* 150.

SALLIS, J. (1979b) Powers and duties of school governors, past, present, future. *Where?* 150.
See also articles by J. Sallis in *Where?* 147–155.

SCRIMSHAW, P. (1980) Making schools responsible. In H. Sockett *et al.* (1980).

SHARROCK, A. (comp.) (1971) *Home and School: A Select Annotated Bibliography*. Slough, Bucks.: NFER.

SIMON, B. and WHITEBREAD, N. (eds.) (1979) Special number. *Forum* 22 (1).

SIMONS, H. (1980) The evaluative school. *Forum* 22 (2).

SOCIETY OF EDUCATION OFFICERS and NATIONAL ASSOCIATION OF INSPECTORS and EDUCATION ADVISERS (1979) *The role of the Educational Advisory Service*. SEO and NAIEA.

SOCKETT, H. (1976) Teacher accountability. *Proceedings of the Philosophy of Education Society*, 10 July.

SOCKETT, H. *et al.* (1980) *Accountability in the English Educational System*. London: Hodder & Stoughton.

STAKE, R. *et al.* (1978) *Case Studies in Science Education* II. Urbana-Champaign, Ill.: CIRCE, University of Illinois.

STENHOUSE, L. (1979) Accountability. *Educational Analysis* (1).

SUGARMAN, S. (1979) Freedom and choice for the family. *Where?* 147.

TAYLOR, F. (1979) What to do when a head doesn't want a PTA. *Where?* 146.

TAYLOR REPORT (1977) *A New Partnership for Our Schools*. Department of Education and Science and the Welsh Office. London: HMSO.

THOMPSON, J. (1967) *Organizations in Action*. New York: McGraw-Hill.

(U) Uplands case study by J. Elliott. In J. Elliott *et al*. (1981).

WATSON, K. (1978) Accountability in English education. *Educational Administration* 6 (2).

WHITE, J. P. (1976) Teacher accountability and school autonomy; a reply to Hugh Sockett. *Proceedings of the Philosophy of Education Society*, 10 July.

WILLIAMS, R. (1977) *Marxism and Literature*. Oxford: University Press.

WILLIAMS, R. (1979) *Politics and Letters*. London: New Left Books.

WILLIAMS, R. (1980) *Problems in Culture and Materialism*. London: Verso.

WOODS, P. (1979) *The Divided School*. London: Routledge & Kegan Paul.

WRAGG, E. C. & PARTINGTON, J. A. (1980) *A Handbook for School Governors*. London: Methuen.

WYATT, J. (1980) Accountability means more than coping: renewing the justification of the liberal education tradition. *Oxford Review of Education* 6 (1).

The National Confederation of PTAs, 43 Stonebridge Road, Northfleet, Gravesend, Kent, produces a number of pamphlets and model constitutions of value to anyone setting up an association.

The monthly magazine *Where?* regularly publishes articles relevant to many of the issues raised in this book (18 Victoria Park Square, London E2 9PB).

Index

18. *Functions of Faith in Academic Life*, p. 112.
19. See, for example, D. Nineham, *The Use and Abuse of the Bible* (Macmillan, London 1976).
20. The text is conveniently available in J. B. Pritchard, *Ancient Near Eastern Texts* (Oxford University Press 1969), p. 421.
21. J. Houston, *Common Ground*, p. 36.

Notes to Chapter Two

1. J. Barr, *The Bible in the Modern World* (S.C.M. 1973), p. 60.
2. c.f. J. Barr, *op. cit.*, p. 55.
3. J. Barr, *op. cit.*, p. 55. For a sensitive appreciation of the Bible in literary terms see T. R. Henn, 'The Bible as Literature' in *Peake's Commentary on the Bible*, ed. M. Black and H. H. Rowley (Nelson & Sons 1962), pp. 8–23.
4. cf. A. C. Sundberg, *The Old Testament of the Early Church* (Harvard Theological Studies 20, 1964).
5. cf. C. F. Evans, *Is Holy Scripture Christian?* (S.C.M. 1971); D. Nineham, *op. cit.*
6. J. A. Sanders, *Torah and Canon* (Fortress Press, Philadelphia 1972), p. x.
7. J. A. Sanders, *op. cit.*, p. xv.
8. R. Goldman, *Readiness for Religion* (Routledge 1965), p. 176. For further criticism of this 'New Testament spectacles' approach see my article 'The Old Testament and the Fourth R' in *New College Bulletin*, Volume VI, Spring, 1971, Number 1, pp. 16–27.

Notes to Chapter Three

1. R. S. Downie, E. M. Loudfoot and E. Telfer, *Education and Personal Relationships* (Methuen 1974), pp. 12 ff.
2. H. Loukes, *Teenage Religion* (S.C.M. 1961), p. 151.
3. See, for example, Deuteronomy 7:4–7; Hosea 11:1–9.
4. R. J. Goldman, *Religious Thinking from Childhood to Adolescence* (R.K.P. 1964); *Readiness for Religion* (R.K.P. 1965).

5. R. S. Downie, *op. cit.*, p. 13.
6. R. S. Downie, *op. cit.*, p. 20.

Notes to Chapter Four

1. e.g. Lancashire Education Authority, *Religion and Life*, 1968. M. Grimmitt, *What Can I Do In Religious Education?* (Mayhew & McCrimmon 1973).
2. *Readiness for Religion*, p. 76.
3. M. Grimmitt, *op. cit.*, p. 56. Some of the material in this chapter draws upon my article, 'The Old Testament and the Fourth R', *New College Bulletin*, Volume VI, Spring 1971, Number 1.
4. *op. cit.*, p. 117.
5. See, for example, T. F. Torrance, *Life and Work*, April 1978.
6. M. Grimmitt, *op. cit.*, p. 205.
7. The *Modern Criticism and the Preaching of the Old Testament* (Hodder and Stoughton 1901), pp. 25, 26.

Notes to Chapter Five

1. Quoted by B. G. Mitchell in *The Fourth R.*, p. 358.
2. J. Barr *The Bible in the Modern World*, p. 119.
3. D. B. Macdonald *The Hebrew Philosophical Genius*, Princeton 1936, p. 26.
4. *The Fourth R*, p. 358.

64